Broken and Battered

Broken and Battered

A Way Out for the Abused Woman

Muriel Canfield

HOWARD
PUBLISHING CO.

Our purpose at Howard Publishing is to:

- *Increase faith* in the hearts of growing Christians
- *Inspire holiness* in the lives of believers
- *Instill hope* in the hearts of struggling people everywhere

Because He's coming again!

Broken and Battered © 2000 by Muriel Canfield
All rights reserved. Printed in the United States of America

Published by Howard Publishing Co., Inc.,
3117 North 7th Street, West Monroe, Louisiana 71291-2227

02 03 04 05 06 07 08 09   10 9 8 7 6 5 4 3

Library of Congress Cataloging-in-Publication Data

Canfield, Muriel, 1935-
   Broken and battered : a way out for the abused woman / Muriel Canfield.
     p. cm.
   Includes bibliographical references.
   ISBN 1-58229-098-9; ISBN 1-58229-296-5 (pbk.)
   1. Abused wives—Religious life. 2. Christian women—Religious life. I. Title.

BV4596.A2 K36 2000
261.8'327—dc21   00-020981

Edited by Nancy Norris
Interior design by Stephanie Denney

Scripture quotations not otherwise marked are from The Holy Bible, New King James Version. Copyright © 1982 by Thomas Nelson, Inc. Other Scriptures are quoted from The Holy Bible, New International Version (NIV), copyright © 1973, 1978, 1984 International Bible Society, used by permission of Zondervan Bible Publishers; The Holy Bible, New Century Version (NCV), copyright © 1987, 1988, 1991 by Word Publishing, Dallas, Texas 75234, used by permission; The New American Standard Bible (NASB), copyright © 1960, 1962, 1963, 1968, 1971, 1972, 1973 The Lockman Foundation.

*D*edicated to
Caroline and Susan
and all abused women
in this country
and abroad

About the Author

Muriel Canfield has a heart for battered women. As founder of several Alcoholics Victorious groups, she has worked extensively with disturbed and abused women. Besides giving years of service as a volunteer counselor at a battered women's shelter, she has cofacilitated a support group and served as a court advocate for battered women. Among the books she has authored are *I Wish I Could Say I Love You* and *A Victorian Marriage*, and she has had articles published in numerous magazines. Muriel has appeared on the *700 Club* and the *Praise the Lord* show.

Contents

Introduction   ix

1. The Lie-Detector Test   1

2. Me Tarzan, You Jane   25

3. Under Daddy's Foot   51

4. When Church Is a Haven of Rejection   73

5. When a Christian Home Is Hell   91

6. Speaking of the Unspeakable: Marital Rape   103

7. Lamb in the Pulpit; Lion at Home   123

8. Give Me Liberty   151

9. The Dangerous Departure   163

10. Sentencing Yourself to Life   181

11. Let's Be There for Her   199

12. Legal Medicine That Helps   221

13. Give Me Some Tender-Hearted Men   237

14. A Last Look at Caroline   255

15. A Last Look at Susan   269

Epilogue   283

Appendix A: The Safety Plan   285

Appendix B: Organizations That Help   301

Notes   305

Introduction

Does an abused Christian woman's story begin with the very first date when the abuser exuded charm or with the last time he threw her down the basement stairs? Or the time he locked her out of the house in the winter and she had to sleep in the car? Or the time he lied about her in front of her friends and told them she had slept around before marriage? Where will it end—in divorce, in captivity forever with him, in separation, in healing, in death by his hand?

The story of an abused woman can follow many sad or brutal plots with details she likely hides because she is afraid that, once again, she won't be believed; because no one wants to believe anything bad about that nice guy who faithfully attends church.

THE VICTIMS SPEAK

But it is slowly being understood within the church that there is a significant number of women who are abused psychologically, verbally, sexually, physically, or any combination of the four. They are beginning to speak out. For instance, "The Secret Scars," an article I wrote about wife abuse for *Virtue* magazine, received more letters from women than any other single article they have published.[1] Here are excerpts from a few letters.

> My husband professes to be a Christian. I don't know any-more.... The physical [abuse] is just the tip. I can hardly deal with the emotional part. He is always telling me I'm in sin, I am not submissive like I'm supposed to be, I'm emotionally disturbed, crazy.
>
> He is always quoting Scripture at me to show me I'm wrong. He is very controlling. He keeps all the money, and I have to go to him for even the smallest thing, like shoestrings....
>
> You mention...that it becomes harder and harder for women to leave because they get worn down and exhausted from dealing with the situation and the brainwashing that goes on (and it is brainwashing). After a while I begin to question myself about whether his accusations about me are correct. I'm always thinking, "What if he is right?"... No one in my circle of friends or acquaintances calls me anymore. They don't speak to me at church. They all believe him. I feel so alone.... Some days I don't know if I will make it one more day.[2]

> Six weeks after [I married my husband] I discovered he had a violent cruel streak. His angry outbursts (throwing a pan through the glass door, kicking the dog, screaming, ranting, and raving) progressed until I left him. He followed me and tried to force me off the road with our newborn in the car.
>
> The church we were attending at that time encouraged me to submit and go back. I did. The [violence] progressed and I decided to leave while he was at work, which meant loading furniture in my car at 2:00 A.M. by myself. The church doesn't want to help me because people don't want to offend him.
>
> Few are willing to sit beside me and feel my pain—to carry it with me. Fears abound as I contemplate the future raising three children on eleven hundred dollars a month.[3]

> Unless you have been there, you don't know what it's

like…. For about three years [my husband has] hit me, pulled my hair, and made me stay home all the time. He raped me several times. We've talked to preachers and counselors, and they all said I should try to make my husband happy and things would get better; he is trying to find himself as a man….

They've told my husband that if I divorce him, I am not in the Lord's will and I will go to hell for it. All the church body has to say is "Have faith and everything will be OK."[4]

THE EXTENT OF WIFE ABUSE

These letters reveal that wife abuse is alive and well in the church. But how alive and how well?

More studies are needed concerning wife abuse in Christian homes, but here are two that suggest the extent: "In 1992, the Christian Reformed Church in North America reported that 28 percent of members surveyed experienced abuse. Eleven years previously, the United Methodist General Board of Global Ministries surveyed 600 Methodist women and found that one in every six [was] abused by [her] husband, specifying battering in at least one-fourth of these cases."[5]

"Whatever form the brutality takes," James and Phyllis Alsdurf, authors of *Battered into Submission,* write, "the fact that it exists unchecked in some Christian homes is a deep affront to our faith."[6]

In America, approximately four million women suffer an assault by an intimate partner annually,[7] and one-fourth of all women will experience domestic violence in their lifetime.[8] This report doesn't cover the unreported cases of emotionally abused women, who are called "sluts, whores, crazy, stupid" and humiliated in every way for control.[9] It is especially disturbing to find women at the shelter where I volunteer who gain absolutely nothing from their marriages. He's on drugs, so he takes her financial-assistance check. She has no rights as a wife. All she possesses is never-ending fear.

Why are there so many domestic-violence victims? Wired into our culture is the idea that men have the right to control and demean women. Don't we laugh during *The Honeymooners* when Ralph

Kramden threatens Alice: "One of these days, Alice—Pow! Right in the kisser"? Don't we still feel that love excuses all in *Carousel* when Julie, the battered wife, says, "It is possible, dear, fer someone to hit you—hit you hard—and not hurt at all"? How about the way Archie Bunker needles poor, befuddled Edith on *All in the Family?*

The O. J. Simpson situation graphically highlights certain complacent attitudes about domestic violence. O. J., like most males who strike their wives, was able to quietly get away with it. On October 25, 1993, Nicole Brown Simpson called 911 twice, saying O. J. was going to beat her. He had broken down her back door. Here is an excerpt of her conversation with 911, taken from the police-department recording:

> *911:* What's the problem there?
>
> *NS:* Well, my ex-husband...or my husband...just broke in...and he's ranting and raving...
>
> *911:* Has he been drinking or anything?
>
> *NS:* No, but he's crazy.
>
> Then later in the conversation, 911 asked, "What is he doing? Is he threatening you?"
>
> *NS:* He's ...going nuts.
>
> *911:* Stay on the line.
>
> *NS:* I don't want to stay on the line. He's going to beat...me.
>
> *911 (At the end of the conversation):* Has this happened many times?
>
> *NS:* Many times. [10]

Many times, and yet O. J. only incurred one small penalty for his *ninth* episode of violence against Nicole: probation, a term of community service, and a seven-hundred-dollar fine.

Nicole's tragic life prompted her father, Lou Brown, to establish the Nicole Brown Simpson Charitable Foundation, which raises money to fund shelters and educational programs for domestic-violence victims. Lou Brown says, "If a single life can be saved as a result of what we have learned since Nicole's death, our efforts will be worthwhile."[11] It is heartening that Nicole's tragic life has produced this positive response.

Abused women need our help—help that has been slow in coming from the church. Currently it is more difficult for many abused wives to find relief at church than in their communities. (Though by no means do all pastors ignore battered women's pleas for help, nor are all insensitive to this tragedy.)

WHAT IS WIFE ABUSE?

Experts define wife abuse as an assault on a woman's mind or body, meant to make her comply with her husband's will. The assault can be physical, sexual, verbal, or psychological. The methods include kicking; choking; twisting her arm; banging her head into a wall; shouting, often using gutter words to describe her body or her inferior intelligence; rationing money; and regulating her every action and move ("Iron my clothes *now!*" or "Get in here *now!*"). He may lock her in or out of her home, destroy her property, force her to do various sex acts (possibly with objects that cause pain), or continually demoralize her through intimidation and threats. An abuser may brutalize pets to terrify her; threaten to kill her, the children, or himself if she should leave him; or actually kill her.[12] (A man can become a murderer when his wife leaves him or he fears she will. He reasons, *If I can't have her, no one can.*)

The threat of physical abuse can be as terrifying as an actual incident and is defined as a form of psychological abuse. Susan, whose story is told throughout the book, says her husband often punched the kitchen cabinet beside her head. "That could be you," he'd say.

According to domestic-violence expert Lenore Walker, psychological abuse includes isolation. The abuser can create "a situation in which the family is isolated and the man's opinions and points of view are the only ones to which family members are exposed." He may rarely let his wife use the car, the telephone, or let her visit friends.[13] Often he times her trips to the store or church and beats her or accuses her of infidelity if she is late.

Caroline, whose story will also be shared, has suffered thirteen episodes of physical abuse in a five-year marriage. She claims emotional abuse distresses her more than physical abuse. "Once physical abuse is over, I never replay the episode—maybe it's too terrifying. But I redo the emotional abuse, ad nauseam. The more I replay it, the more real it is. I keep hoping to figure out why he said it."

The National Woman Abuse Prevention Project reports that a physically abusive event usually consists of three predictable phases:

Tension building: Stress causes him to start in on her, wanting to destroy her morale to raise his own. ("She's crazy, seeing other men, a terrible cook.") He blames her for all his problems, real and imagined.

Acts of violence: It may start with a gentle push, but physical abuse worsens over time. Wife beaters typically feel males are supreme, that they possess the right to "discipline."

The honeymoon: An abuser suddenly becomes sorry, crying real tears, promising to go to church, saying he will get counseling. He buys his wife gifts and she relaxes, thinking that finally everything will be all right. It probably won't. Now he's just one step away from repeating the cycle, the next time, more intensely.[14] His contrition may be genuinely felt, or it may be a ruse to get her back under his control.

Some men, inured to their violence, skip the honeymoon phase and switch between building tension and striking.

Unfortunately the cyclical nature of abuse feeds hope in a woman that *This time, finally, he's changed!* Good-time hopes can override the bad-time horrors. One woman says, "It was really cyclical actually, really incredible. And the odd thing was that in the good periods I could hardly remember the bad times. It was almost as if I was leading two different lives."[15]

But eventually a wife's faith that the abuse will stop withers, as do his statements of remorse. If she stays, a kind of emotional self-death occurs as he blames her for his abuse and she concurs.

In this book we will explore how victims and perpetrators alike can be treated and taught to maintain healthy relationships; though frankly, therapists report that perpetrators' reform rates (from all forms of abuse) are low. We will talk about what this low cure rate means to abused Christian wives, who dearly want to uphold their marriage commitments before God.

We will discover why women cling to abusive men, denying or

minimizing the extent of the abuse. Once women understand their own motives, they can work to break their obsessive attachments. Then we'll look at how the church, in a strange kind of two-step, joins these women's dances of denial. Churches deny because they reject the idea that their men (supposedly Christlike) would hurt women. Actually, we have a threesome on the dance floor. Abusers dance their denial to the lyrics, "It's not my fault. She's rebellious. She provokes me. I had to lose control!" Tragically, this dance is often misjudged as authentic.

Throughout the book, you will hear honest words about real people and their horrors. You will read some unpleasant information. But how can you really help if you don't know what abuse looks like, feels like, and tastes like deep down in the gut?

The first time I encountered wife abuse, I thought the wife provoked it. Vivian and Clark attended my Alcoholics Victorious group—Clark because he kind of wanted to sober up and Vivian because she was desperate for a sober husband. Vivian phoned one day, sobbing that Clark had kicked her down the stairs and was threatening to hit her with a plate. While Clark grabbed the phone to explain his side, I heard her screeching at him. I thought, *If Vivian wouldn't yell at Clark, he'd leave her alone.* Not true!

Christ says, "And you shall know the truth, and the truth shall make you free" (John 8:32). The truth will help women say no to abuse. The truth will educate pastors and laity on how to help victims and perpetrators of abuse.

We will explore two tales of abuse from two women: Caroline and Susan. Caroline, a mother of five, is married to a misogynist (one who hates, dislikes, or mistreats women) and lives in a million-dollar house. She would give all her possessions for one moment of love and peace. Susan is the ex-wife of a popular pastor who abused her physically and sexually for more than thirty years. Afraid to ruin his reputation, she never told a soul.

Throughout the book names and identifying details are changed to protect the safety of the women who have confided their stories. I thank each one for her help. They told their stories, although it hurt to remember, not for themselves but for you.

Rock meeting rock can know love better
Than eyes that stare or lips that touch.
All that we know in love is bitter,
And it is not much.

—Conrad Aiken, "Annihilation," st. 8

One

*T*he Lie-Detector Test

Fourteen months after Ed and Caroline Stuart married...

I closed the door of Miller-Dover, Inc., a professional polygraph service, feeling as if I had spun through a laundry cycle—detergent, bleach, and all. The corridor glistened from end to end, and I breathed deeply of its waxy scent, feeling relief. *Where there is wax there is order, cleanliness: signs that normality exists in this world,* I thought.

I wiped my hand over my forehead, still damp from the strain of the lie-detector test. I felt reassured by my perspiration as well. I was here—me—intact. But even though I had passed the test, I knew its graphed truth was not considered "proof positive" by all authorities.

While I waited for the elevator, I clutched Miller-Dover's nine-by-twelve envelope, fearful I would drop it, lose it, or fling it at someone and say, "Let's trade lives. You be me!" *It's so unfair,* I thought, tears stinging. *Why must I suffer the indignity of a polygraph to prove to my minister I have been beaten, while Ed sails along, a scot-free darling at church?*

1

Yet I also felt I had betrayed Ed by taking the polygraph. I hated to act against him.

I recalled the incident from the previous week with my pastor, Doyle Morris, that prompted me to take the polygraph. After I told Pastor Morris that Ed had kicked my chest black and blue, I pleaded with him to confront Ed. Doyle placed his hands on his desk edge and rolled back his chair until it, along with his grandfatherly frame, touched the wall. I knew in that process he had separated his mind as one would separate his legs, one half of his brain in my camp, the other in Ed's. I didn't know how he did it, but he could also both believe and disbelieve a person.

"Well," he started, "you say and Ed says—"

I couldn't listen to all that again. I didn't think I'd ever do this in front of any man. My face burned with shame as I fumbled with the buttons of my blouse to reveal a little of my chest. "Look at this."

Doyle looked. He winced. He then stared at his desktop. "I just don't know, Caroline. I've talked to Ed on two occasions about your claims of abuse. He says that you lie or exaggerate what happens. He says you sometimes self-inflict your wounds. I don't know who to believe."

"But isn't it obvious I've been attacked?"

"You may have provoked Ed. He tells me you behave like a wildcat sometimes, and he has to wrestle you in self-defense."

I quickly buttoned my blouse. I felt like trash. Tears flooded my eyes. "I'm not perfect, but I've never done a thing to cause Ed to hurt me like this."

"Does he ever hit the children?"

"No—but he almost hits them. I'm afraid one day he'll lose control."

"We have to be thankful that they've not been hurt."

Doyle hadn't quite said it, but his implication was that it was okay to hit me, but not the kids. Nearly hysterical, I rushed from the room, drove to the office of the chairman of our church board, told him that Ed was physically abusive, and opened a bit of my blouse. Though Porter was Ed's best friend, I hoped his role as a church leader would supersede his role as Ed's friend. "Ed beat me, Porter. I need you to talk to him about how wrong it is to hurt me."

"There are two sides to everything," Porter said, barely glancing at my bruised skin.

I studied his desk so I wouldn't break down. No clutter there. It held only an in-out file and an onyx pen-and-pencil set. A few papers lay before him. No clutter around anywhere. Not even a picture on the wall. Even Porter's gray eyes looked as if they were never cluttered with emotion. "I'm physically hurt. Ed can't possibly have a credible side."

Porter spoke kindly, but his eyes remained cool. "Ed's my friend. I don't want to get involved."

I felt as humiliated as I had in Doyle's office. *But it's Ed who should feel humiliated,* I thought. And Doyle. And Porter. Every last person who had not believed me should feel shame. I decided then to have the polygraph.

I stepped into the elevator and hit the first-floor button. High heels clattered along the shiny floor as a slim woman with a briefcase ran up. Her dress was tailored, yet it showed her curves. Her blond hair swung rhythmically, every hair cut in classy orchestration. Perfume and allure poured from every cell of her body. *She has it all together,* I thought. "Hold the door!" she called.

I watched the door slide shut. *Sorry, but I can't face you. I'm so glad Ed's not with me,* I thought with relief. He'd love that woman. She had just the kind of figure he couldn't take his eyes off. I realized I suffered from sick thinking, but Ed's constant leering had damaged me. I hated myself for looking at other women through Ed's eyes.

The brass elevator walls glittered like a golden cage. The walls seemed to represent my life. I lived in a similar cage, a million-dollar house overlooking the Ohio River in Louisville. Tears welled in my eyes as I stared at my blurry reflection on the golden wall: blond, a size-twelve figure, big eyes, and a wide mouth—vivid features that brought compliments. I was still all-right looking for forty-one, though what I looked like meant little. What good did it do to look okay if your husband abused you?

I hurried from the building to my car, where I calmed down enough to read the lie-detector results. "I, Caroline J. Stuart, voluntarily—without threats, duress, coercion, force, promises of immunity or reward—agree and stipulate to be interviewed and/or take a polygraph examination for the mutual benefit of myself and Miller-Dover, Inc."

Specific Investigation Questions

1. Are you lying when you say that without physical provocation, your husband has suffocated, choked, slapped, and kicked you in the past? NO. (Look at this, Doyle! No provoking! No wildcat!)

2. Are you lying when you say your husband has thrown you down and banged your head repeatedly on the floor on more than one occasion? NO.

3. Are you lying when you say that your husband has told you that he would kill you? NO.

4. On February 13 of this year, did your husband make you have sexual intercourse against your will? YES. (That is rape, Doyle!)

5. Have you ever in any way stalked your husband's ex-wife? NO. (Ed lied to you, Doyle!)

Tears spilled on the paper. Certainly only a fool would subject herself to the described abuse. I apparently was half-nuts, as Ed said. One thing I would not admit; I didn't deserve to be abused, as Ed said. Nobody deserved to be choked and bashed nearly to death.

I read the examiner's assessment of the test. "Throughout Mrs. Stuart's polygraphs there were definite indications of her truthfulness when she answered her test questions. It is the opinion of the polygraphist, based upon the polygraph examination of Mrs. Stuart, that she was truthful throughout the testing procedure and that she has been physically abused by her husband in the past."

I started the car and turned up the air conditioner, breathing in cold air to snap me into action. The kids had to be fed. The house had to be spotless before Ed returned from his business trip, or we would all pay. As owner of a commercial real-estate brokerage firm, which Ed had expanded throughout Kentucky, Indiana, and Ohio, he traveled frequently, but he seldom left his itinerary with me. The reason I knew he'd be back was that his tennis buddy had phoned to say they had a 7:00 P.M. court time at the club.

At home, I telephoned for an appointment with my pastor, cleaned for three hours, and said hi to Ed at 11:00 P.M. as he strode through the living room with his garment bag, briefcase, and gym bag. He looked tired, and I wondered where he had gone after tennis. He muttered hello and continued up the stairs to his bedroom, leaving a trail of hate. I ran upstairs to my bedroom and flung myself on the bed, weeping. At least he could have said, "How are you and the kids?" What was wrong? Why didn't I matter? Wasn't the house clean enough? Had the kids left something in the yard? Did I look awful? "Oh-oh," I moaned. You'd think I'd be used to this treatment. Not react! Not care! But I did care.

I wished that we didn't sleep apart at all, but Ed swore at me so often in bed that I lost more sleep than my health could take. Now we slept together only when he was in a decent mood. That would not be tonight.

The next morning, I watched my pastor with alarm as he read the lie-detector report in three minutes flat. *It's a bad sign that he whizzed through it*, I thought. His eyes turned wary.

"It shows I've never provoked Ed," I said quickly. "He hits me out of pure malice."

"Who is Miller-Dover, Inc.? Are they—ah—reliable? Not all these places are."

His disbelief stung. I had prayed all morning that Doyle would make Ed stop his violence. "No!" I cried in despair. "They operate in a shed and use a twenty-year-old machine!"

He spoke patiently. "I'm just trying to get the facts straight."

"This test is reliable!"

"I'm sorry, Caroline. It's difficult when I hear your side, then Ed's." He reached over his desk and patted my hand. "As a pastor, I'm very busy, and I wear many hats for many people. You realize we have twelve hundred members in this church, don't you? It really isn't easy for me. Everyone expects something different from me. I can only spread myself so thin, but I do the best I can. I'm sure it's like that with your five children. You do the best you can with all their demands."

My whole body was going crazy inside. I was almost losing faith in my story. I had to hear Pastor Morris tell me that I was abused and that I didn't deserve it. "Please believe me!"

"I'm sorry, but Ed's just as credible as you. I don't know what to think."

"Then pray to know the truth."

His facial lines deepened. "It's not a simple situation. I have to drop this matter. I don't want to discuss it with either of you again. I'll give you the name of another therapist. I suggest you and Ed try harder with this one."

"Never mind." The one Ed and I had previously consulted had listened to Ed, not me. I remembered how calm Ed was, how self-assured. I was crying and ranting on and on. No wonder the therapist believed Ed. He was the picture of mental health and civility. I was on the edge.

My legs plunked toward my car. I poked along the road, too discouraged to press the gas pedal with much force or even cry. *What do I do now?* I thought. My husband hated me, my pastor had rejected me, and (this was the part that disturbed me the most) my love for Ed was as strong as ever. I really had to be crazy!

Then I thought about how gorgeous Ed was (tall, a face like Paul Newman's) and how loving he had been while we were dating and how wonderful he still was at times, though infrequently. I would never get Pastor Morris's help, but somehow I had to find help for Ed and me. I remembered how Ed used to say, "You're so much woman, I have my hands full just looking at you." I wanted that Ed back full-time. When Ed was loving, my world could be no better.

Two years before Caroline married Ed…

I remembered the evening I had met Ed, when Dad and I walked along the hallway of a church, looking for a codependency meeting. Dad wore a suit and tie, and he had polished his shoes to a shine that reflected the hall walls. Dad, a retired professor who was as socially inept as he was brilliant, hoped to find a woman to date at the meeting. He had divorced my mother twenty years earlier because he couldn't stand her, then later he called it the biggest mistake of his life. I couldn't figure out his sudden urge for female companionship after living like a hermit for twenty years. He had worried me a lot in the past year. His memory had slipped, and he sometimes forgot where he was supposed to be going.

"You'll only meet dependent women here," I warned. "Some dependent women are real basket cases."

"I doubt that. We'll more likely find improved women here. Anyhow I like a little dependency in a woman. Your mother was too self-directed."

"No, she wasn't, Dad. She did everything for you, but you scorned her."

"Well, that's the past, little lamb. Let's look ahead."

I was there to support Dad and get a few tips on codependency, but certainly not to find male companionship; my divorce was not yet final. I still reeled from the breakup of my eighteen-year marriage with Pete. Although Pete and I were well known for our pro-life ministry, for years no one had known that he emotionally and physically abused the children and me. I had urged Pete to seek help from our pastor (at a former church) or a therapist, but he flatly refused. I finally gained the courage to tell our pastor about the abuse, hoping he could help Pete and me. Furious that I had broken our privacy, Pete became depressed and bitter, and he told the church board that my lack of submission had forced him to severely discipline me. The board and pastor believed Pete and drafted rules of marriage for us to live by. My list was long, detailed, and degrading, while Pete's was short, task-oriented, and businesslike.

My worst rule was, "I will limit my outside activities, beyond home and church activities, to five hours per week, and I will tell the pastor each week how I intend to spend those five hours. Any of the following activities will count toward the five-hour limit: political activities, meetings, media events, article and letter writing, speeches, and telephone activity." I was even told which rooms I had to clean each day of the week and given the names of seventeen men in our ministry and political circles to whom I couldn't talk unless Pete were present. That one really hurt, as I was utterly faithful to Pete in thought and deed.

As a result of the degradation I experienced through my church and my husband, I was diagnosed with posttraumatic stress disorder, depression, and codependency. Pete, in turn, fell apart before my eyes then walked out on the children and me.

Little did I know that night with Dad that at the end of the corridor was a man who would control me, beat me, ignite hostility in me, and turn me into a codependent basket case that would make Pete's abuse look like playtime.

After Dad and I found the meeting, I glanced around the group: Dad; five women in the blush of youth; several men, including one with an earring, one whose huge body slid beyond his chair, and on my right, Ed. I thought he was gorgeous: athletically built, gray-headed, and distinguished. Our leader read from our text, *Codependent No More* by Melody Beattie, then we discussed it. Afterward I was relieved that Dad didn't venture toward the youthful women. Instead he turned with me to talk to Ed. After a twenty-minute conversation, Ed invited me out for pizza.

"But can you take me home?" I asked Ed. "Dad drove me here."

"Certainly—of course."

"Have fun, sweetheart," Dad said.

"I'm sorry it didn't work out for you," I told Dad.

"It's just as well. I didn't like the meeting."

At the restaurant I learned that Ed was forty-nine, well-to-do, and a gourmet cook who could make boeuf bourguignon, a dish that I adored. He was separated from his second wife, had three children (two by his first wife, one by his second), had just invested two hundred thousand dollars in a farm venture, wore a Rolex, drove a Mercedes, had a boat, had totally white teeth (all real), and he was a committed Christian who sang in a choir. The one unpleasant fact we revealed (and glossed over) was that neither of us had received our divorces yet. Mainly, I felt flattered that this Adonis seemed to like me.

My relationship with Ed zoomed forward. He told me I was beautiful, intelligent, interesting, the most extraordinary woman he had ever met. On the second date Ed stated, "If I had met you first, I wouldn't have suffered two bad marriages with two ungrateful women." He bought me flowers and dresses and telephoned daily, sometimes talking until 2:00 A.M. I felt adored, and my mind lived somewhere over the rainbow. I even accepted an engagement ring from Ed when my divorce was final, though it disturbed my conscience terribly. How could I, a devoted believer, be officially engaged to a married man?

That was bad enough, but I became worried that Ed wasn't the Christian he claimed to be. After our engagement, he insisted we have sex, something I felt a believer wouldn't ask. I resisted, pleading that he not ask me to sin. He expressed a heathen philosophy that chilled me. "I want you." Followed by, "We're married in the eyes of God." Finally, I gave in, afraid I'd lose him. As a result, I refused to take communion, crying while the plates were passed, while Ed ate his bread and drank his grape juice in pagan peace.

Other events concerned me about Ed's profession of Christianity. One night at a seafood restaurant, under a romantic canopy of net and shells, Ed said, "Did I tell you about the most marvelous time of my life?" I supposed he referred to an experience with God or me. Instead he said, "I was at a real-estate convention [while still married to his second wife, Betsy], and I had an affair with a knockout broker." He elaborated on her incomparable features.

Shocked, I cut in. "That's immoral! What about Betsy?"

He said, "I had invited her. I suggested she get a baby-sitter. She should have hired one."

A Christian would not describe his best day as the day he had engaged in extramarital sex. Nor would he use one woman (the real-estate broker) to punish another (his wife) for not finding a sitter. The canopy lost its romance.

Another time at a pro-life banquet, Ed pointed out a speaker on the program sheet. "She went to my [former] church," Ed said. "She's really a hot number."

I expected a beautiful woman to walk to the microphone; instead, a teenager appeared and told us how she had given her baby up for adoption. Goose bumps broke out all over me. Had he lusted after this child?

As much as I hated Ed's brand of Christianity and lust for women, I kept his ring. If I broke up with Ed, God might present a truly fine man. But could I take the chance? What if God didn't? What if I couldn't get a job to support the kids? (My alimony would end in three years.) Certainly Ed would never lust after women when we married, I reasoned. After all, he had said that I was his ideal woman at least one hundred times. He loved me so much; it was incredible. He had even hired a full-time nanny so that I could be free to attend his business dinners and negotiations. He wanted me with him all the time.

But ultimately, what most bound me to Ed was love, full-blown Eros love: a mix of passion, heat, jealousy, anxiety, admiration, and addiction. I was as addicted to Ed as an alcoholic to his bottle. I shook at the thought of withdrawal. The rationale that buoyed me was that deep down Ed was good because he *sacrificially* would support my five children.

In June, two years after I met Ed, we invited one hundred guests to a lawn wedding at our million-dollar house. (We had bought it six months earlier, and Ed lived in the guest cottage, for appearances' sake). I wore a white gown, hoping its purity would cleanse my mind of the shame of marrying a man I had slept with. My guilt was not assuaged.

A wedding card from a close friend didn't help either. It was from Frances, who knew everything about my relationship with Ed, including his affairs and his aspiration to be richer than Donald Trump. Frances despised Ed's character, saying he would drag me to hell with him. She designed the card as if it were a contract between the devil and me. The devil, the grantor, gave me in marriage—for a price.

> This is a business deal that you are willingly entering into. I promise for the rest of your born days you will travel and meet many interesting people. You will partake fully and freely of all the pleasures this world has to offer. I conditionally promise you at least thirty or forty more years of this wonderful existence on earth. Then at the end of your days, you will join us and we will entertain you for all eternity. You don't have to sign this; all that we ask is that you keep doing what you are doing, keep going the way that you have freely chosen.

I tingled with horror. I knew my friend was absolutely right. Yet I banked on the fact that, as a Christian, God would forgive me for my sin. I also knew full well that we reap what we sow. I thought of that letter often in the years that followed.

CAROLINE'S ADDICTION TO ED

A woman's lack of money or dislike of being alone may tempt her into a relationship with a questionable man, but for Caroline, her major draw to Ed was her physical love; even the sight of him transfixed her. She was flattered that a wealthy man loved her—a mother of five, abandoned by her husband and a church. Only later did she learn that Ed was a narcissist, a person who loves only himself. He desired Caroline because it fed his ego to win a beautiful woman who attracted male attention.

Caroline's story is that of a love-addicted woman. Even now, after years of pain, she told me, "I will always love him. I am embarrassed to be this woman. I'm weak. My brain knows that Ed is a narcissistic personality type, and he will always justify himself by shaming and blaming me. He won't change. If there is such a thing as a classical love addiction, then I have it for Ed. Just like the alcohol addict, the only healing will come when I am geographically removed from him. His substance is still interacting with me and intoxicating me."

Dr. Susan Forward and Craig Buck state that love-addicted women like Caroline reduce or stop activities and friendships to devote themselves to their partners. Then, "as their world narrows, their need for their lover increases accordingly."[1] Pleasing Ed will become the most important activity in Caroline's life, replacing pro-life ministry, political speaking, and valued friendships. Then as her world shrinks, her need for Ed's love will intensify, driving her to desperation.

Following is a checklist that describes traits of abusive males. It is designed for women who are dating, but it can also help married women identify abusive husbands. You can also work through the following checklist for a friend or relative whose relationship you are worried about. If you answer affirmatively to eight or more questions, the man you specify is highly likely to be abusive.

Caroline answered the questions as if she were dating Ed. She responded yes to thirteen questions, but she says that if she had responded yes to all twenty-three before she married Ed, she would not have canceled the wedding. "I would have rationalized, *It'll be hard, but far better to be taken care of and loved than to be alone.*" Caroline's responses follow the questions.

Checklist for Spotting an Abusive Personality

___1. *He was physically or psychologically abused in childhood, or his father battered his mother.*

Yes, but not directly. He had a strict, Christian upbringing in the South, yet aspects of his rearing had to have harmed him psychologically. He was never allowed to be dirty. If his shirt was dirty, he was told in hateful bigotry that other races lived like that. Neither of his parents graduated from high school, and they felt their cleanliness differentiated them from the poor and especially the blacks whom their families had historically hated since slavery. Even today Ed is far more interested in one's cleanliness and race than one's character. He is not a college graduate, by the way. Yet most of his business associates are.

___2. *He has a violent streak or temper that is out of proportion to the incident in question.*

Yes. One time we were at a PGA tournament, and I had a tag sticking out of my blouse—unknown to me. Ed blew up and cursed like mad. "You've got a tag hanging out! You look like Minnie Pearl."

___3. *He makes contemptuous remarks about women.*

Yes. He never had anything good to say about his other two wives. The first was "stupid, lazy, messy." The second was "not supportive, a witch." He called women bitches or broads. He leered at young girls. He showed his contempt toward women when he reduced them to their body parts.

Author's note: Abusers commonly use vile language to degrade their wives. I have sanitized their language in this book to avoid sensationalism, but believe me, it is animalistic and vulgar.

___4. *He has a fetish for guns and other weapons and claims he keeps them around to protect himself from others.*

Yes. He had weapons: two rifles and bows and arrows for deer hunting. The arrows had four razor blades on the end, and I shuddered thinking how much pain they must cause a deer.

___5. *He uses drugs or abuses alcohol.*
No.

Author's note: But if you answer yes to this question, realize that when a man is drunk or drugged, the part of his brain that controls judgment and reason is impaired. Anything might happen to a woman if the man is predisposed to be abusive. Not all men who batter drink, but one study of four hundred battered women found that 67 percent of their abusers frequently abused alcohol.[2] As to drugs, in Contra Costa County, near San Francisco, police report that 89 percent of domestic-violence incidents to which they responded involved the increasingly popular drug methamphetamine.[3]

___6. *He commits acts of violence against objects or animals.*
Yes. A cat crossed Ed's path, and he went out of his way to kick the cat and hurt it. He caught a mole, and he snapped its neck. Cruelty to animals was fun to him.

___7. *He is jealous of you and questions you about time spent away from him.*
No. He was totally atypical here. He had no signs of jealousy, then or now.

Author's note: If you answer yes, realize jealousy is not a sign of love, but of distrust and insecurity. After marriage, a jealous husband may limit his wife's freedom, fearing infidelity. She may have to account for every moment apart from him, or else.

___8. *He becomes enraged when you don't listen to his advice.*
I don't know. When dating, I always listened to his advice. I was so codependent I wanted to please him and do all he said. Now he commands. He never advises.

___9. *He has a dual personality. One minute he's cruel and critical. The next minute he's kind and loving.*
Yes. He could be cruel to strangers and service people, but he

wasn't cruel yet to me. I was like a Mafia wife: "He's cruel to all, but me he loves."

___10. *He has a whirlwind style of courtship: getting real close, real fast. He sweeps you off your feet.*
Yes. It was totally whirlwind. Lots of cards, presents, phone calls, and vows of love.

___11. *His anger so frightens you that you try hard not to make him angry.*
No. He didn't get angry with me then. But, on the other hand, I tried to not make him angry because I loved him so much.

___12. *He considers himself a macho man.*
Yes, definitely. He had the guns and bows and arrows. He's a man's man. He does not believe in sweet talk and mush talk now that we're married. It was just for dating purposes.

___13. *You sense that you're being treated abusively.*
Yes. We lived fifty minutes apart. He never came to my house because he was such a busy man. His charm was so great I drove to his house and didn't see that he abused my time.

___14. *He's not above pushing or shoving you around when he's angry. Abuse during dating usually guarantees abuse during marriage.*
No. Nothing physical then.

___15. *He's extremely critical of you.*
Yes. Particularly of how I dressed. I have my own style of dressing: a variety of skirts, jumpers, and tops that are conservative and that I like to combine with colorful scarves. He took me to a fine dress shop and said, "Get what you want." I tried on Pendleton skirts, elegant Shetland sweaters, and wool jumpers. He said, "No, no." So I said, "You pick it." He chose *Dallas* and *Dynasty* dresses: and they were expensive and too revealing. He said, "Those are Mrs. Stuart outfits, and you are going to be Mrs. Stuart. The others are Caroline Johnson outfits, and they must go." This was three weeks after we met.

___16. *He's had a string of unsuccessful relationships or marriages.*
Yes. He had two wives and two long-term mistresses. He con-

vinced me that his other wives were horrible and that he never had the right woman before me.

___17. *He has very low self-esteem.*

No. If he had low self-esteem, it was well covered. Currently he thinks he is the best real-estate broker in the world. He believes he is gorgeous and invincible. For all the world, he looks like Mr. Together and Mr. Wonderful.

___18. *He believes men are superior and rule the roost; they don't have to consider women's ideas.*

Yes. He pressured me to sleep with him, thereby causing me to violate my relationship with God. My ideas didn't count; his needs did. I realize I gave the consent and didn't have to, but believe me, the pressure was intense. I was afraid I would lose him if I didn't give in. I lusted after him, and that did me in too.

___19. *He believes his angry outbursts should have no negative consequences.*

No. I loved him so much I never made him angry. I do remember him blowing up because I messed up a few things in his workshop, but he put aside his anger quickly. Immediately after marriage he started to blow up all the time. He says Billy Graham and the pope would have the same actions and outbursts; it's just human nature. No negative consequences are due from sin if you are a Christian.

___20. *He has an unusual relationship with his mother that borders on love-hate.*

No. I doubt he would define it like that, though he might hate her and not know it. He is not in touch with his emotions. But his mother is a martyr. She had outpatient surgery recently to correct a hernia. When they wheeled her into recovery, Ed's dad said, "I think I might go fishing this afternoon" (which is typical of how rotten he treats her). She said, "But I don't think I can skin the fish today." I got mad and snapped at Ed's dad, "For goodness sakes! Don't go fishing!"

___21. *He tries to control your life—what you do, whom you see, and what you think.*

No. Not then or now. He's too self-preoccupied, too busy with his own life.

___22. *He has used violent language or called you obscene names.*

No. Not until after we married.

___23. *He twists Scripture for his own purposes.*

Yes. He considered himself a born-again believer, totally forgiven. When he wanted me to have sex, he'd say, "Don't be so hard on yourself, Caroline—Jesus forgives." I never could buy his idea that God can forgive and expect no accountability in return.

If this checklist indicates that you date a potential abuser, share this information with a sympathetic pastor, professional counselor, and/or Christian friend. At this point don't panic over anxious thoughts about separation. Simply be willing to share your test results with someone you trust. Consider sharing an exploration. As the book proceeds, you will learn how to leave a dating relationship or marriage that threatens your safety.

PROFILE OF ABUSIVE MEN

You wonder what kind of man attends church on Sunday, attends a Bible study on Monday, and slaps his wife senseless on Tuesday. You're not likely to spot him in a group.

He can be a man like Ed, who is admired at church. He can be a doctor, a pilot, or unemployed; a salesperson, a drug addict, an actor, a teacher, a truck driver, or even a minister. Researchers, though, have identified two traits that wife abusers like Ed hold in common. First, they use fear tactics to control their wives and dominate them. Second, they aim to rule the world—at least their world—and their women according to rules of their kingdom. If you miss *their* mark, you get hit or yelled at.

The following are tactics abusers may use to force compliance, most of which Ed has applied to Caroline.

Tactics Abusers Use to Force Compliance

- *Coercion and threats:* If you don't comply with his demands he threatens to kill himself, harm you, or kill you. Ed (who has been identified as a narcissist) loves himself too much to die, so he threatens only Caroline with death.

- *Intimidation:* He puts on frightening displays of power: points guns, kicks pets, destroys your property, rants. Ed doesn't point a gun, but the other hostilities are standard behaviors for him.

- *Emotional abuse:* He humiliates you and puts you down. He blames you for everything wrong in his life. He tries to convince you that you're crazy. His aim is to call all the shots. That's absolutely Ed!

- *Using isolation:* He monitors your visits to friends and relatives—or forbids them altogether. You must account for time apart from him. This is typical behavior of abusers, according to residents of the shelter where I volunteer. Ed differs, apparently loving himself too much to care where Caroline is.

- *Minimizing and denying his abuse:* "I simply touch you and you bruise," he says. "I had to hit you to calm you down." Absolutely true for Ed.

- *Using children:* He threatens to report you for child neglect. He threatens to kidnap or harm the children. Ed criticizes Caroline's method of child rearing, while actively abusing her children.

- *Using male privilege:* He's the boss; you'd better comply. You'd better get his Cokes and beers. That's definitely Ed. He must rule Caroline for her benefit, in the same way whites had to own slaves for the slaves' benefit.

- *Economic subjection:* He decides who spends the household money and for what. He may refuse to let you work. You must plead for money. Ed seldom gives Caroline any money.[4]

These tactics do the job. Abused women tiptoe around the house to avoid wrath. One abused woman says, "I'm always wary. My husband plays 'gotcha.' He can hardly wait until he decides that I blew it so he can get me. The trouble is, I never know what act will *get* me."

Ed's number one specification for Caroline is "Be neat!" Caroline says, "Often his swearing woke me in the middle of the night. 'You're rolled up in the covers like a dog,' he'd scream when we slept together. We'd have to get up, refold the covers, slide carefully under them, and lie straight so they wouldn't mess up. Windows open at various levels bother him too. He nailed shut the girls' bedroom windows so he wouldn't see a jagged line. 'What if there's a fire?' I asked. He didn't care. Just so the windows were straight."

An abusive man strikes his wife or rages at her because he feels she is not meeting his needs, as he perceives them. For instance, he sees her talking to a friend on the phone. This means she doesn't put him first. Rage builds. If she doesn't put him first, he can't control her. More rage. As he strikes (either with words or fists), his inward thoughts might be: *Why is she treating me like this? I deserve better than this.* Afterward he might rationalize: *She provoked me. It's her fault. If she didn't spend all her time talking on the phone, I wouldn't have had to hit her.* Remember O. J. Simpson's comment about Nicole in his suicide note: "I felt like a battered husband." His domestic violence was her fault, not his. Her infractions were behind her *nine* calls to 911.

Men work up their rage on their own steam; the women they hit or humiliate do not cause this rage. They not only provoke themselves, they are in control of the anger and violence they have provoked. Rolf Bauer, Nicole Simpson's cousin, says, "O. J. beat [Nicole] up and put her in the wine cellar. O. J. then watched TV for a while and went back and beat her up some more."[5] Who was in control? O. J.? The anger? Circle O. J.

If anything, abuse is coldly premeditated, for it is not unusual for an abuser to disable his wife's car or rip out the phone wires before he beats her, thus trapping her before he attacks her. Note that Simpson had time to sit and watch TV and meditate upon when to go back and hurt Nicole again.

Though abusers retain control of their anger, they apparently have lost touch with many of their feelings. Dan Keller of the Indianapolis Salvation Army has led therapy groups for abusers for twelve years. He says, "Everyone knows that big boys don't cry. Abusers have been taught not to feel or have compassion. They shut down their emotions:

If I am jealous, I get angry. If am hurt, I get angry. Anger is my reaction—period."[6]

So when the mental rope the abuser used to tie his wife to himself slips, he gets angry.

Three Types of Abusers

Due to a variance in batterers' behavior and mental health, Amy Holtzworth-Munroe, a psychologist at Indiana University, identifies three types of abusers:

> Group one: men who infrequently hit women, who are usually sorry afterward, and who may at times feel empathy for their wives. These men are coercive and controlling though, and they blame their mates for their violence. Estimates are that 50 percent of [abusive] men fall in this group. These men are most likely to respond successfully to batterers' intervention programs.
>
> Group two: men who are intensely jealous of their wives and fear abandonment. They depend on their women, as do men in the first group, but have an additional need to control them through fear tactics. A husband of a woman at the shelter where I work is typical. He constantly accused his wife of sleeping around and phoned her ten to twenty times a day to be sure that she was home. He finally stuck Scotch tape outside of the door as he left for work. If that tape was broken, she was beaten.
>
> It is estimated that 25 percent of batterers fall in this group. They are most likely to threaten to kill themselves or their wives if they leave. These men are dangerous and most likely to stalk their wives after separation.
>
> Group three: dangerous men with antisocial personality disorders. These men display a pattern of violence beyond abusing women: violence that may have caused trouble with the law. Neil S. Jacobson, a marital therapist at the University of Washington, points out that acts of violence do not agitate these men but calm them and drop their heart rates. He says,

"They're like cobras." Twenty-five percent of abusers appear to be in this group.[7]

What kind of backgrounds do abusers usually have? Keller says, "Eighty-five percent of abusers in my groups have been abused as children or have seen it in people of authority." Children raised in violent households learn that violence is normal in relationships. As one abuser stated, "My parents had a horrible relationship. So it's kind of hard now to learn to have a good one."

PROFILE OF WOMEN WHO CHOOSE ABUSIVE MEN

Who are the victims, the women who endure physical and emotional violence? A bachelor I know defined them like this: "They're all masochists. I've known three abused women. I tried to help them, but they all stayed put. They wouldn't take it if they didn't like it." He expressed a view that I have heard often, from Bible study groups to casual lunches with friends.

Certainly Freud would have endorsed this bachelor's sentiments. Freud thought women suffered an innate masochism, a sexual perversion where one enjoys pain and humiliation. "Masochism...became for him an essentially feminine behavior and an expression of the feminine nature. As a result of Freud's influence, masochism, passivity and femininity became closely associated and were for many years widely accepted as accurate descriptions of basic female character."[8] Though Freud's view has been discredited, the effects linger in too many therapists' offices, endangering the minds and bodies of abused women who call.

In reality, one important reason women endure abuse is because they have little sense of what an appropriate male/female relationship is. Imagine that you are cutting out a dress for the first time without a pattern. You'd probably end up with a mess or at least a defective product. Similarly you need a good pattern to establish a good male/female relationship. As children, many abused women had fathers or other males who only displayed abuse of and contempt for their femininity. They had little opportunity to develop responses to love, approval, and fun with men. They may have learned at home that females were secondary to males, a lesson subtly displayed in derogatory comments ("Women: you can't live with them and you can't live without them.") or brutally displayed in blows to their mothers or themselves. Their fathers may have used their daughters' bodies as deposits for their lust, semen, and disdain for women. The lesson was: You are inherently unworthy because you are female. You are here for men's use, not for yourself, nor for God.

Why, you may wonder, does a woman marry an abuser? Dr. Vietta Keith, director of counseling at Cincinnati Bible College and Seminary, explains, "She may on a conscious level try to find someone who will give her what she didn't have from her father. But unconsciously, she is looking for someone just like her father so that she can recreate the relationship where she was traumatized."[9] Only this time around she will make sure things come out right.

Other factors that draw women to abusers are a high desire for love and approval (abusers usually pour on the charm initially); addiction to alcohol or drugs (which diminish judgment); dependent personality (they think his controlling manner means he is taking care of them); and passivity with males. As one woman says, "I felt I had no choice. Others had always run my life." Experts find that a psychologically healthy woman may marry an abuser as well; she may be blinded by love or by the man's importance, be pregnant, or need financial help. Even loneliness may be a factor. And of course, she may have no idea at all until after the vows are exchanged and his first verbal or physical blow rocks her to the core.

Although women of all social classes suffer abuse, women with family incomes under $9,999 experience more domestic violence than women in higher-income groups.[10] Dr. Rich Meyer, director of the Christian Counseling Center, notes also that women with higher incomes are more likely to hide domestic violence than lower-income women. "Abuse is the same animal with different spots, depending where the person's social/economic realm is. In a wealthy area abuse is more invisible to others but inwardly just as painful."[11]

Abuse toward women will not end until abuse is understood as obscene and the censure and punishment for abusers is raised to more appropriate levels. Abuse won't end until women feel free to tell. It is a bizarre dichotomy in our culture that an abused woman feels denigrated, a candidate for ostracism, while her abuser feels powerful, often beyond legalities and rules of conduct.

VIOLENCE IN OUR LAND

What motivates an adult male to victimize his wife or girlfriend? We know he may have experienced violence during his childhood, but he also may have learned how to be violent through the media, sports, and even his toys. The average child, for instance, views "8,000 murders and 100,000 acts of violence on television before finishing elementary school."[12] Children's cartoons "are among the most violent shows on television, often exceeding 24 acts of violence per hour and earning a 'high violence' rating from the National Coalition on Television Viewing."[13] Some cartoon shows are rated as "very high violence shows. *Looney Tunes*, for instance, has eighty acts of violence per hour and *Bugs Bunny and Pals* has sixty-eight.

Not all violence on TV, though, is equally graphic or cruel. And what one person considers violent another may not. It is true, as well, that old-time classics, fairy tales, and Scripture contain violent content. But the violence created for TV is more gruesome, graphic, and geared to reward the perpetrator. Formerly, it was common for negotiation, kindness, love, or forgiveness to bring satisfactory endings to a story, but now, fireworks of violence often signal *the end*. George Gerbner, dean emeritus of the University of Pennsylvania's Annenberg School of Communications, talks about "happy violence" that pays no price for brutality, giving the idea that evil is okay. "The historical, limited, individually crafted, selectively used and often tragic symbolic violence has been swamped by 'happy violence.'... Happy violence shows no pain or tragic consequences. It is a swift and easy dramatic solution to many problems, employed by good characters as much as bad, and always leading to a happy ending."[14] Happy violence even has a resurrection element; hitting hurts momentarily, and death doesn't kill forever. Cartoon animals and TV characters that were battered or killed last week rise again to play in a subsequent episode or a different show altogether.

What is the result? An elementary teacher says that several of her pupils thought it was okay to use physical violence at school because the Mutant Ninja Turtles were violent.[15] When some of these students marry, might they hit their wives to end arguments because the Mutant Ninja Turtles did? And might they look dispassionately at their bruised wives because they represent just one of more than one hundred thousand incidents of violence they have already seen? One abusive man said, "I didn't think the hurt lasted, so I didn't feel guilty."

It is likely today that the influence of parents and Sunday-school classes runs second and third to TV. In fact, a National Research Council study found that violent offenders watch an abnormally high amount of TV violence.[16]

Another source of violence is movies, where children may watch Arnold Schwarzenegger as the Terminator, as well as horror films and slasher films. And there are MTV videos, a hot item with teenagers. The majority of these videos portray a male-fantasy type of world, where women enjoy sexual cruelty and even rough handling by strangers.[17] Some of the women are portrayed as nymphomaniacs, and others give the message that "no" to sex really means "yes." After adolescents' brains are bombarded long enough with this trash, sexual cruelty to women seems normative.

Sports that emphasize winning at all costs rather than fair play may contribute to male violence as well. In some high schools, football players are instructed to "take out" (injure) an opposing player in an attempt to win. Certainly if this attitude inculcates itself in a male, he may later feel justified in "taking out" a woman, should she get in his way. In college sports a study of ten NCAA Division I colleges and universities showed that student-athletes composed 3.3 percent of the male population, but committed 19 percent of on-campus assaults.[18] This information is scary. Fortunately, many good coaches instill in student athletes the desire to win fairly, enjoy the challenge, learn teamwork, and have fun.

Finally, toy stores are hotbeds of violence. An advertisement on my desk promotes video games containing pictures of bared-toothed monsters and evil-eyed aliens that curdle my blood. Even some of the titles scare me: "Mortal Kombat," "Maximum Carnage," "Punch Out," and "Rebel Assault." To play these games, children maneuver a control pad or joystick. While children manipulate their control pads, they learn to control life through vaporizing their targets (often people) to win. Will male children absorb a control-pad mentality that okays hitting their wives to control the game of marriage?

We permit this display of "fun" violence to run rampant in our land because we want it, we love it, and it is cathartic. Christian psychiatrist Paul Tournier says, "Has not man always been fascinated by violence? Would violent shows be put on if they were not popular? And how could they be popular if there were not in the human heart an extreme thirst for violence, which in default of real violence which the law forbids, is satisfied to some extent by proxy, by identification with the criminals of stage and screen and the fighters in the arena?"

Two

*M*e Tarzan, You Jane

Caroline's honeymoon…

For our honeymoon we chose a little coastal town in Maine that could be walked from one end to the other in thirty minutes flat. It had a sandy beach, a fleet of fishing boats at the dock, and a gourmet restaurant tucked in a Victorian house, typical of the architecture of the area. I held Ed's hand as we walked along the beach, both of us clad in shorts. I had never been happier. The noonday sun perched above, burning bright, but cooled by the Maine air. As I swung along in step with Ed, I loved the day, I loved the air, and I loved being married to Ed.

I paid little attention to the female sunbathers until I noticed that Ed kept glancing at them. I fell silent as he completely turned his head to gaze at the young women we passed, apparently forgetting I was at his side. I felt hurt—and worried. I remembered the young girl he had called a "hot number" at the pro-life banquet. Ed suddenly stopped and glued his eyes on a curvy woman as she rose from her towel and stretched her arms to pull off her T-shirt, revealing a voluptuous form. I tugged at his hand.

"Stop it!" he said.

"Ed, let's go."

He shook his hand free and continued to stare.

This was our honeymoon. He should have been looking at me. Why wasn't he? I felt shut off from his love. "Come on, Ed."

He didn't move. Feeling jumpy and jealous, I stepped in front of him to block his view. *I'm being silly*, I thought. *He is my husband. Countless times he's said he loves me more than any woman on earth.* I hoped my voice was reasonable. "When we're together, could you please not stare at other women's bodies?"

"It's all in your mind," he said, starting to walk with me.

"It's not. You were at a dead stop—staring."

"You're letting your imagination run wild."

Well, maybe I was, I thought, as we continued toward the car to find a restaurant for lunch. In the parking lot we passed a young blond, bent into a paper clip form to apply suntan oil to her legs. Ed turned his entire body around to stare at her. *This isn't my imagination*, I thought angrily.

In the car I exploded. "You outright stared at two young women! Don't you realize how much this hurts me?"

"I don't want to talk about it."

"Ed, we have to talk about it. It's important to us."

I was vaguely aware that his face was red. More prominent in my mind were anxious memories of his prior affairs. I feared that he might one day be unfaithful to me. I remembered his first wife saying, "I got so desperate I sat outside a motel room waiting for Ed and his girlfriend. I left because the owner said, 'Honey, go home. Confronting him here won't help you.'" I remembered as well how Dad had divorced Mom because she wasn't ideal enough. *Will I end up like Mom?* I thought, my mind unglued. "Your eyes should be on me!" I cried. "I'm your wife."

Ed lunged at me and shook me like a rag doll. He then threw me against the car door. I yelled in pain. "You're sick!" he shouted. "Do you understand how sick you are?"

My shoulders throbbed. My mind could barely absorb that the man I loved had injured me.

He stared coldly. "I'm sorry, but you were hysterical. I had to quiet you down."

He reached into the glove compartment for the tape recorder he used for business comments and pressed the record button. "Speak. I want to prove to you later how sick you are."

I was too distraught to comprehend how crazy his recording idea was. "Staring at young women is a sin," I insisted.

"Nothing is wrong with looking, as long as there's no touching." He related a story about flying his plane over a boat containing three naked teenagers. He buzzed them several times while they waved in wild excitement.

I felt sick as I pictured the scene. "That moment didn't belong to you. You were a voyeur."

"Let me tell you reality. If Billy Graham or Pat Robertson or Jerry Falwell were piloting an airplane, every single one would circle that boat."

I shook my head. "Some men live for God. They put aside lustful thoughts. They don't spy."

Ed moved the recorder close to his mouth. "It's no different than looking at a magazine with nudes. You forget that humans are human. Everybody sins—look at Adam and Eve. We all screw up and lie, and, yes, feel lust—and don't tell me you haven't. What do you call sleeping with me before we married?"

"I call it sin!"

"Let's suppose it was, though certainly an understandable one. God forgives sin, as long as we say we're sorry. That's what the gospel is all about. Ease up, Caroline."

I stared at Ed, chilled by his manipulation of the gospel. *This theology, more than anything else,* I thought, *caused his affairs during his two prior marriages—and might in his third.* "There's more to the gospel than love, mercy, and forgiveness. There's accountability for sin, endeavoring to be holy."

"You can't possibly be so self-righteous, judgmental, and anti-Christian as to think God would kick anyone out of the kingdom who fails a little."

He pushed the recorder near me for my answer. I shoved it away.

Would his sick theology allow him to look, lust, and sample forever? I buried my face in my hands. I loved him. I wished today had never happened. "Let's go," I said.

I was too upset to eat out, so Ed ordered lunch through our hotel's room service. I showered while we waited, hoping to ease the pain in my shoulders and comprehend the last hour. *Most of the honeymoon has been sheer bliss*, I reasoned. *It's just the 1 percent in the car and on the beach that hasn't been.* I rationalized that bachelors notice pretty women, and Ed, newly married, had momentarily reverted. It wouldn't happen again. He loved me far more than his wives that he had cheated on.

I toweled myself dry, ready to eat, expecting the honeymoon to become perfect.

Caroline's first year of marriage...

We returned to the house we had bought before our marriage, a remodeled nineteenth-century Victorian with gingerbread-trimmed gables, a heated pool, and a master bedroom suite with a library tucked in an alcove. The state-of-the-art bathroom held two toilet stalls, a Jacuzzi for two, a shower stall, a sauna, and mirrored walls. It was as if the house were built for us. At the end of a trellised walkway was a maid's quarters that Ed had expanded and outfitted into a first-class office. What I loved most was our view of the Ohio River, narrowly curving by, a one-lane road for the boats and barges I never tired of watching. The library was next best, for I loved to read.

I was eager to buy umbrella tables for the poolside, install creative lighting for night swimming, and refurbish a few worn rooms. I had lived a middle-class life with Pete, and this house represented opulence. When we bought it, Ed insisted I supply the down payment, the one hundred thousand dollars I had received from my divorce settlement. It was all the money I had except child support. This bothered me, for he said he made well over a half-million a year. He said, "This makes us partners. I need my funds for my business—your business too, baby. It'll make us rich." So we bought the place in both our names with my money.

My honeymoon bliss (except for the car/beach scene) withered quickly as I learned that my children and I lived with a tyrant. Ed had specifications for the pool; no toys left in it, no leaves in the water, no splashing, and no talking loud because that would bother his clients. So my kids picked leaves from their feet before entering the water and swam in a soundless form of fun. Furthermore, all bikes and toys had to be stored in the garage immediately after use. He seldom spoke to the kids except to bark orders that widened their eyes in fright. He expected an equally spotless house: never laundry on the floor, never toys in the living areas, never dishes in the sink, and never kids using his copy machine, scanner, computer, or any other equipment in his office.

"Your demands that we be spotless are impossible with five kids," I said at breakfast one morning.

"It's how my mother kept house. If she could do it with hardly any money for cleaning products, you can."

"But there was only one child."

"She worked her fingers to the bone. You read too much." He tweaked my nose and smiled with his full lips, winning my assent to try harder.

Another requirement cropped up; he had to grocery shop with me because he considered me a spendthrift, specifying such extravagances as wheat bread. "Wheat bread costs twice as much as white bread," he said. "White bread is perfectly fine. My mother served white bread, and I was a healthy child."

I hated shopping with Ed. He snatched out food items from the cart that he considered frivolous, even cleaning products that would have shined up our house like his mother's. Ed also canceled my credit card and checking account because I forgot to give him my credit bill twice and we were charged interest. "This will teach you that a penny saved is a penny earned," he said, glaring up from his desk. "When you learn the basics of financial management and shopping, you can have a credit card and checkbook again."

Before I met Ed I had valued helping others; now I counted it an achievement if I pleased Ed. Wondering if my former character traits still existed, I would look in the mirror, especially into my eyes, to see how much humanity remained. My eyes looked hollow, I noticed, and new, faint lines radiated from the corners. I looked unhappy. Yet I loved Ed, and if it took climbing Mount Everest to please him, I would attempt it.

Before a business dinner one evening, Ed eyed me with disgust as I zipped up a plaid rayon dress with a white collar. "With all the effort you spend on clothes, how do you always end up looking like a total frump? Did you get that dress on a rack at a street sale? Put something sexy on."

I felt humiliated, yet stubborn, for I had bought the dress at a good shop especially for tonight. I twirled around, thinking he had missed its beauty. "Really it's cute, don't you think?"

"Take that dress off."

"But I spent a lot of time finding it."

"Knock it off! These contacts are important."

His demanding personality crushed me. I couldn't let him strip me of every right I had. "I'm wearing it."

His face flushed. He reached for my neck and plucked at the skin around my Adam's apple, like you might pluck a chicken's neck to find the vulnerable spot. Wincing, I stepped back. He grasped my arm and ran his fingers up and down my throat in a robotic action that scared me. He gathered my long hair and yanked it. "Go change, Caroline!"

"I love the dress," I insisted as tears fell. "The saleslady loved it, and Linda [my girlfriend] was crazy about it."

"Then you're not going." He left the bedroom, and I heard a door slam downstairs then his car starting up. I ran to the bathroom and watched my mascara draw black lines on my cheeks. Oh, I did look awful, I thought, seeing for the first time that the dress hung too loosely. I could have—oh, I should have changed!

Ed didn't speak to me for three days, and he slept in the adjoining bedroom. After work, he would leave in his car and return between 11:00 P.M. and midnight. Ed's withdrawal drove me mad. Did he know how much his abandonment hurt? I anguished as he walked by me as if I were invisible. *Will he ever love me again?* I thought. I returned the dress and put the money aside to choose one later with Ed, should we speak again.

About to go crazy, the fourth day of his silence I ran into his office, grateful that his assistant, Ridly, was out. I threw my arms around Ed. "Darling, I love you so much. Please tell me you love me. Please speak to me."

He kissed me and life felt like heaven again. "I love you, too, sweetheart. I've missed you. Let's stop all this ridiculous stuff. You're beautiful, you know." He fingered my hair. "I love the way it shines like gold."

In the following days I printed love notes in calligraphy, bordered with tender artwork. I dressed to please him, I hoped; at least he didn't comment otherwise. I carried snacks to his office. I cooked complicated dishes with unusual spices. He seemed happy. Life seemed grand. I lay in the hollow of his arm at night and slept like a baby.

One day I worked hours on a spaghetti sauce that required hand-peeled tomatoes. At dinner I said, "Please say you like it. It took a lot of time."

He tasted it, while I sat in suspense. His mouth screwed up. "It's horrible, Caroline. You put in too much garlic!" Judy, my five-year-old, who had hung around the kitchen while I prepared it, started to cry. I couldn't eat.

Ed finished his spaghetti, even though he thought it was horrible, then stomped out to his office. He returned in an hour and hugged me. "Oh, baby, let's not do this," he said.

"I should have put in less garlic. I forgot that you just like a bit." My world was perfect again.

Some days Ed spent the evening with me, but most nights he worked late. "I'm setting up a big business, baby," he explained, "so just stick in with me. Pretty soon I'll have more time for you." But he had increasingly less time. He started eating lunch in his office, which had a galley kitchen, fixing gourmet meals for himself and Ridly. "Sorry, baby, but I have to go over details with Ridly. You know he's my right-hand man." I'd smell the rich scents and think painfully, *Before we married he invited me to business meetings.*

Yet Ed said the magic words, "I love you," often enough to keep me hoping our marriage would work.

Nine months after we married, I inwardly groaned as we headed to grocery shop, an experience that I hated. In Kroger my tension mounted as he plucked out half the items I had put in the cart. I thoughtlessly grabbed four loaves of wheat bread.

"No wheat bread! " he barked, replacing them with white bread. "For Pete's sake. Can't you remember anything?"

I put in a name brand of spaghetti noodles. He replaced them with a generic brand.

"But they get sticky."

"Not if you add oil."

I put in two boxes of chocolate bars for the kids and me.

He grabbed them out. "Chocolate is expensive and addictive."

I put in diet soda.

"It causes cancer."

"But I'd like to stay slim."

Out it went.

I put in olives for the children's tuna salad.

Ed grabbed them. "I hate olives. You know that—you stupid idiot!"

At the checkout counter he snatched several more items from the cart. "We won't need these," he told the clerk.

I was furious. I needed those items for recipes and would have to buy them later from my child-support money; I still had no credit card or checking account.

Ed smiled at the clerk and swiped his credit card through the machine. The action tipped me over the edge. He had a credit card. He had the power. He had the money. He had the groceries he wanted. That big swipe told me, "I'll always win, Caroline, and you'll always lose."

I walked to the end of the checkout lane. *I'm a bright person,* I thought. *I run the household, not this dictator in his eight-hundred-dollar suit.* I had to prove that my inner self existed. I felt hot and weird, my head spinning like a top. I thought what I planned to do was crazy.

As the clerk loaded the cart, Ed looked my way. I raised my arms and did a perfect cartwheel. People gawked as I flipped to my feet. I ran to Ed and grabbed his arm so that everyone would know I was his wife. *Look, folks,* I thought, *this rich-looking man is not all he appears! There's trouble here!*

Ed's face was livid as he wheeled out the cart. In the car he screamed, "Anybody who does a cartwheel in the middle of Kroger is psychotic. I'm putting you away, for good!"

"I'm not a dimwit!" I yelled back. "I know what food products I need."

"You just wait, Caroline. One day, you'll flip your lid entirely, and I'll have you committed. You'll never see the light of day."

I felt horrible about the cartwheel, yet also relieved that I had announced my existence to myself. I flirted with the idea of saying I was sorry then ruled it out. Then Ed would never respect me. He would control me even more than he did now. I could not let him break my spirit.

Yet worried that the cartwheel meant I was losing my grip, I visited Dr. McClure, my psychiatrist, who had counseled me during my last marriage. He was thin, kind, and intense, with a habit of wiping his fingers across the lenses of his glasses. I told him about Ed's strict control over me then about the cartwheel. I started to cry. "It was a crazy thing to do. I'm frightened about myself."

"You were acting out, but it was an act of defiance that makes sense."

"It does?"

"God gives us a core sense that we're worthwhile. When Ed swiped the credit card, he represented ultimate control over you. He had the money, the power—you felt devoid. The only way you could fight back was nonviolently, so you chose to embarrass and shame him. It's called passive-aggressive behavior, a mild form of retaliation. Once in a doctor's office I saw a picture of a mouse shaking his fist at a huge eagle. It was titled 'The Last Great Act of Defiance.' Your act was brave but ineffective."

"Brave?"

He smiled. "Yes, and creative." Dr. McClure paused, his eyes darkening. "Has Ed ever hit you?"

"On the honeymoon, but it was a one-time thing." A rush of tears came. "It hasn't been easy with Ed, but I love him so much."

He touched my hand. "Caroline, he *is* abusing you."

"That's hardly possible. Ed and I love each other. It's so good at times."

"You need to consider your safety. If Ed hit you once, he'll hit you again."

"It's been nine months since he has. I'm sure he won't."

"At least learn the facts about domestic violence." He handed me the business card of a women's crisis agency. "Give them a call."

I took the card. "I don't know if I'll call. I do feel depressed, though, all the time."

Dr. McClure prescribed an antidepressant. I threw the business card in a trash barrel on the way to my car but filled the prescription that day. Little did I know the terrible consequences of that careless toss.

The next evening I carried a slice of pound cake to Ed's office. The trees wore the first fringe of spring, indicating that we'd soon be able to swim. The lighting I had wanted had not been installed: "Business first" was Ed's stand. I heard Ed's TV, and on impulse, I peeked through a crack in the curtains to see what he was watching. I was horrified. Ed sat on his couch masturbating while a sex scene played on the TV screen.

All the nights I had lain in bed wanting him, I thought, *and he was probably doing this.* The plate fell, shattering on the walkway.

After picking up the pieces, I dashed to our bedroom, threw on a gown, and sobbed in bed. When it came to sex, I had given Ed my all. In exchange for that, I expected him to be faithful. Finding out he masturbated was doubly hideous, for he had no excuse.

I can't fight an eighteen-year-old body on TV, I thought. *I'm starting to sag, and ahead lies more deterioration.* I ran into the bathroom, stared into the mirror, raised my hand, and slapped my face over and over. My cheek turned red and ugly. *If he hates me, I hate myself*, I thought. *I hate myself! I hate myself!* I sank to the floor, cradled my knees, and rocked and rocked.

Worn out, I got a can of soda and a cookie. I lay in bed and tried to read. In two hours I read half a page.

When Ed entered our bedroom after 11:00 P.M., his face was bland, no sign of unusual activity. As he put on his pajamas, I jumped from bed and brushed out a few cookie crumbs; Ed didn't allow food in bed.

"Did you eat in bed?"

"Yes."

"Pigs eat in bed. At home we never ate in bed. What kind of stinking pigpen were you raised in that you would eat in bed!"

"And you?" I looked directly at him. "Were you brought up to masturbate?"

His eyes burned on mine. "What are you getting at?"

"I peeked through your curtain." Tears fell, and I wiped them away. "I'm here for you—every night!"

"Every man does it. You're making a federal case out of nothing."

"Please don't cite Billy Graham and Jerry Falwell!" My voice broke, and I pleaded, "You know you could have come to me, Ed." He didn't speak. "We're practically newlyweds. This shouldn't be happening!"

He shrugged.

"You don't even feel guilty?"

He flipped off the lamp. "If I find one crumb, you're changing these sheets!"

A rocklike feeling that remains until today gripped my chest. I knew it was masochistic, but I'd stand in the walkway at night when the TV light flickered behind Ed's curtains, thinking, *I'm so old, a joke to him.* I began to doubt my womanhood. I trained at an exercise club, used a facial cream with vitamin A, and had a tummy tuck to tighten muscles from a prior surgery. My skin glowed as it hadn't in years.

One morning, I had overslept, and I scurried around with uncombed hair and no robe over my granny-style nightgown to get the kids off to school. After they left, I sat down to eat breakfast with Ed. He took one bite of bacon, chewed it vigorously, and glared at me. "You look worse than a dog. You even smell like a dog. You look at least fifty years old. I wonder why I ever thought you were pretty. You'd never be on any man's short list of looks."

I dropped my toast, ran, banged our bedroom door shut, locked the bathroom door, and slapped my face until my hand tired. My face stung badly, but the physical pain was preferable to the emotional pain it replaced.

A week later, Ed was all honey and compliments. Even the intimate evening at the Derby Dinner Playhouse across the river was Ed's idea, and as he reached for my hand over our table, I tingled like a schoolgirl. "I love you," I said.

Our server appeared, a tall, lovely blond. Ed's eyes went wild, and his gaze followed her from table to table. Our evening was totally wrecked because of his infatuation with the waitress.

I confronted Ed at home. "You went nuts over that Swedish giant!"

He hung his pants, then ran his fingers down the seams to preserve the crease. "Your mind's in the gutter as usual. If I'm not absorbed with you every single minute, you go crazy! I've told you before—if you're polite to a waitress, you get good service."

"It's common courtesy to look at whom you're dining with—not constantly at a waitress!"

"Cut it! Now!"

"You ignored me!" I screamed.

He called me every possible degrading name, forging me into the lowest dominator of human life. His neck veins pulsed. He grabbed my arms and yanked me to his chest. He placed his hands around my neck and pressed his thumbs on my windpipe. I couldn't breathe. My vision blurred. I dug my nails into his face, then my strength failed and my arms dropped feebly. *Let him do it*, I thought. *What use is life if the man I love wants me dead?* The room darkened. Lights flashed in my head. Then my body floated away in darkness.

When I regained consciousness, I was on the floor, sitting between Ed's legs. I gasped for air, but it didn't reach my lungs. My windpipe felt raw and constricted, as if it were badly damaged. I felt the fear of knowing I would never breathe again. I continued to struggle for air. Ed pounded my back to revive me. Finally, a thin stream of air reached my lungs.

Ed cradled me. "Dear God, I almost killed you." His tears bathed my face. "Are you all right, baby?"

I coughed and threw up.

"Forgive me, sweetheart," he begged. "Oh, darling, I love you so much and look what I almost did. Please, please forgive me. It will never happen again. I don't know what got into me. It just hurt me that you didn't trust me at the dinner theater."

I forgave him immediately. He was so contrite. *He must truly love me*, I thought. The man who choked me was not the real Ed, but a man exhausted from overwork.

My neck was swollen and purple. I felt ashamed—inferior because my husband had choked me—and I wore a scarf to hide the bruises. For three weeks Ed brought me flowers and candy, and one day he presented me with a figurine of a dancing couple. The figurine represented a night we had waltzed under the stars, looking in each other's eyes, totally in love. I placed the figurine on my nightstand. *That figurine stands for the truth*, I thought.

If so, then why did I visit Dr. McClure and tell him that Ed had almost strangled me?

Dr. McClure's response was to contact Ed and demand he attend my next session. At that session, Dr. McClure coolly appraised Ed. "You could have killed Caroline in three seconds flat. If your thumbs are placed correctly, you immediately crush the windpipe."

Ed's gray eyes hardened. "While I have you here," he said, "can I ask you a question? Why does my wife always dress like hell?"

I stared at Ed in shock. Dr. McClure's mouth dropped, unable to speak through Ed's rampant indifference to me. Finally, Dr. McClure stuttered, "I—uh think she dresses just fine."

At home, Ed led me to his office and handed me a photograph of the scratch marks I had left on his face when he choked me. "I had it taken the next day. I've shown it to my friends to prove you're a madwoman. You hurt me far worse than I hurt you, baby. Show this to that shrink. It's this photograph against the word of an insane woman. Ask any clerk at Kroger, sweetheart, if you're not deranged!"

I felt as if Satan stood before me. The air got thick and hot.

"I've got copies in my safety-deposit box. It won't do you any good to destroy it, baby."

My world fell apart. Sobbing, I ran to our bedroom, locked the door, phoned my mom, and told her Ed had almost killed me.

"Are you sure?" she asked. Mom believed that a wife must love her husband, no matter what, and that's why she had loved Dad, even when he treated her like dirt. She also believed Ed was a king of the world—so handsome, so rich.

"Mom, I *am not* making it up."

"Of course not, sweetheart. But sometimes little scuffles seem more than they are. You have a lovely life, and if I were you I'd devote myself to enjoying it. Arthur [her second husband] gets testy, but I humor him."

"Arthur's an alcoholic—a total waste." Mom had a compassionate nature that saw the best in everyone, even Arthur. He had a prize in Mom but didn't know it.

"You're only saying that because you're hurt over Ed." Mom paused. "You're not calling the police, are you?"

"No."

"Did he really hurt you?"

"Yes."

She continued vaguely, "Be careful and don't scuffle anymore, and if Ed hurts you again, then you should call the police."

That support from my passive mother showed real caring. "I don't think this will happen again. It was too extreme."

"I hope nothing happens to your marriage. Ed's such a nice boy."

It was at this time, when my emotional pain level skyrocketed, that I started to overeat. I'd bring a sack of cookies or another food into the bedroom, lock the door, and eat. That took care of the pain for a while.

Ed assaulted me twice in the next few months.

On the first occasion, he ordered me to the pool after the children had finished swimming, interrupting my telephone conversation with a friend. I followed him out with my hand over the receiver. "Look!" he yelled. "There's a water raft and goggles in the water. There's food on the table. Pool toys and food cannot be left in the yard!" he yelled. "Your filthy kids have violated that rule three times in four days! Where are the dirty little pigs?"

"The children are cleaning their rooms. Just let me finish the call."

"Clean up this mess now! Hang up!"

"Just give me a minute."

"I knew we shouldn't buy a place with a pool, not with that rattrap group you're raising."

"Ed, just let me say good-bye."

"Say it."

"I want some privacy to say it."

It was just a chat with a friend, but his controlling manner drove me to protest. While I ran to the kitchen, Ed followed so close behind that his foot hit my heel.

"Just one minute alone."

"No."

As I pressed the off button, I anxiously watched Ed's neck veins enlarge. "I'll clean the pool now," I said.

It came so quickly. I didn't expect it until he raised his leg. He kicked me to the floor and banged my head against the tile like a vase he swore to shatter. I screamed. Then fearing he would kill me, I made my body go limp, hoping to startle him into thinking I was dead. He released my head. As I heard his footsteps retreat, I opened my eyes a crack to see if he looked back. He didn't.

I struggled dizzily to my feet. *He doesn't care at all about me,* I thought. Though my head throbbed, his disregard hurt more.

Ellen, Kay, and Judy, my youngest children, ran in crying and screaming.

"I'm okay," I said. "I just can't talk very well. I'll lie down, and I'll be all right. If I'm not okay, I'll ask you to call the doctor. But please let me lie down alone." I looked at Ellen. "Please bring me some aspirin."

My pain lasted for three days. I didn't go to the doctor, because I was afraid he would ask questions that would lead to Ed's arrest. If that happened, I knew Ed would leave me. During this time, Ed never mentioned the incident. *What have I done to make him hate me?* I thought in anguish. *What can I do to make him love me?* The questions drove me mad.

The next assault occurred in our hotel room at a Christian convention in Dallas, attended by one thousand Christians. The night's talk and banquet had been the final events of the three-day convention, which had been great so far. After the talk, Ed rushed for the exit with me hurrying after him, wondering why he didn't stay to talk to our friends. He slammed shut the door to our room.

"You embarrassed me to the maximum," he yelled. "Everyone gawked at your clapping and shouting, 'Yes, yes! That's right!' Particularly Mel. [Ed hoped to sell Mel an office complex.] Your antics identified me as one of the foolish husbands of golf widows the speaker joked about."

I dropped into a chair and sighed. "I wasn't identifying you. I was simply enjoying the talk. So were the other women."

"You shot the hell out of my chance to get Mel's business. Did you see how he went the other direction from us immediately after the talk?" Ed threw his suit coat on the bed.

"I wish golf were your problem! I would love it if you paid half the attention to me that golfers pay golf widows!"

"I *am* demanding you apologize *right* now, Caroline!"

"No! I did nothing wrong."

His face swelled and turned red. "Apologize!"

"All the other women were clapping. I would love to apologize, but I can't think what for."

His large frame tensed, ready to pounce. My heart thumped with fear. He yanked me from the chair and socked my chin, snapping my head back. "Please," I begged, "please don't."

He threw me on the floor and pinned down my arms with his knees. I yelled for help. He clasped his hand over my mouth, while his other hand sought my throat. I thought, *This time for sure, he will do it.*

My head roared as the air turned black. I vaguely heard someone knocking. The next clear image was of two security guards with pulled guns. The shorter one lifted me from the floor and sat me in a chair. "What's going on in here?"

Ed said, "Nothing."

I spoke in raspy voice. "When he gets mad, he hurts me."

"Are you all right?"

"Yes."

"What happened?"

"He choked me."

"Do you want another room?"

Ed snapped, "She does not!"

"We can call the police."

"No, I'll be okay," I said, certain their intervention would prevent further violence. "How come you came?"

"A guest heard you scream and phoned."

The guard curled his lips at Ed, as if he were scum. "If there's another incident, we'll have you arrested."

The guards left, and Ed changed for bed. "You told the security guards that when I get mad, I hurt you. A more truthful statement would have been: You acted like a fool during the speech to ruin my image. You do that *so* often that you ignited such anger in me that you made me explode. Even when I begged you to apologize, you didn't. You tricked me into a rage, and I had to hurt you to stop your hysterics. You're a masochist and very sick!"

"How can you talk like that?" Tears falling, I grabbed my pillow, grabbed the key off the dresser, ran from the room, and lay in the stairwell, sobbing well into the night. Then I returned to bed. Ed was sleeping quietly.

Three days after returning home, Ridly, Ed's assistant, phoned. "Ed left for a business trip. You can pick up an itinerary in the office."

"But he didn't say good-bye!"

"Perhaps he was rushed. I'm sorry, Caroline—truly."

I slammed down the phone, ran to my bourbon bottle that I'd hidden in our bedroom, and gulped at it. It stung, and I choked. The habit was new. I had bought the first bottle after Ed banged my head in the kitchen. I had never drunk hard liquor before this marriage.

I curled up in bed in the fetal position and wept until the liquor lowered my pain level. I hated that I had not prayed to God for peace but had given that job to liquor.

WHY DOES AN ABUSED WOMAN STAY?

Why does Caroline stay? Why does any abused wife take all that pain? *Why?* The fact is that abused women stay for a variety of reasons, a mix as individual as each woman.

Caroline says, "When the abuse gets bad, I don't stay because of remembering the good times. I don't stay under the delusion that he'll come back. I stay because I'm terrified of abandonment, of being alone, of not being able to make it alone. Anything, even staying with this man, is better than being alone. My fate would be on my own shoulders. It would just be my kids and me. That's so terrifying that I stay. Then I justify why I stay. That's where the good-memory stuff comes in. I tell myself, *Ed's not always so bad. If I could just keep my mouth shut, he'd be better. If I could keep the house cleaner, he wouldn't be so mad at me. If I were slimmer, he would love me more.* It is not a deluded love but rather a justification of my fears of abandonment. It's a misplaced hope that, if I tried harder, things would go more smoothly, and at least I wouldn't be alone. But I'm embarrassed to be this woman who can't face life alone."

The majority of abused women hate to tell us the magnitude of their abuse because we then demand to know why they stay. If an abused woman is unable to explain *why* to our satisfaction, she feels judged, stigmatized—a weakling without the backbone to act on her own behalf. If we leave the encounter at this point, we have not helped her a bit. Our first question when a friend confides abuse should not be, "Why do you stay?" but, "What can I do to help you?"

It is reasonable to try to determine why a friend stays with her batterer, but it is important to process this information in a nonjudgmental way. The following material should help you better understand an abused woman's reasons for staying. The priority is to support her, whether she decides to stay or leave. For instance, if a friend stays for economic reasons, you or your church can offer her the financial help she needs to separate from her husband. If she stays because she is addicted to her abuser, then your best help is to provide information on wife abuse and allow her to decide to stay or leave without your input.

SHE IS ADDICTED TO LOVE

Caroline states, "I'm a love addict. I would rather be with Ed, even though he hurts me 90 percent of the time, than any man on earth. The 10 percent of the time he's nice is the closest to heaven that I've known. My soul latched on to this man, and I am praying that he will keep me. But he has no heart, no soul."

Pia Mellody, author of *Facing Love Addiction*, describes love addicts. They "focus almost completely on the person to whom they are addicted; they obsessively think about, want to be with, touch, talk to, and listen to their partners, and want to be cared for and treasured by them."[1]

A love addict craves a total bonding with her husband that no person can give, much less an abuser who by rule avoids intimacy. But in her obsession to be intimate, she may relentlessly question him; cling; cry; read his personal papers, letters, and checkbook; or telephone his friends to learn about his past. Her primary terror is not his violence, but his departure. She doesn't adore a real man with his faults and attributes, but an ideal man, one she fabricates, invests with power, and worships like a god. She well knows the reality of the cruelty of her creation, but she ignores it.

Ultimately, though, it is likely that his unrelenting violence will destroy her addiction and love.

She's Hooked by the Cycle

It is not usually wham, bang, pow right in the kisser, ma'am. It's usually flowers, charm (abusers can pour it on), love, declarations that "You are the most ideal woman in the world"—then pow.

Susan Forward and Joan Torres, authors of *Men Who Hate Women and the Women Who Love Them*, say, "Nothing bonds a woman to a misogynist more addictively than his swings back and forth between love and abuse.... The mixture of not knowing when she will be loved and when she will be abused keeps a woman hooked in and off balance."[2] She hopes against hope that the honeymoon phase will settle in permanently.

Marianne, a victim of emotional abuse, graphically states this hook. "Whenever my husband was cruel, he would drop to his knees and beg for one more chance. My nerves would be shot. I would think, *If I just say okay, then this tension will go away. He'll be nice for a while—maybe for good.*"

Eventually the honeymoon phase shortens as a husband becomes habituated to his violence and his conviction that his wife provokes it. If he also convinces his wife that she is to blame, he has her hook, line, and sinker. He can discard the honeymoon phase altogether. He doesn't need it. The honeymoon was simply a ploy to regain control of his wife after his violence broke that control.

He Threatens Her

She believes him when he says, "I will kill you if you leave!" Her belief is, in fact, well-founded. Barbara J. Hart, staff counsel for the Pennsylvania Coalition against Domestic Violence, says, "Women who leave their batterers are at a 75 percent greater risk of being killed by the batterer than those who stay."[3] My local newspaper carried the story of a woman who had stated on a court questionnaire that her estranged husband would eventually kill her. She was right; he did.

While serving as a court advocate for battered women, I attended an arraignment at which a man's grisly description of how he would kill his wife terrified me. I can only imagine the fright this woman felt continually. If her abuser later pressured her to come back, might she have complied to try to avoid a horrible death?

Some men threaten to kill themselves to prevent their wives from leaving. Abby McFarland, an actress during the nineteenth century, described her fright over her abusive husband's suicide threats. "He would snatch my scissors from my work-basket, and, tearing open his [shirt], he would brandish them about, swearing he would 'let out his heart's blood' before me."[4] For a while his ploy worked. Eventually she divorced him, but not without paying a terrible price. He later killed her fiancé.

Abusive men may even threaten to kill their children if their wives leave. This device to entrap often works, for wives know their abusers' brutality, so they know these men mean business.

HER CAPACITY TO ACT ON HER OWN BEHALF IS DIMINISHED BY ABUSE

Caroline explains how verbal abuse so debilitates a woman that she can't plan for her children's or her own safety. "It's like a ramrod on your psyche all the time when someone is telling you how stupid, old, fat, and ugly you are. It's like the Chinese water torture, as it wears away at your self-esteem, and you are too paralyzed to leave. All your energy is going toward your survival, and there is no energy to think about moving or making a move. You are always coping with what he has defined you as then. You are always boomeranging from the hurt. I don't think anyone can just say, 'Honey, leave.' She just may not be able to do that."

The ties that bind Caroline to Ed are not formed in love, but are braided from fear and battering and control and an obsessive infatuation that Caroline calls love. Her attachment to Ed has become so nearly instinctual that it is almost as if her mind has been kidnapped— and in a way it has. Trauma expert, Judith Lewis Herman, M.D., explains what it is like to be held captive, whether by gun or by abuse. "In situations of captivity, the perpetrator becomes the most powerful person in the life of the victim, and the psychology of the victim is shaped by the actions and beliefs of the perpetrator. He enslaves his victim through exercising despotic control over every aspect of the victim's life."[5]

Barbara Hart speaks about this despotic control, citing a dentist's four-page list of rules for his wife. Among them are: "Look adoringly at me when we dance, no matter how you feel. If you're sad, don't ever let me see it. You can't use the phone, unless I say so. You can't leave the house, unless I say so." Later, his list convinced a jury that he was a wife abuser, and he was sentenced to jail. Hart says, "It is extraordinarily shocking that most batterers know all of these rules of coercion, of degradation."[6] These ties that bind.

Martina, a frightened-looking woman at the shelter where I volunteer, tells about her tyrant. "My husband wouldn't let me have a dresser drawer. He broke my brushes so I couldn't fix my hair and look nice. He was afraid I'd cheat. He smashed my glasses, and at the grocery store he led me around like a blind woman. He wouldn't let me have a purse." She blinked helplessly. "I'm afraid to leave the shelter. I can't remember how to take a bus. I worry I'll have to go back to him just to get along."

She's Financially Dependent

"I'm just about tired of living," Bobbie told me, fighting back tears. Though only twenty-seven years old, Bobbie had already undergone three miscarriages, an operation for cancer of the cervix, and five years of physical abuse from her husband, Ray. Finally, after he opened his pocketknife and threatened to kill her, she fled.

"The hardest part is finances," she says. "When I had the cancer operation, I was left with a bill of three thousand dollars. I've tried to pay it off at fifty dollars a month from my paycheck. [Bobbie nets two hundred dollars a week from her waitress work at a country club.] I don't see how I can pay the hospital. I don't see how I can pay rent or keep up my car. I have an appointment at Welfare. I hope they can help. I want so much to leave Ray and go up in the world. But can I?"

The average woman's standard of living drops by 73 percent in the first year after her divorce. In addition, only 58 percent of mothers with custody of children receive child support. Of these, only one-half receive the full amount the court awarded. A woman will only earn seventy cents for every dollar a man earns.[7]

Moreover, an abused wife may be reluctant to live with relatives, not wishing to burden them or endanger them if her abuser stalks her. A woman may see no recourse but to remain with her abuser.

SHE WANTS TO PRESERVE HER MARRIAGE

Far too frequently, a woman's church expects her to work out her marriage, even if it's abusive. One woman says, "I am a Christian woman who is still feeling the judgment and criticism of the church for leaving an abusive relationship. My husband was welcomed by the church with open arms. When I left, my name was taken off the roll. My pastor never asked why I left until years later. He still felt I should have stayed and worked it out."[8]

James and Phyllis Alsdurf, authors of *Battered into Submission*, surveyed pastors to learn what level of violence would justify a woman's separating from her abuser. "One-third felt the abuse would have to be life-threatening. Almost one-fifth believed that no amount of abuse would justify a woman's leaving, while one in seven felt a moderate expression of violence would be justification enough. The remainder interpreted 'occasional' violence as grounds for leaving.... However, only 2 percent of the pastors said they would support divorce in situations of violence."[9]

The Alsdurfs note that to expect a woman to endure abuse sacrifices the humanity of women to the institution of marriage, a type of viewpoint Jesus condemned when he said, "The Sabbath was made for man, and not man for the Sabbath" (Mark 2:27).

Marriage was created for mankind, not mankind for marriage. A person's basic needs for food, housing, peace, and safety always outrank any institution. David illustrated this when he ate consecrated bread, lawful only for priests to eat, because he was hungry and in need of food, a policy Christ endorsed (see Mark 2:25–26).

She Feels She Deserves Abuse

The National Council on Child Abuse and Family Violence reports, "Some women feel they 'deserve' mistreatment. They have been brought up to believe that women are weak, inferior, and should submit to men in return for financial support."[10] These women may have witnessed domestic violence as children, and they think, *This is the way life is meant to be for a person like me.*

At the shelter where I work, one of the most important things we tell women is, "No one deserves to be abused."

She Wants to Preserve His Reputation

A woman married to a professional may fear she'll ruin him if she exposes his abuse. Susan secretly endured sexual and physical abuse to protect the reputation of her husband, a respected pastor. She says, "He was looked upon as able, articulate, and well-organized. Everyone thought he kept in touch with God. I didn't dare pull that down." As we will see, her protection brought her to the brink of suicide.

If Susan had sought help, would she have been believed? Probably not. Many pastors are thought credible after their wives report misconduct, while their wives are often considered liars and troublemakers—and they are blamed for maligning their husbands. This subject will be covered in another chapter.

She Hopes to Reform Him

In James and Phyllis Alsdurf's study of nearly one hundred abused women, they found that "seventy percent...agreed that it was their responsibility to save their husbands from themselves."[11] Subjugating their own needs, the majority of abused women returned love for violence, hoping their love would cure their husbands. Constance Doran, who counsels battered women, comments on this missionary syndrome. "It keeps women locked into an abusive relationship. They feel that if they just hang in there long enough and turn the other cheek one more time, then he will change. And women are particularly encouraged to do this in the Christian community."[12]

Glenda, the product of a happy childhood, felt she had a reserve of love from which to redeem her abusive husband. Whenever he hit her, she forgave him on the spot. But she miscalculated her abuser's ability to hate. For all her efforts, when she finally left him, he nearly stabbed her to death in retaliation.

An abusive man is not violent because he is deprived of wifely love, but because he chooses to be violent. Deuteronomy 30:19 states this choice to do good or evil: "I have set before you life and death, blessing and cursing; therefore choose life, that both you and your descendants may live."

It is the abuser's choice to hit or to use coercive tactics to control his wife. Trying to love a violent man into meekness is like trying to spoil a spoiled child into goodness. The abuser and child think, *What I do must be okay because I still have my power and I'm still so loved.*

SHE NEEDS MONEY FOR DRUGS OR ALCOHOL

An alcoholic or drug addict may endure abuse because her abuser supplies the money for her addiction. Kelly, a mother of three, now sober for nine months, says, "I was always drunk and mixed up with an abuser. I don't remember a man who didn't hit me. My mind was in a fog most of the time. Basically, I stayed because I needed the drugs."

Let me warn you: If your husband is an addict, his judgment is impaired when he is high, and he is dangerous. Rose Marie, a director of a shelter, notes how crack (commonly used by drug addicts) affects abusers. "Crack abuse causes abusers to inflict more serious injuries. The women we house today are more violently abused than formerly. Their bruises are often visible. We have women with gunshot wounds, women on crutches."

If you live with a violent addict, seek immediate help. A list of organizations that help is found in Appendix B.

On the other hand some women turn to alcohol or drugs in response to their abuse, then become addicted. If you suspect you have a substance-abuse problem, ask yourself the following two questions:

1. Do alcohol, drugs, or prescription medication interfere with any aspect of my life?

2. Do I feel I must have alcohol, drugs, or prescription medication on a regular basis?

Yes to either question indicates an addiction problem. In this case, Alcoholics Anonymous, Narcotics Anonymous, or private therapy can help you kick your addiction. You cannot effectively deal with your abusive situation if drugs confuse your mind.

SHE BELIEVES CHILDREN NEED THEIR FATHERS

The price of staying with an abuser for the children's sake—because he's reasonably good with the children or because, though he's a terrible father, that's better for the kids than no dad—can be high. The National Coalition against Domestic Violence reports that as violence increases in a home, children "experience a 300 percent increase in physical violence by the male batterer." In addition to danger to the children's bodies, there is danger to their minds as they absorb their dad's relationship tactics: *It's okay to yell and hit to get your way. It's okay to mistreat people.*

Even if children are not directly struck, watching their fathers violate their mothers physically or verbally is a terrifying form of abuse in its own right. Horrible pictures and words sear children's minds that can affect them negatively forever or until they undergo a healing process.

And, fathers, do not provoke your children to anger; but bring
them up in the discipline and instruction of the Lord.

—Ephesians 6:4 NASB

Three

*U*nder Daddy's Foot

Sixteen months after Caroline married Ed...

Ed's swearing startled me awake. He stood at the foot of our bed in his
terry robe, the golden sun haloing the red fury on his face in a weird
kind of splendor. Hanging from the tips of his fingers, as if they were
poisonous, were my brown flats. (Lately, he had been sleeping with me
in the master bedroom. Officially his room still adjoined mine.)

"Slut!" he roared. "You dropped your shoes on my bathrobe."

I pushed up on my elbows. Last night I had returned late from a
wedding shower. As I negotiated my way through the dark bedroom, I
set my shoes on a chair, where he wouldn't trip over them, a pet hate of
his. "I'm sorry."

"Because of you, I am wearing a filthy robe."

"I said that I'm sorry. It was dark."

"I always put my robe on that chair. You know that!"

"I guess I forgot. I didn't want you to trip over my shoes."

"You could have put them under the chair or under the bed. You are as stupid as____!" He made a horrid racist comparison. Because I had been active in civil rights, Ed's racism particularly infuriated me.

I stuck my feet in my slippers and plodded toward the bathroom, knowing the day would be difficult. I flinched as Ed roared, "Your kids left their bikes out last night. Get them in the garage now, or I'll whip their rear ends off!"

Last week, for the first time he had used a switch on Kay, Judy, and Trent for leaving their books in the living room. Their scarlet welts sickened me, and I feared a repeat performance.

I ran outside and rolled the bikes into the garage. Then spotting Trent's weights on the floor, I lifted the light ones to a shelf and pushed the heavy ones into a corner. Panting, I sat on a stool. I had recently been diagnosed with chronic obstructive pulmonary disease (COPD), a potentially fatal lung disease that had diffused throughout my lungs. Because my clogged lungs processed only 40 to 60 percent of the oxygen I needed, I had IV treatments three times a week to clear them of fluid.

I returned to the house and fixed pancakes, which the children ate in silence while Ed carried on about their bikes. Surprisingly, Ed kissed my cheek before he left for his office. The kiss perked me up. *Maybe it will be a wonderful day after all*, I thought. As I loaded the dishwasher, I decided to do something special for Ed: roast a turkey for dinner.

Though Ed loved turkey, he hated *that* turkey. "Half the meat's overdone, and the other half's underdone. You roast turkey like a [racist remark]! People die from rare poultry. You're from the bottom of the mental barrel, Caroline. Your brains are fried!"

My stomach churned. The kids stared at their plates and picked at their food. Then we struggled up like a flock of stormed-on birds and cleared the table in silence.

Judy, my five-year-old peacemaker, said, "Mom, I loved the turkey. I really loved it."

"Thanks, honey." I turned to Kay and asked, "Would you load the dishwasher?" At thirteen, Kay was a thin, leggy child who blew out her words, as if verging on hyperventilation. She craved male approval, since she had received so little, and hung out with fast boys who gave it. I had grounded her a few times for sitting on boys' laps at football games and for smoking marijuana. I worried endlessly about her, afraid that she would get pregnant and addicted to drugs.

Kay slammed dishes into the dishwasher. "Why do you use so many dishes? Why did you cook turkey? Ed hated it, so what's the use? You do everything for him. Why don't you do something for us!"

"I'll cook what you want tomorrow. Just tell me what."

"I don't care what. If you really cared about me, you'd leave Ed. I hate that dunkhead. Why do you let him slap you silly? If any guy ever hits me, he'll get killed—just like that!" She pointed her finger like a gun.

"I wish he were easier on you."

"Is that all you've got to say?"

"Just try to stay out of his way."

"He'd better stay out of my way!"

Bottles clattered as Judy put them in the refrigerator. Judy was a quiet, little child who loved the Lord. To date, it seemed that Ed's obnoxious behavior had failed to damage her.

The kitchen had heated up, so Kay slipped off her sweater and set it on the counter. Ed strode in to refill his coffee cup, eyed the sweater on the messy counter, and exploded. "Whose sweater is that!"

"Mine," Kay said, grabbing it.

"You dirty little pig. Sweaters do not belong on a filthy counter. Look at those spills!" Kay didn't look. "I said *look!*"

Clutching her sweater to her chest, Kay looked. "Leave me alone," she yelled. "I'll wash it."

"I'll stop you from sucking eggs. [His favorite pejorative to the kids. I had no idea what it meant.] I'll take a hammer and break your fingers. I'll teach you to keep your clothes clean—I'll kill me a kid!" His face was blood red.

Kay trembled, her bravado caving. Her knees shook beneath her short skirt.

Horrified, I shielded Kay. "She simply set her sweater in the wrong place. That's hardly a crime. You're driving her to insanity. She's having trouble in school. Please, please leave her alone!" I begged. "She's never hurt you, never once."

Ed pushed me aside and closed in on Kay. I tugged his arm, and he kicked my anklebone, filling me with bone-deep pain. He grabbed Kay's head and pressed it into the roaster of turkey drippings. The roaster rattled as he rubbed her hair and face in it. She coughed and gagged. I screamed and uselessly pulled at his wrists. Our wrestling knocked over the pan, and grease flowed down the cabinets.

"That'll teach you what a pig looks like! Go look in the mirror!"

Grease trickled down Kay's face and hair. As I looked at her white skin and dilated pupils, I knew she represented the epitome of my failure to protect my children. If dying could have reversed that, I would have died on the spot.

Kay wiped her mouth with the back of her hand, gagged, then threw up in the sink. Ed walked out the kitchen door.

I dampened a dishtowel and handed it to Kay. I put my arms up to hold her. She knocked them down. "Leave me alone!"

"Oh, darling," I said, "that was so horrible! Honey, I love you so much. Are you all right? Let me take you upstairs. We'll get you cleaned up." She stared at me. I added weakly, "I tried to stop him."

She continued to stare. I feared that Ed had destroyed her ability to be a normal child or adult. *It's my fault*, I thought. I knew I had to leave Ed to protect my children. *But not yet*, I thought. I wasn't ready to leave, even though I knew I loved a monster, which meant I was a monster.

"Please let me hold you," I said helplessly.

Her eyes flamed. "You could have stopped him!"

"I tried. He's too strong for me."

"That's what makes me so mad. You don't know how to try. You're a doormat. I hate you. I can't count on you!" She dashed from the kitchen.

I ran after her. Sobbing, she flung herself flat on her bed. She allowed me to put her head in my lap and stroke her hair. When she had calmed down, I ran a tub of water so that she could bathe.

I then went to finish cleaning the kitchen. Through the window, I saw Ed's office lights glow. Judy and Ellen, my nine-year-old, helped me. It was hot work, and when we finished Judy's hair strung around her thin face. I sat at the table. She stood beside me, her eyes serious. "Mommy, don't be so sad. Dad probably is real sorry."

Stunned, I looked at her, wishing that were true.

She sat. Her small hand patted her lap. "Here, come sit. You be the little girl, and I'll be the mommy."

I pushed my chair against hers. She stroked my hair. It felt so good. It felt like when my mother comforted me after a hurt. But Judy shouldn't have seen what happened. She shouldn't be caring for me. It should be the other way around.

Judy jumped up. "I'm going to Kay."

I started for my bourbon bottle then remembered I no longer drank. My sister had convinced me I was headed for alcoholism and a face full of red veins. The red veins worried me the most. If I had red veins, Ed would hate my face. Instead I locked myself in the master bathroom and banged my head against the wall until it throbbed like a boil. I did not take aspirin. I needed the physical pain to relieve my emotional pain.

Ed returned from his office after midnight and didn't say a word while I pretended to read. He stripped and climbed in bed. I was surprised that he didn't go to his own room. *Does that mean he's sorry for what happened?* I wondered, and despite all the horror of the night, I felt a little hope.

"Good night," he said.

"Good night. Kay—" I started.

"Some kids have to learn the hard way."

He certainly isn't sorry, I thought painfully. I would have to keep the children and Ed separated as much as possible.

Kay's art teacher phoned the next morning. "Never in my life have I experienced in a classroom situation what happened with Kay. I'll remember it until the day I die," she said. "All of a sudden Kay stood in class and pulled a doctor's glove over her head. The fingers were on top. Kay blew hard and sucked in. The fingers ballooned and pulsated, and it looked like a chicken's head. Kay then flapped her arms like chicken wings. There was dead silence. The class was in shock. I thought, *She's breathing in carbon monoxide; she could die.* But I was so startled by her bizarre appearance that I was locked in my chair."

"Oh, I'm so sorry. She had a hard night last night."

"I've reported this incident to the principal. Dr. Schwartz, the school psychologist, will be calling you."

When Kay came home, she threw her book bag on the stove, flopped in a chair, crossed her arms, and dared me with her eyes. I grabbed the book bag, knelt, and put my arms around her waist.

"You want to know why?" Kay screeched. "I'll tell you why. I can't be myself here. If I do one thing out of line, I get my hair rubbed in grease, so school is the one safe place I can let myself go. I hate Ed. I wish he would die! Why do you kiss up to such a sick, horrible man? Thinking about it drives me *crazy!*"

"The school psychologist insists we see him."

"What do I care? What I can't understand is why you don't leave Ed."

"Kay, it's hard. I love him—though I shouldn't, and I'm sick—my lungs. I don't think I could hold down a job."

"That just it! You love him. You don't love us. Let's get out of here! I don't care if we live on the street. At least we'd have our dignity."

"I will promise to try to think of how I could leave."

In Dr. Schwartz's office, Kay stared out the window, refusing to participate. Ed (obviously worried he would be reported for child abuse) had warned Kay and me not to mention the grease incident. "You'll be out on the street if you do."

"Good," Kay had said.

Ed told Dr. Schwartz, "As the incident with the glove shows, Kay is often uncontrollable. It's difficult for a stepfather to discipline children that aren't his own. I feel the children have been somewhat deprived of normal family relationships. They went through some rough years with their biological father, and when I took them on, I really wanted to better their lives. They were lovable, and I was very fond of them. Due to business and marriage crises, I've not been the father I would like to be. Caroline does a great job of giving positive strokes to the kids, but I'm of the opinion that kids also need firm discipline. I was raised that way, and I've never regretted it. Caroline lacks the ability to discipline, and because of that, I've overreacted at times with the children, but it's always been in their best interests. I promise to do my utmost for Kay. You have my absolute word on this."

I nodded, convinced Ed meant to help Kay. Surely the turkey-grease incident had shaken him up.

"Kay's acting out was a cry for help," Dr. Schwartz said. "Mrs. Stuart, you need to be firmer, and Mr. Stuart, you need to spend quality time with Kay—develop interests in common. Have you and Mrs. Stuart been in therapy?"

"I'm not so hot on therapy," Ed said, "but if Kay continues to act up we'll go."

"I'll be meeting with Kay on a regular basis. I need to see improvement in her behavior at school. If I don't, we'll have to work out a different strategy." Dr. Schwartz looked in Kay's direction. "All right, Kay?"

She gazed out the window. "Yeah."

On the way to the car, I hooked my arm in Ed's. "Your help will mean the world to Kay."

"I said I would help Kay, and I will. I guard my word and my integrity, and if you ask me where I value integrity, I would rate it high."

"Honey, Kay needs you desperately."

A week later, I felt happy as Ed drove Kay and me to a clothing outlet. This week he had given her several motivational books about how to succeed in life and had helped her with math homework. At the outlet, she pranced from the dressing room wearing a new sweater and Levi's then turned to model them. She made the most positive statement she had in weeks. "I love my new clothes. Things are looking up."

"Oh, what new clothes did you get?" Ed asked.

"I have them on," she said.

"You have them on!" he said. "Those pants look fourteen years old."

Her face fell. Ed had gone in for the kill. Kay burst into tears and ran into the dressing room.

"What got into you?" I cried. "You were so good with her this week. You know she doesn't have the emotional resources to fight comments like that."

"I told the truth. I can't lie."

"You could have said you didn't like the clothes in a nice way."

"There's no nice way to say it."

"You mean you can't force yourself to say something nicely, even to save a little girl's life?"

He said flatly, "I can't lie."

That night as I lay awake, I heard a cow moan downriver, reminding me of Kay's cries for help, which would become fainter and fainter if Ed didn't ease up. And Kay wasn't my only child who needed help.

Vivian, nineteen, lived in an apartment, worked as a draftsperson, attended night school, and exhibited lesbian traits. She hung around in a lesbian bookstore and had taught the kids that pink triangles stood for lesbians. Whenever the kids used the word *gay* derogatorily, she snapped at them. She looked like a man—purposely, cropping her hair and buying her clothes in the men's department. I believed she was deliberately fat to turn off men so that she wouldn't have to deal with them. Her father and stepfather had taught her that men were cruel.

Trent, twelve, was abusive toward his sisters, though he appeared to love me. Even though Ed treated him like dirt and had spanked him, the male in Trent tapped into the animalistic part of Ed. He admired that Ed was vicious, a survivor, powerful, successful, and terrifying. I believed Trent had a hard row to hoe, because he had four sisters and a mother who distrusted men. Preserving his male identity would be difficult. He hated me to be angry at Ed. "He gives us a roof over our heads, so don't make trouble, Mom. Don't mouth off too much." He tied into computer bulletin boards from 4:00 P.M. until 11:00 P.M. (he had his own telephone line) and had no close friends at school. Impersonal relationships suited him best. His grades were poor, even though his intelligence scores were superior.

Nine-year-old Ellen was a tall, beautiful child. She read her Bible nightly and prayed for Kay, even though Kay was verbally and physically vicious toward her. (Kay hated Ellen for her beauty.) Ellen had tapped into the Lord's grace, allowing her to survive Kay's and Ed's mean behavior. She did everything with diligence, maintaining an almost straight-A average. Even though she considered Ed extremely mean, she wanted to like him. Like Trent, she urged me to keep the peace with Ed. I thanked God that she was okay.

Judy, at five, was shy and frail looking, yet she was the kingpin of my world, the one who hugged me when Ed blew up. I sensed that

Judy's role of comforter was too heavy a load for so little a child, but I needed her and adored her. Like Ellen, Judy loved the Lord and always forgave Ed.

I burrowed into my pillow, hating Ed, and I allowed my mind to plan his funeral. *He dies*, I thought, *and I arrange the visitation. His clients come, all the bigwigs, but the kids and I do it our way. I hang a life-sized drawing of Ed choking me above his coffin. I hang another of him battering my head on the kitchen floor. I hang one of Kay with her hair dripping turkey grease. Everyone looks from the angelic face in the coffin to the evidence.*

CHILD ABUSE CONNECTED WITH DOMESTIC VIOLENCE

Knowing that your children are in an abusive situation yet feeling for personal reasons that you must stay with your husband is one of the most difficult things imaginable. Telling others what really happens to your children in your home is excruciating. I attempted to interview Caroline five times about Ed's abuse toward her children before she could talk about it, and even then she spoke quickly, finishing in about half an hour. Pieces came in later interviews, always with stress and grief. One day, Caroline assessed her situation. "I tell myself God gave me these children knowing their lives would be rough. I really believe God has allowed the kids to have this environment for a particular reason, and they can have gifts beyond what a functional family would have. My sister says that's a codependent cop-out to justify why I stay when I shouldn't." Caroline sighed. "Maybe it is. But it's my rationale now."

Experts would agree that children can develop strengths as they cope with mistreatment, but they also stress that many children carry scars all their lives unless they undergo a healing process. Unfortunately, domestic violence and child abuse often go hand in hand. A national survey of more than six thousand families revealed that 50 percent of the men who frequently assaulted their wives also frequently assaulted their children.[1] It has been found that children who live with stepfathers and their mothers' boyfriends are more sub-ject to abuse than those who live with their biological fathers.

Specifically, child abuse is an action or a lack of action that endan-gers a child's physical or emotional safety or development. Children, for their own vital reasons, don't usually tell us what's bad at home.

They may fear that their bad behavior caused their beatings. They may also fear that exposing the abuse will destroy their family, annihilating their only source of security. (Even tenuous security is better than none.) Because children often keep abuse secret, it is hoped that adults outside the family will be alert to signs of child abuse in domestic violence situations and act to protect abused children. Wives of abusers need to look for signs of child abuse as well, for it can occur when they are not present.

We'll look at five types of child abuse that can accompany domestic violence: physical, sexual, psychological/emotional, negligence,[2] and witnessing domestic violence. This is helpful information that points out how to identify child abuse and how to help abused children in homes where there is domestic violence.

1. PHYSICAL ABUSE

A father who physically injures his child does not do so randomly, but with intentional malice—to vent his anger, but predominantly to exercise power and control over the child. Because younger children are defenseless, they are in the most danger of an abuser's wrath. One resident of the shelter where I volunteer reported her husband had rolled their baby down a hill because it wouldn't stop crying. Some abusers have been known to shake their babies to stop their crying until they are brain-damaged or dead. Childhelp USA literature states, "Head trauma is the leading cause of child abuse death among babies. This includes shaken baby syndrome in which 25 percent of victims die and the majority of survivors suffer brain damage."[3] Even a child in the womb can be kicked or pummeled as his father's fists or feet strike his mother's belly, sometimes resulting in birth defects or brain damage. Estimates are that 15 to 25 percent of pregnant women are battered,[4] either because the father is frustrated about the pregnancy, repelled by his wife's appearance, or attempting to abort his child.

Signs of Physical Abuse

- *Bruises and burns* shaped like the objects that caused them: round cigarette holes (often applied to a child's hands, buttocks, forearms, and soles of her feet), long strap marks, a series of welts from a switch, hairbrush shapes, iron-shaped burns.

- *Water scalds*, where the child was dipped into hot water, or donut-shaped scalds, where a child was forced to sit in hot water.

- *Friction burns* from ropes or cords.

- A *large number of bruises* that have various colorations, indicating they have been inflicted on different occasions. Look for bruises in spots where a child doesn't usually fall: the mouth, back, genital area, and thighs.

- *Unexplained fractures or injuries* in any part of the body, but particularly the mouth or the head. Investigate if you leave your baby with his father or your boyfriend and return to find his mouth cut or arm bruised.

- *Isolation* may signal physical danger in the home. Note parents who regularly miss church events, school events, or family gatherings.

Much controversy surrounds the issue of spanking. Is it abuse, or is it discipline? I can understand why public child-protective agencies and battered-women's shelters prohibit spanking. Shelters house mothers who are angry at their abuser's violence, angry to be at a shelter, and angry that they may lose their hopes and dreams, and perhaps their possessions. If these mothers do strike their children in anger, they demonstrate that hitting when you're mad is okay. The child thinks, *Dad gets mad and hits Mom, and Mom gets mad and hits me, so it's okay for me to hit.* The child will likely carry this attitude into adulthood.

At the shelter where I work, Shirley teaches mothers alternate forms of discipline: giving a "time-out" (as sitting on a chair) or initiating constructive behaviors to replace destructive ones. These are excellent forms of discipline. Yet I believe that spanking is appropriate under certain circumstances and must be reserved for parents who are gentle, loving, and wise—diligently training their children to be sensible, responsible, and godly. Ephesians 6:4 defines a crucial parental attitude in child rearing: "And you, fathers, do not provoke your children to

wrath, but bring them up in the training and admonition of the Lord."
Parents must not create angry children through speaking or spanking
in anger. Rather, act toward children according to Proverbs 29:15,
which defines the goal of correction: "The rod and rebuke give wisdom,
but a child left to himself brings shame to his mother."

Debbie Morgan, mother of nine, describes her use of verbal correction and spanking, which I believe is not abusive but part of a discipline process.

> I want my children to understand why they are spanked and
> to learn from the experience. They have to be old enough to
> understand right from wrong—about two years old. I won't
> spank in anger. If I'm angry with the child, I tell her that I will
> deal with her later. I try to be consistent and do a spanking the
> same way every time.
>
> First, I explain to my child what she did wrong and why it's
> wrong. "You can't run out in the street. A car could hit you and
> you'd be badly hurt." I tell her that, if it happens again, I'll need
> to spank her to show how serious it is to run into the street. I
> never spank her the first time she disobeys. I always explain the
> problem then tell her that she will be spanked the next time.
>
> Then, if she runs into the street again, I bring her to a pri-
> vate room and lovingly explain again about the dangers of
> streets. I invite her to talk to me about these dangers. Then I
> remind her that I had said she would be spanked, and I spank
> her. I never leave a bruise.
>
> After the spanking, I hold her and tell her I love her. I don't
> let her run off all upset. Sometimes the older children won't stay
> around, but I try at least to give them a loving pat on their way
> out.

2. SEXUAL ABUSE

Sexual abuse can be nonphysical or physical actions that sexually
gratify the perpetrator and satisfy his need to have power and control.
Nonphysical abuse includes sexual remarks, indecent exposure, and

showing the child pornography. Physical acts include fondling a child's sex organs, actual intercourse, sodomy, beatings during the sex act, cult sexual sacrifice of the child, and prostituting the child. A child is either forced or manipulated into participating in sexual abuse. If a father forces sex on his child, he may threaten, "Don't tell or you'll pay for it!" If he manipulates her, he may promise her gifts or favors. Melissa, a mother of six, said her father manipulated her. "He would say, 'There, there, honey—just give your daddy a little loving. Shush, I'll get you that coat you been needin'—a real nice one with fur on the collar.' I'd never get the coat or anything else he promised."

A child whose body is fondled or penetrated can suffer polar emotions. She may be aroused, a good feeling. Yet she knows the act is wrong, a shameful feeling. It may be the only time that her father is nice to her, a positive feeling. She feels that she provoked it, a dirty feeling. She often blames her mother for ignoring her plight. Melissa says, "I'd hear Mom moving around in the next room, and I'd think, *Why didn't she help me?* I felt she had let me down. I didn't trust her or anyone."

Shirley says, "We assume that every child we shelter is sexually abused, and then we work to prove that the child hasn't been." Shirley examines the children's artwork and their play activities for signs of sexual abuse. "We had one girl of six who would babble rather than speak. We observed her in the playroom with Ken and Barbie dolls. She had Ken doing oral sex on Barbie. Later we found the child could speak, so emotional trauma had made her revert to infantile communication."

A very young child may tell her mother she is sexually abused in naive vocabulary. "Daddy plays a game in my panties that makes me feel bad." Often when a child doesn't tell her mother that sexual abuse occurs, there are suspicious signs. But a mother may ignore the all-too-obvious signs because the reality would be too painful and would shatter her family.

Indications That a Child May Be Sexually Abused

- stains on panties
- injury or irritation to the rectum, vagina, or penis

- venereal disease signs of itching, blisters, and discharge

- discharge from the rectum

- fearful reaction to a male voice in a baby or young child

Dealing with Sexual Abuse

If you discover that your husband has molested your child, your reaction is vital to your child's safety and emotional security. Experts recommend the following responses to a child's report of abuse:

- *Believe your child.* Remember how difficult it is for a child to specify sexual abuse.

- *Don't panic.* That will scare her or him. Tell your child it was right to tell you. Never blame your child for the event: "If you were quieter, nicer, neater, or didn't sit on Daddy's lap so much..." Say, "It's not your fault." It is vital that your child recognizes his or her own innocence.

- *Promise your protection.* If the abuse has been chronic, ask your child to forgive you for not intervening and assure him or her of your protection. For your child's sake, separate from your husband until he has reformed. On visits, do not leave your child alone with his or her father. Once men establish a pattern of child molestation, they rarely stop until they have been through a recovery process, and even then, the cure rate is low. Due to the stigma attached to sexual abuse, your husband will likely deny it, even when presented with irrefutable evidence. How do many molesters deal with their consciences? Some believe they are entitled to have sex with their children. Others insist their children enjoy the "special" sexual relationship. Others rationalize that they are teaching their daughters how to have sex.

- *Report the abuse to a child-protection agency* that will help you do what's best for your child. If you do not report child abuse, it is likely someone else will. Professionals, including ministers, who are aware of child abuse, are legally obligated to report it. It will appear that you have failed to protect your child.

- *Arrange a medical exam*—but only if the abuse was severe. You don't want to put your child through an exam that is uncomfortable and embarrassing unnecessarily. As a rule, penetration of the child's vagina is considered severe, while fondling is not.

- *Assure your child of God's love* and that he has not deserted him or her. Awful thoughts surely torment your child. *God must hate me! Why did God allow me to be born in this family? Why didn't God keep Dad away from me! I wish Dad would go away or die.* Explain that, though we don't know why defenseless people are victimized, we do know that God will bring good to all victims who trust him. "And we know that all things work together for good to those who love God, to those who are the called according to His purpose" (Romans 8:28).

- *Do Bible studies with your child* to build trust in God. It is important to help your child verbalize concerns and fears as you study the Bible; then look up scriptures that offer hope. (They will offer you hope as well, for this is a terrible time for you.)

- *Invite your child to ask you questions anytime.* Recognize that your child may not trust you to have answers. You likely appear to be a victim, just as he or she is. So be patient, willing to answer questions again and again.

- *Teach your child how to protect him- or herself from the father's advances* if ever alone with him despite your efforts to guard your child's safety. Tell your child to run, scream, and call 911. Explain that if a sexual assault occurs, he or she must tell you what happened, even though the father has threatened him or her. Promise your child that you will report the abuse to the child-protection authorities and increase your efforts to protect him or her.

- *Find a Christian therapist* to help your child recover from trauma. Some children have a natural resiliency and bounce back from sexual abuse, even if they are not counseled. But you don't know for certain if that describes your child, and it is better to err in the direction of more therapy than less.

3. PSYCHOLOGICAL/EMOTIONAL ABUSE

A child who endures psychological/emotional (p/e) abuse feels crazy. Never knowing what might happen next, the child is always on guard. Suddenly the worst happens. Dad is kicking the dog around the living room because the dog barked at the sound of a horn. Feeling tortured, the child breaks out in a sweat. That is what p/e abuse is like for a child. Other examples of p/e abuse are delegating adult-sized responsibilities then blaming a child for not fulfilling them perfectly, not speaking to a child for a long period, demeaning a child ("You'll never amount to anything."), expecting perfect behavior (Ed's parents expected that of him.), humiliating a child in front of others, locking a child in a dark closet, denying a child food, forcing a child to lie or steal, blaming a child for the father's wrong, or putting a diaper on an older child because she wet the bed at night.

Although p/e abuse doesn't break bones, it breaks spirits. Unfortunately, we cannot fix a spirit as easily as a bone. We can't x-ray it to identify the fracture. We cannot put it in a cast. Dr. Byron Egeland, professor of child psychology and affiliated with the University of Minnesota's study of emotionally abused children, says, "These kids had the most serious psychological problems of any kids in our study. Some showed signs of severe psychopathology."[5] The children tended to withdraw into silence, avoid close social contacts, and suppress their tears and feelings.

Signs of Psychological/Emotional Abuse

- Shyness and shame over simple matters, such as being called on in class.

- Unwillingness to talk about her family and to invite friends over.

- Rebellion or overcompliance.

- Abuse of drugs or alcohol.

- Low self-esteem.

- Acting out, like Kay, Caroline's middle child.

- Perfectionism as a top student or underachievement as a terrible student too depleted to function in school, like Trent, Caroline's son.

4. Negligence

By definition, neglected children lack adequate emotional and physical care and protection, situations that frequently coexist with domestic violence. Care that should be given to children often is not. Abusers may spend most of the family money, leaving children without adequate clothes and food. Abusers might lock their families out, forcing them to sleep in the car, even in cold weather. Mothers can be so depressed over abuse that they do little but sit and stare, unable to give children the attention they need, leaving them to fend for themselves. A distressed or battered mother may fail to take her sick child to the doctor.

Signs of Neglect

- The child is extremely thin, poorly clothed, listless, or sleepy.
- The child is left alone for long periods of time or put in dangerous situations.
- The child is dirty and lives in a filthy home.
- The child's behavior may be extreme, such as overly affectionate to strangers or overly aggressive and disruptive.
- The child is withdrawn and anxious around adults and other children.
- The child is often on the sidelines, unable to make close friends with children or adults.
- The child's medical needs are obviously neglected.
- The child may be rigidly obedient. The neighbor of a woman facing a fourth conviction of child endangerment describes her neighbor's children as "always respectful, never cussing."

5. Witnessing Domestic Violence

Witnessing domestic violence is a distinct form of child abuse, and although it occurs obliquely, it is every bit as traumatic as direct abuse.

A child is paralyzed with fear as he watches dishes fly, hears parents scream, and watches his mother's face bleed. The child's home is never safe. He never knows when the storm in the form of Dad will strike or humiliate his mom. The child experiences intense fear of his father and anger at his mother for staying with him. Although witnessing abuse may start out passively, the experience can turn deadly if the child intervenes. Shirley says, "A little girl staying in the shelter told me that her father knocked her mother to the floor and was about to stab her. The girl threw her body over her mother and said, 'You're not going to do this to my mom.' The girl was lucky. Her father didn't stab her or her mother."

Often mothers believe young children are not affected by the violence. "They'll be all right; they're so young." "Oh, she was in bed and didn't hear." But 87 percent of children do hear and do know.[6] Interviews with children of battered women "reveal that they...can describe detailed accounts of violent behavior that their mother or father never realized they had witnessed." Experts find that younger children are often the most seriously traumatized. Lacking adult logic to explain abuse, they usually blame themselves for it. "If I were good, Mom wouldn't be hit." The next time violence occurs, children may think, *I've got to be better.* When children finally learn they can't save their mothers, they may become depressed, build walls, run away, or turn to drugs or promiscuity to forget the violence.

Shirley showed me pictures children at the shelter drew, innocently created, but graphically highlighting how violence looks to them.

A four-year-old said his picture was about a tornado hitting his house. It showed an outline of a man's face surrounded by a page full of squiggle lines. Shirley said, "It was a sunny day when he drew it. Afterward he drew a picture of himself cleaning up the mess from the tornado, showing he assumed responsibility for the trauma."

A six-year-old boy drew a person who was nearly all chest with crosses and lines comprising the chest's innards. The child explained to Shirley, "These are all a person's broken hearts." The boy repeatedly drew the same picture for three days.

A six-year-old boy filled his paper with bold faces. To the side of the paper was a boy, drawn in pale pencil. In the middle loomed a monster face, bigger than all the other faces. The boy said, "The faces are people trying to push me at the monster [Dad?]."

Indications a Child May Have Witnessed Abuse

- The child seems hopeless about the future. "I won't grow up." Or, "When I grow up, my life will be as bad as Mom's."

- The child can't function well at school.

- The child has physical or emotional problems. One source states, "Of children who witness their mothers being abused by their fathers, 40 percent suffer anxiety, 48 percent suffer depression, 53 percent act out [destructive behavior] with their parents, 60 percent act out with siblings."[7]

- A young child cries more than normal. Crying is the only effective outlet available to his inexperienced mind.

- The child is aggressive. At the shelter where I volunteer, a four-year-old girl bit another girl. The child smiled as the staff advocate described how she had hurt her victim. "My flesh crawled at the sadism she'd learned at home," the advocate says. "I explained that it was wrong to hurt people and that there were other ways of solving problems. The girl looked blank. She didn't have the experience to comprehend."

MOTHERS REPORTING CHILD ABUSE

It is important that mothers of abused children understand that physical abuse, neglect, and sexual abuse of a child are criminal offenses. If you confide that any one of these abuses occurs in your home to a pastor, psychologist, doctor, women's crisis center, childcare worker (and many other professionals), they are required by law to report the abuse to the appropriate authorities. The intent of the reporting law is not to hurt or to punish the family, but to supply help to children and families in need.

When child abuse is reported, child-protection agencies focus on the child's safety and urge the mother to leave her abuser. One advocate in child protection says, "We want to see the mother act responsibly and remove the child from physical or sexual abuse. If the abuse has been chronic, we determine why the child has been left in such circumstances and if the mother could now protect the child. We consider it best if a child has her mother for a support, but if the mother can't protect and emotionally support the child, it is best that the child be placed elsewhere."[8] She notes that each case of child abuse is assessed individually.

If a mother doesn't report her husband's child abuse, she can be convicted in court for "failure to protect her children." The court may rule that the mother is 50 percent responsible for the abuse because she didn't stop it, report it, or remove the children from it. Courts are beginning to take a harder stand against mothers who do not protect their children from abuse. In two landmark cases, adult children successfully sued their parents for sexual abuse, and both parents were held jointly liable to pay the judgments (one for $2.4 million, the other for $3.4 million).[9]

In the event you suspect your husband will harm you or your children if you seek help from children's services, take them to a shelter or other safe place. Let experts in domestic violence and child protection inform you about the best way to protect your children.

What if you participated in your child's abuse? Call a children's services agency. Authorities will count it in your favor that you telephoned on your own. If you show willingness to recover through attending groups such as Parents Anonymous (they meet anonymously like A.A. and share how they have conquered child abuse) or a church parenting group, you will likely retain custody of your children.

I know firsthand that feeling of guilt that a mother has when she fails to be the mother she would like to be. When I was an alcoholic, I often agonized about my neglect of my children. When I became sober, I asked my children to forgive me, and I believe it helped them to hear my admission of failure and determination to change. They have grown up to be happy adults.

Most mothers recoil at the thought of losing their children due to their husbands' abuse, but it can legally happen, even when a mother is doing her very best to protect them. It's important to know how vulnerable you are and how much you need advocates to assist you as you seek your children's ultimate welfare.

OUTSIDERS REPORTING CHILD ABUSE

If you suspect a child is abused, contact the mother and urge her to report the abuse to child-protection authorities and to her pastor, who can be involved as an adviser and a support. You might say to her, "I'm worried about your child's welfare. We both want your child to be safe, but we need help. We can't protect your child alone."[10] If you follow up with an offer to support the mother through subsequent proceedings, she may feel less afraid of stepping forward.

If the mother refuses to make a report, inform her that you must. Then offer to "stand by her during the investigation and any court proceedings that result." If you don't speak up, your silence may contribute to a child's suffering or even death. Some of you may wish to report the abuse but don't want to be identified as the informant. Shirley says, "You don't have to give your name when you call, and you don't need a parent's permission to call. But by all means call. Give as many facts as you can. 'I heard screaming. I heard the mother say.... I saw bruises on the child.' At the least give the child's address and the reason you suspect abuse. Your report will be confidential, and even if the parent should phone and say, 'I know who reported this! It was that nosy Mrs. Brown!' the agency will refuse to comment." Importantly, 70 percent of child-abuse reports come from third parties.[11] After you make your report, the child-welfare agency will decide an appropriate course of action.

He that drinks will get fat; he that loves will be healthy;
and he that beats his wife will be saved.

—Polish proverb

Four

*W*hen Church Is a Haven of Rejection

Caroline's church is conservative and upscale, attracting mainly professionals and executives from the greater Louisville area. Mainly white people attend, but there are a few blacks, a few Hispanics, and several foreign students from the University of Louisville. There are two Sunday services, broken by a half-hour coffee time for socializing. Sunday-school classes for adults and children meet during the two services. In addition to Pastor Doyle Morris, four assistant pastors, ranging from a youth pastor to a seniors' pastor to a business administrator, run the affairs of the twelve-hundred-member organization. The building began as a two story with a bell tower, but as membership increased, wings were added on the first and second floors so that it is now necessary to hand newcomers maps to negotiate the maze.

One wall of the sanctuary is constructed of glass to display a courtyard of flowers, shrubs, and fountains. In warm weather a group (mainly businessmen) meets in the courtyard at 6:30 A.M. for a weekly prayer meeting. The church's main emphasis is growth. Caroline says,

"Doyle loves to stand up front and count the sheep as they arrive. He loves to see his numbers go up. But should one of those sheep trip up, he doesn't want to know about it." The church also emphasizes missions and sending groups to Haiti to build churches and provide clothing, food, and school supplies to the needy.

Pastor Morris's sermons follow such themes as forgiving, loving, and being a stronger Christian, and he considers the Bible infallible. Lighter problems of everyday living are featured sermon topics, while heavier topics like domestic violence are downplayed or ignored.

The church atmosphere is so upbeat that you absorb the idea that Christianity is easy, lighthearted, and problem free, and that all you have to do is attend meetings and you'll be happy. There is the Wednesday-night dinner, followed by a Bible study that Pastor Morris leads. There are thirty care groups that meet weekly to allow members to relate intimately and discuss questions that Doyle has developed from his sermons. A church rule is that care-group members can share personal concerns if they wish, but they cannot discuss anyone else's sins. "I can't attend a care group," Caroline says. "My problems with Ed are too serious. How can I say, 'Things are bad at home,' without saying why?"

Caroline does attend a support group, which Pastor Morris reluctantly permits to accommodate a few women needing emotional support due to marriage problems. Pastor Morris warned the group leader to avoid husband bashing. He also said, "Frankly, I'm not all that comfortable with your meeting in a manner that differs from the care-group format."

Caroline says, "We don't go out of our way to point fingers at our husbands, but when we are upset we do say, 'He did this...' I'm getting well through the group. They validate me. They believe me. Their facial expressions show sympathy and understanding when I share something awful Ed did. No one warns, 'Don't gossip!' When the group started, I was terribly depressed. There were times in the beginning when I would think, *If only I can make it to Wednesday.* I had been on Zoloft, which is stronger than Prozac, but through the group I'm off it."

Church activities comprise Caroline's life. She doesn't participate in country-club activities, bridge clubs, tennis matches, or engage any longer in the pro-life movement (except for an occasional speech), due to marital stress. Her closest friend at church is May, the pastor's wife, a giver who helps myriad needy people. "She's one of my best friends in life," Caroline says. "She thinks I provoke Ed into beating me, but she has done so many nice things for me that I just put up with that. She's invited me to holiday dinners and on a three-day vacation, paying my expenses because Ed wouldn't. We honestly share our struggles with our faith. I adore her. I do hope that one day May will believe me. Maybe then Doyle will hold Ed accountable for abusing me and that will cause him to reform."

Hurt at church…

I put my plate of cake down to answer the phone. It was Yvette, a member of my Sunday-school class and the leader of the women's retreat. Her voice was thickly Southern and cultured, placing her in my imagination on a veranda in a hoop dress that spanned two columns. That was actually close to reality; Yvette wore furs and jewels, marks of her husband's rank as a CEO, and she had perfect kids, marks of parental surveillance and love.

My life was so different from hers—falling-apart kids, falling-apart marriage. I remembered that I had mentioned in Sunday-school class that Ed abused me, only because I was crying over a rough night. The class was strangely hushed, including Yvette, indicating I had violated the rule not to point fingers. Since then, no one in the class had asked me if I was all right.

Yvette said, "Honey, I hate it, but I'm forced to call you at the last minute. I know you'll understand because you're sooo deep in the Spirit."

"What is it?"

"Betsy [Ed's second wife] has agreed to lead worship at the retreat."

"What!" Hot shock waves hit me from every direction. Betsy wanted Ed back, and whenever Ed and I picked up his son, Glen, for our weekly dinner, she blatantly flirted with Ed. The procedure was that my kids and I waited in the car while Ed went to the door for Glen. Betsy always opened the door painted to the hilt, wearing an outfit that exhibited her curves. She always touched Ed's arm and smiled into his eyes, while I died of jealousy in the car.

"Is it all right?" Yvette said.

"I—ah. You obviously know Betsy is Ed's second wife."

"Yes." She paused. "But I didn't know it at first. The retreat speaker suggested Betsy. When I phoned Betsy to invite her, she told me she was Ed's ex-wife. She said it could be awkward, but she'd pray about it. She later agreed, convinced her leading worship was of the Lord."

I paced wildly around the kitchen. "Betsy and I don't have a good relationship."

Her voice perked up. "I see why this is of the Lord now very clearly. This is to be a time of healing, where you and Betsy can forgive and forget."

Thoughts bombarded me. Yvette was right about one thing: It did me no good to be bitter about Betsy. Yet I had not been consulted. I felt like a nonentity. I would die of humiliation if I went to the retreat. "Yvette, Ed and Betsy still have an attraction to each other. When Ed hears that Betsy led the worship, he'll gloat. I really, really hope you can cancel Betsy."

"I've worked hard on the retreat, and I feel I can't cancel out Betsy two days before the retreat. Really, Caroline, if one soul is saved, it's worth it all, even if it hurts you a little. I honestly can't see what's upsetting you so much. I know it wouldn't upset me, and it isn't upsetting Betsy."

"There must be six hundred women in Louisville who could lead our worship at a moment's notice. Would you please call one of them?"

"I don't want to hurt Betsy's feelings."

"Please," I begged.

"All right. I'll check with the committee."

"Will you phone me this afternoon with the committee's decision?"

"All right."

Yvette never phoned, and that evening I called her. "This is Caroline."

"What? What? Oh, I can't hear. My phone must be out of order." She hung up, and when I phoned back, her recorder was on. I left two messages, which she didn't return. Finally, I reached a member of the committee, a schoolteacher who edgily conveyed the committee's decision to have Betsy as planned. She then added as salve, "We love you, Caroline, so believe me, this is hurtful for us all."

I felt desperate. *I must be an awful person to be treated this way,* I thought. Ed was right about me. I ran to the bathroom and banged my head on the wall. I hit and hit. I had never been so empty. I had never been so low.

I skipped the retreat and Sunday service. I paced the house, hurt and angry, wishing someone from the committee would phone and apologize. (May had phoned the day before the retreat but said it was too late to intervene. She promised, though, to speak to Yvette.)

Sunday night I lay in bed, Betsy on my mind. In a way I felt sorry for her. *She went through hell with Ed too,* I thought. Ed's son, Glen, had said that Ed had thrown a glass of water at Betsy, then locked her in the laundry room. That probably wasn't the only violent incident. Yet Betsy was obviously as addicted to Ed as I. *What quality in Ed magnetized two women to him,* I wondered, *despite his violent core?*

The next week Maria Lopez from my church phoned. "Juan and I heard what happened to you about the retreat," Maria said, "and we are angry. We want to give you a present. You said your kitchen cabinets were disorganized, so Juan and I want to organize them."

"Why that's just great!"

"Is tonight all right?"

"Perfect."

They arrived in jeans and T-shirts about 7:30 P.M., and I sent their three children to play with mine. Maria was short, as was Juan, but soft and chubby from indulging in American ice cream, which she judged far superior to Mexico's. I had told Juan and Maria in detail about Ed's abuse, and they had responded with love and help, qualities learned in their Mexican village, where everyone helped everyone. Maria was a homemaker, and Juan was an engineering consultant, a success that made his village proud. After May, Maria and Juan were my closest friends at church.

I served coffee, and we got to work. While I organized a drawer of papers, Juan pulled out a dagger from the drawer he worked on. "What is this dagger for?" Juan asked.

"I never saw it. It must be Ed's."

"Why would he keep a dagger?"

"I'm not sure." Then I remembered his arrows. "I know he's obsessed with bows and arrows and guns. He has arrows that have four razor blades on the end. Maybe he started to collect daggers."

Juan's brown eyes darkened with alarm. "Maybe he would use this dagger on you?"

"No, he's a macho man. He uses his hands and strength. I can see him shooting animals or knifing them, but not a woman. I really think it's something old of his that he's forgotten about."

"*Quiza.*" Juan said.

"What's *quiza?*"

"It's *maybe.* May I have this dagger? I would like to photograph it for evidence, then I'll dispose of it. But I want to show the actual dagger to Doyle."

"It won't do any good. I've shown him a lie-detector test. I've shown him bruises. He won't believe there's any problem with Ed having a dagger."

"I have to do it—so I can sleep at night. I must get our pastor to confront Ed."

It was comforting to have this couple's love. Maybe they were right. Maybe Ed was capable of using such a weapon. I had seen murder in his eyes often enough, and there were those vicious arrows. "Okay."

Juan phoned me after his visit with Doyle. His voice raged in Spanish. When he got to *"Esto es,"* he abruptly switched to English, apparently remembering I spoke no Spanish.

"I showed Doyle the dagger. He held it for an instant, then said, 'Well, it's not unusual to have a knife in the house.'

"'This is not just a knife,' I said, 'it's a dagger. I'm telling you, Doyle, Caroline is in danger. You need to speak to Ed. If you don't, you'll be responsible if something happens in the Stuart house.'

"Doyle said, 'Caroline dramatizes things, and I wouldn't be surprised if she excited you about this dagger. My brother has a dagger because it's an antique. He's not planning to stab his wife. You'd be better off to relate to Ed than be so suspicious. Take him to lunch and be his friend. That's how to change lives. I know the Staurts have marital problems, but we can't always be looking for trouble. We need to show them both love.'

"I left in disgust. I photographed the dagger and threw it in a dumpster."

My eyes stung with tears. Though I basically thought the dagger was harmless, it hurt that Doyle called Ed's violence "marital problems" and believed loving Ed would solve them.

"Then I telephoned Ed and met him downtown at a coffee shop. I showed him the photograph. 'It's a very dangerous weapon,' I said. 'Why do you keep it in the kitchen with young children around?'

"Ed really glared. 'Why did you photograph my dagger? Where is it?'

"'I threw it away,' I said. 'I know you have abused Caroline, and I have grave feelings of worry about this dagger.'

"He told me that he could have me arrested for stealing his property.

"I told him, 'I wish you would. I would tell those police what you do to Caroline.'

"Ed said, 'I'd like to talk about Caroline, as long as she's the subject. If someone incites another to riot, shouldn't he be jailed?'

"I said, 'Yes, but in Mexico it seems almost everyone goes to jail all the time.'

"Ed said, 'It's the law that if you incite someone to riot, you are guilty, not the person who riots. It's the same thing with Caroline. She incites me to hit her. She's the guilty one; I am not!'

"'That's crazy,' I said. 'The one who riots or hits is guilty.'

"'Not in all cases,' he said, 'and certainly not in Caroline's. I have photographs to prove she's a vicious wildcat.'

"Ed ranted about you for a long time," Juan concluded.

"Please don't tell me any more of what he said," I pleaded.

"Maybe I said too much?"

"No. I just can't handle it. He's so twisted."

"I told Ed that if he hurt you again, I would call the police to arrest him. I told him that he was accountable to me. He's an evil man. My hands are shaking even now."

I started to cry.

"*Lo siento mucho.*"

"What?"

"I'm so very sorry for your pain. You're not safe, Caroline. I wish you would leave. You and the kids can stay with us as long as you need."

"Thanks so much, Juan, but not yet."

I felt desperate. Obviously Ed hated me and Doyle cared nothing about my welfare. I ran to the bathroom and banged my head on the wall.

The next Sunday I switched Sunday-school classes to avoid Yvette.

At dinner the kids choked down their food while Ed raged about the dagger. "You and your comrades are paranoid—totally insane. The dagger was a souvenir from a holiday in China. I've wondered where it was. Only a madwoman would see murder in a souvenir. Kids, your mother is nuts. Absolutely nuts!"

The children all stared at their plates.

"Okay," I said, "I'm sorry. Let's just forget it."

He jabbed a damning finger at me. "I will never forget it! You're lucky that I've decided not to have you and Juan arrested."

Ed ranted about the dagger for days. During one of the fights, I blew up and yelled at Ed for flirting with pretty choir members. "I'll never trust you. I'll never forget you had an affair with a choir member while married to Hildy [his first wife]."

"I regret the day I told you that. I must've had too much to drink."

"You did. You told me a lot." (Rarely did Ed drink too much, evidently because he played this kind of "true confessions" when he did.)

"I have never been unfaithful to you."

I hoped that was true.

A few weeks later, a member of my new Sunday-school class said, "Did you know about the letter inside the choir-room door?"

"No, what letter?"

"Ed's resigned from the choir. It's an awful letter!" Her pale eyes blazed with the injustice that explained why she was a social worker.

"How long has it been there?"

"Two weeks."

"And nobody told me!"

"I should have. But I thought you knew about it. I'm sorry."

Why hadn't someone on staff taken it down? Why hadn't one single member of this twelve-hundred-member church contacted me before this?

I ran into the choir room and ripped Ed's letter from the door. I read with disgust:

> It has been the best experience of my life, singing with this choir, and I feel I have made friends with all of you. I am sure that all of you have experienced trouble in your marriages and can understand that difficult times can befall a couple. Caroline is in the midpoint of life and very subject to hormonal swings. She feels jealous and worried that I pay attention to the ladies in the choir. For this reason, I am forced to resign.
>
> I cannot tell you how much regret this brings me, as I so highly regard each one of you ladies and have never on any occasion been anything less than a gentleman and helpful person. I remember that once I started Marge's [an elderly lady] car because her battery was dead. That is the closest I have been to being alone with any one woman.
>
> I will miss you all. I hope you will pray for Caroline and me—that our marriage can overcome this jealousy of hers.
>
> I can't sing with you up front, but my voice will join yours from the audience on Sunday as you sing.

After church, I stormed into Doyle's office. To his credit he was upset. "This letter should never have been posted or have remained posted. There should never be public accusations in our church. I didn't know about the letter. I'm very sorry, Caroline. I'll speak to the choir and to Ed."

"Why did you put that awful, lying letter up!" I yelled at Ed at home.

"How does it feel to have your image tarnished?" he asked. "Just like you try to tarnish mine."

He stalked off, leaving me in mental shreds.

The next Sunday Doyle asked me to come by his office, where he told me he had chastised the choir members, and he planned to speak to Ed.

Buoyed by his support, I left his office thinking, *Maybe he's turned the corner and will believe that Ed is abusive.*

My elevated spirits lasted only moments. Marge, the older woman with battery problems, confronted me in the hall. Her lips curled in indignation. "Ed never flirted with one woman in the choir! How could you accuse that nice man of that! I was alone twice with Ed in the choir room and once when he fixed my car, and he acted like a perfect gentleman. I think you should tell Ed to return to the choir. He would come if he knew you were over your jealousy. We need him. He has a lovely baritone voice, and he's a lovely man; the most faithful Christian man in the choir!"

I wanted to scream, *Of course, he didn't flirt with you! Why, he'd never look at any woman who was twenty years older than he, and not even one his own age. Why, he hardly looks at me, and I'm forty-three, ten years younger than he. It's young girls he likes.* But I didn't. "Oh my Lord," I said, and I dashed to the rest room in tears. No way to bang a head in there though. Oh, how I hurt!

I asked Doyle the next Sunday after church if he had spoken to Ed.

"Yes," he said, "but the conversation must remain private."

I wished I had not asked.

Spring came, my favorite season. As the forsythia bloomed and the river craft ploughed downriver, I just knew my life would improve. I was so quickly wrong.

Ed and I attended the Wednesday-night dinner at church, and after the meal, Allan, a retiree with crippling arthritis, hobbled up to ask if he and a few people could pray for our marriage. I liked Allan; he was a nice guy. Because he had one of the sweeter hearts at church, I had once confided the extent of Ed's violence. Allan had responded, "It is very wrong."

Allan prayed, "Dear God, draw these two people together and give them peace, healing, and joy." He prayed for a quick settlement of our "marital problems" and happiness together in Christ. He said, "All marriages experience valleys, but if a couple turns to Christ, a stronger relationship is formed." I trembled all over. "Domestic violence" was a term unable to stick in Allan's nice, kind mind. I believed then that 99 percent of the congregation did not believe domestic violence occurred among Christians. They thought we Christians only suffered marital valleys, out of which one easily climbed. Maybe only people personally familiar with violence, such as criminals, murderers, and battered wives could relate to the truth.

I opened my eyes and stared at Ed. He glowed like a star. He loved the prayer. He was vindicated, elevated to the status of a typical Christian husband who had failed a little here and there.

Once again, I found myself in the church rest room, sobbing.

OBSTACLES TO FINDING HELP AT CHURCH

Caroline agonized over Pastor Morris's failure to hold Ed accountable for his abuse. She believed Pastor Morris should revoke Ed's church membership, an act that might shock him into reforming. At least the pastor should inform him there are repercussions to wife abuse. She cited Matthew 18:15–17: "Moreover if your brother sins against you, go and tell him his fault between you and him alone. If he hears you, you have gained your brother. But if he will not hear, take with you one or two more, that 'by the mouth of two or three witnesses every word may be established.' And if he refuses to hear them, tell it to the church. But if he refuses even to hear the church, let him be to you like a heathen and a tax collector." Since Pastor Morris believed the Bible is infallible but ignored Matthew 18, Caroline concluded that he believed she exaggerated Ed's abuse or incited it. This tormented Caroline.

Jeaneen Watkins, an evangelical adviser on domestic violence and a crisis counselor, says that when she asks women in her support group, "'Is the church a resource for you right now?' and I'm not stacking the question at all, they will burst into tears. They love their church and are absolutely tortured that the church is not there for them in the way that they need, in a caring, loving, open-armed fashion."[1]

It hurts Caroline that so many women at her church discount her abuse. She would have expected common gender to draw them to her side. Yet that tie is not necessarily in force when it comes to domestic violence. A jury study found that female jurors have difficulty relating to women prosecuting their boyfriends or husbands for domestic violence. "They tend to comb the testimony for any indication why this unsettling woman before them is exaggerating—why she could never be them."[2]

I have often witnessed this same attitude. If someone tells me they wouldn't take it—that they'd be out in a minute—I explain that I felt like that once. But through my volunteer work with abused women, I have realized that I don't know what I'd do in every given set of circumstances. If I had little money, if my husband threatened to kill me, or if my health were poor, would I leave? Would you? We can't answer that question when we live on the other side of the fence. Abused women need us to help them, not ignore, condemn, or feel superior to them.

Here are a few issues that I feel prevent women from seeking help from their pastors, church leaders, and fellow Christians.

AN UNQUALIFIED VIEW OF SUBMISSION

In Ephesians 5:21–33, two verses talk about wives submitting to their husbands, while six verses discuss husbands' obligations to love and nurture their wives. Yet women often tell me they hear volumes on the two and next to nothing on the six. Why don't we highlight the six? And qualify the two? If we'd do that, abused women wouldn't be afraid that if they ask their churches for help they would be told they failed to submit and certain churches wouldn't cling to the idea that a lack of submission is the root cause of domestic violence.

Let's examine this Ephesians passage.

> Submit to one another out of reverence for Christ.
>
> Wives, submit to your husbands as to the Lord. For the husband is the head of the wife as Christ is the head of the church, his body, of which he is the Savior. Now as the church submits to Christ, so also wives should submit to their husbands in everything.
>
> Husbands, love your wives, just as Christ loved the church and gave himself up for her to make her holy, cleansing her by the washing with water through the word, and to present her to himself as a radiant church, without stain or wrinkle or any other blemish, but holy and blameless. In this same way, husbands ought to love their wives as their own bodies. He who loves his wife loves himself. After all, no one ever hated his own body, but he feeds and cares for it, just as Christ does the church—for we are members of his body.
>
> "For this reason a man will leave his father and mother and be united to his wife, and the two will become one flesh." This

is a profound mystery—but I am talking about Christ and the church. However, each one of you also must love his wife as he loves himself, and the wife must respect her husband. (NIV)

I suggest that we qualify the verses that speak to wives in light of the verses that speak to husbands. Husbands who abuse their wives usually exhibit characteristics that are the exact opposite of the husbands described in Ephesians 5. These husbands:

- emulate the devil, not Christ

- control, but don't lead

- display indifference as to whether their wives read the Bible

- beat their wives but don't beat themselves ("Husbands ought to love their wives as their own bodies")

- rage at their wives but never exhibit self-directed anger (again not treating their wives as they would themselves)

- humiliate their wives but see no faults of their own

The fact that God invests a husband with the responsibility to lead his wife does not license him to subject her to psychological or physical agony. There are obligations placed on his leadership, which if ignored, disqualify him as her leader. He is obligated to love and nurture his wife as Christ does the church and to lead her toward holiness through setting a holy example. A husband bears the greater scriptural responsibility for meeting his wife's needs. A husband's love is commanded to be the antithesis of violence and berating.

A wife is called to submit to a husband who strives to model Christ, not the devil. If she submits to an evil husband, she will likely be led into evil practices. Proverbs 4:14–17 states: "Do not enter the path of the wicked, and do not walk in the way of evil. Avoid it, do not travel on it; turn away from it and pass on. For they do not sleep unless they have done evil; and their sleep is taken away unless they make someone fall. For they eat the bread of wickedness, and drink the wine of violence."

When a Christian husband stands before God, he will be judged both for the quality of his life and his wife's life (implied in Ephesians

5:22–33). So if he abuses his wife, what will he say to God? And what will God say to him?

I believe that putting a no-restriction sign on the two verses in Ephesians 5 concerning wifely submission, more than any other factor, leads Christians to suppose that wives must endure mistreatment.

How common is it for a church to apply pressure to wives to submit to abusive husbands? James and Phyllis Alsdurf, authors of *Battered into Submission*, found in their survey of one hundred battered women that more than "one-third...felt pressure from their churches to submit to their husbands despite his violence." Yet experts in domestic violence agree that violence accelerates when women submit to it. The Alsdurfs state, "Accumulating clinical evidence suggests that the single-worst action a victim can take is to submit to an abusive partner."[3] Certainly submission does not protect abused women, but lays them out like doormats.

Research indicates that "the probability of abuse increases with the rigidity of a church's teachings, particularly teachings pertaining to gender roles and hierarchy."[4] Churches that emphasize gender roles also emphasize the husband/wife hierarchy. But Scripture says, "There is neither Jew nor Greek, there is neither slave nor free, there is neither male nor female; for you are all one in Christ Jesus" (Galatians 3:28). The emphasis here seems to be on the bond between *believers*. Actually, the marriage bond dies when one party in the marriage dies. In heaven the couple will join a population of gender-neutral believers, cluing us as to which is the more important tie. We must stop using the secondary tie to urge women to submit to abuse to maintain their marriages. Instead we should focus on the primary tie of believer to believer, thereby guarding a female believer's safety, sanity, and precious femininity.

Importantly, the command for believers to submit to believers, regardless of the sex of the believer (see Ephesians 5:21), prefaces the description of husband/wife roles (see vv. 22–33). It is clear that husbands cannot lead wives unless the husbands are first submitted to their wives as fellow believers. The abuser, with his lust for power and control, cannot submit to his wife, but can only dominate her. Don't mistake an abuser's kneeling and calling himself a worm and crying tears of sorrow for submission. This display is only meant to get his wife's affection so that he can control her again.

Finally it should be noted that many churches do not consider Scripture infallible, and the concept of submission has little meaning. Still, in those denominations, and in society in general, the view prevails that it is the wife's responsibility to make her husband happy enough that their marriage will endure. The spotlight is on her behavior when there are marriage problems. One woman from a liberal church says, "I'm not abused, but if I were, I wouldn't go to my church. They wouldn't tell me to submit. They just wouldn't know what to do about wife abuse. They would just hope I'd try harder and that marriage counseling would help."

A MIND-SET THAT BLAMES THE VICTIM

The parties involved in a domestic-violence incident (victim, perpetrator, as well as pastor, friend, or family member) often blame the victim for the assault. The victim thinks, *If I hadn't done that or said that, he wouldn't have hit me.* The perpetrator says, "You were hysterical, and I had to hit you." The pastor or friend says, "If you stopped putting red flags in front of your husband, he wouldn't hit you."

If it were true that a wife had the power to compel her husband to abuse her, we could draw several bizarre conclusions. A victim is more powerful than a victimizer, for her acts cause his violence. An abuser has no will power to control his violence, but he is his wife's puppet. Ultimately, the sin of violence lies at the victim's feet, for she incited the assault. The perpetrator is never responsible for his violence and should never be jailed, taken off church rolls, or be held accountable in any way. We need victim-reform programs to halt the epidemic of victim provocation! Of course, these statements are crazy, yet they have excused men for rape and domestic violence in and out of the church. We allow perpetrators to continue on as pastors, elders, deacons, choir members, and Sunday-school teachers, and as admired executives, sports figures, and senators.

Scripture tells a different story, one of personal accountably for sin. For example, when Cain killed Abel he tried to hide his crime, telling God he didn't know where Abel was. God penalized Cain by driving him from the land on which he killed his brother and consigning him to struggle for a livelihood (see Genesis 4:11–12). Cain's excuse didn't fool God. He had to pay for his crime. Neither does an abuser blaming a victim for his violence fool God.

Chillingly, if we blame the victim, we participate in the abuser's sin of violence. The next time the abuser strikes, he will be more certain it is his victim's fault because we have blamed her. What if he decides to murder her? Are we then oblique participants in a murder? Cain's sin.

Even a nationally respected Christian psychologist blamed the victim, accusing a minority of abused women of baiting their husbands into violence with an eye to doing them in. He noted that by taking a beating, a woman might instantly achieve a moral advantage in the eyes of neighbors, friends, and the law. He knew of women who belittled and berated their husbands until they had to react, just as the scheming wife wished. The beating might even help her justify a divorce. He then described a woman who paraded a black eye in front of the entire congregation.

I would not want to be counseled as a domestic-violence victim if that viewpoint judged my experience. I have talked to countless battered women, and I have never believed that any baited their husbands into blackening their eyes to gain a marital advantage or a divorce. They considered their bruises badges of shame. They covered them with scarves and sunglasses. They stayed home for days if the bruises were intense. Many thought they were somehow responsible for the assault, and their attitudes were of culpability and shame, not victory.

This prominent Christian's comments were made several years ago, and maybe he wouldn't speak so caustically today due to current secular indignation over domestic violence. But he, at least, shows a frightening attitude just around the corner of his past, an attitude still lodged in the minds of many in the church.

Whenever we blame the victim, we abuse her, resulting in a double victimization. We may heap more blame on her than she can bear. Diane, a Christian with two children, endured regular beatings from her husband, an engineer who claimed Christ. He punched and kicked her torso, thighs, and hips—places where bruises wouldn't show. When she approached her minister, she was told it was her fault: "Obviously, you are not fulfilling your husband's sexual needs."

Diane left his office, doubting everything Christian she had ever believed. We cannot allow our sisters in Christ or any other woman to suffer like this. Wife abuse is always the abuser's fault.

SEXISM

Male sexism, the prejudice of a male toward a female based on sexual differences and nothing more, has crippled women in and out of the church from ancient days to the twenty-first century. Aristotle wrote that the "male is by nature superior, and the female inferior," with a lower level of ability to think intelligently. Saint Thomas Aquinas stated that women, insane people, and children were incapable of giving evidence due to their "lack of understanding."

In the twentieth century, Freud stated that women "show less sense of justice than men…they are less ready to submit to the great exigencies of life…they are more often influenced in their judgments by feelings of affection or hostility."[5] In 1995, in Oslo, Norway, the courts acquitted a man who beat his girlfriend, ruling she deserved it because she habitually berated him, causing him to lose control. The decision was a regression for Norwegian women who had gained equal status to men.

In a locker room, Penn State football coach Joe Paterno, who had lost an upsetting game, commented, "I'm going to go home and beat my wife." When New York Mets manager Dallas Green lost, he took the same tack. "I'll just beat Sylvia and kick the dog and whatever else I've got to do to get it out." The two men apologized when accused of gross language, but Paterno went further afield, rationalizing that his comment was "just part of sports culture, locker room talk, harmless, a joke that did not mean anything."[6]

Dan Trujillo, director of Amend, a program for abusers, states how men generate sexist suspicions about women. "Men tell each other myths about women. A young husband in a locker room tells about a problem with his wife. His friend responds, 'That's not the worst of it. She will do that and more.'" The young man is primed for the worst, ready to act to prevent it. Trujillo says, "This kind of talk goes on all the time."[7]

These sexist beliefs, which are mythologically absorbed from the culture into male minds, form sexist convictions that they carry into churches. Ollie and his pastor are prime examples of sexism in full flower at church. Ollie had hit Sally in the chest before they left for church, causing her to speak and breathe with difficulty. After she panted out her story to her pastor, he said, "You must have done something wrong, or Ollie wouldn't have had to hit you."

"That's right," Ollie said.

This minister really believed that a man's power over his wife was absolute, a kind of dog-to-master view of women, with which he felt comfortable. You can have this comfort level only if you put a sexist twist to the Ephesians 5:21–33 passage.

Certainly neither gender is superior or inferior to the other, nor has Christ delegated men to angrily discipline women. Rather the sexes are equal. "But you, do not be called 'Rabbi'; for One is your Teacher, the Christ, and you are all brethren. Do not call anyone on earth your father; for One is your Father, He who is in heaven. And do not be called teachers; for One is your Teacher, the Christ. But he who is greatest among you shall be your servant. And whoever exalts himself will be humbled, and he who humbles himself will be exalted" (Matthew 23:8–12).

But if we are equal, then why does abuse and sexism exist in the church, the last place you'd expect to find it? James and Phyllis Alsdurf say that "one of the primary reasons so little serious attention has been given to the problem of wife abuse, both from a biblical perspective (for there is much within Scripture which directly addresses this problem) and from a psychological one, is that it has been men who were the writers, preachers, counselors, interpreters of the Word and authorities on family life. The selective inattention to this problem within the Christian world may reveal the inability of many men in leadership positions, accustomed to view life from a position of power and control, to remove the blinders of bias they wear and actually see what life looks like from the bottom side up."

For I have sworn thee fair, and thought thee bright,
Who art as black as hell, as dark as night.

—William Shakespeare, Sonnet CXCVII

5
Five

When a Christian Home Is Hell

Four years after Caroline married Ed…

I sat in the kitchen, staring at the clock over the sink, as if mesmerized by the way the hand inched along, driving home the point that this day would soon end without any anniversary present from Ed. The hands hit midnight, the dividing line between the day of our fourth wedding anniversary and the day that would follow. I had a gift and card in a bedroom drawer, but I wouldn't give them to Ed unless he gave me a present or card. I couldn't go through the hurt of last year. He had tossed my gift to him aside, saying he would open it later, which turned out to be the next day. I looked at the light in Ed's office, crazily hoping that he would yet come through.

The office light was extinguished. He entered the kitchen, his eyes fatigued. "Going to bed soon?" he said.

"Not yet."

"See you tomorrow."

Tears streaming, I watched his back retreat, listened to his shoes pad on the carpet, then heard his bedroom door shut. I opened my own anniversary present, a card I had bought for me. It showed a cartoon of a kitchen in chaos, dishes piled in the sink and on the counter. Black paw prints and spills splattered the white floor and walls. All the cabinet doors were open. A little white creature with one horn and little white paws cringed in a chair at the kitchen table, its eyes bulging with fright. Looming nearby was a black creature with two horns who was twenty times the size of the frightened creature. The little creature ventured, "I can explain everything."

I was the little creature, the black creature was Ed. Our house was never as messy as that kitchen, I thought, but my thoughts and life were.

I stuck my card in its envelope, threw it in the trash, then collapsed into a chair and sobbed. Four years was far too short a time for a marriage to become this miserable. But it had. So why did I long for the love of a man who was obviously incapable of giving it? What was the use of hoping he would love me again, when the agony of his rejection physically harmed my lungs, causing me to cough often and gasp for breath?

I found a pad of paper in a kitchen drawer. *If I list the black prints that stain our marriage*, I thought, *maybe I can stop loving him so much*.

1. You choose not to be soul mates! You break plans and don't include me in trips or meetings I specifically am invited to. You often go out to dinner alone, not inviting the children or me. At least I assume you are alone!

2. You choose pornographic pictures and videos over me! You say I am not on any man's short list of looks.

3. I am so upset by your behavior that I have sinned in many ways. I am addicted to a terrible habit of hitting my head on the wall to dull emotional pain rather than depending on the Lord. I hate my addiction to you.

4. The children are filled with pain. Trent won't get out of bed many mornings because he is so depressed. Kay is running wild, and I'm afraid she will get pregnant.

5. I curl up in the fetal position, cry, and agonize about how you hit me or rejected me. I can't get over the bone-deep pain of rejection I feel from the man I would give my soul to.

6. I cling to you. The faster you retreat, the harder I hang on. I know that you shove me away, but I can't help it. I adore you so much. I'd do anything for you—anything! I'd tear up the card, if you would just come in and say, "Happy Anniversary."

7. I've gone from involvement with causes for Christ to dragging around the house like a zombie.

8. I obsess about what you do out of town and worry you're having an affair. I don't pray, and that is my biggest sin before God. I hate you for making me so angry that I can't think of anything but my hurt.

9. What is wrong with me! Why won't you let me have you!

If listing my pain had served as a catharsis, fine, but I didn't think it had. I felt worse. The paper was spotted with tears, but I folded it carefully and stuck it in my skirt pocket. I hoped that the nine items were meaningless notations—that somehow, if I loved Ed enough, he had to love me back.

Six months later, Christmas season…

I perched on the top rung of a ladder outside a window, the last place I should be, while coughing heavily to expel fluid from my lungs. Pain shot through my chest. I quickly nailed the last red bow under a gabled window, climbed down, and made an appointment to see my doctor that afternoon. I had contracted double pneumonia the previous winter, and I prayed I didn't have it again. On that occasion Ed had taken off to visit his parents in Tennessee, leaving me so weak that I had to send the children to their father's and spend Christmas alone.

When it was time to leave for my appointment, I couldn't find my car keys and went to Ed's office to get his key for my car. Ridly, at his computer, waved and then continued to work. Ridly was strictly business, and whenever Ed and I argued, he remained as still as a statue.

"Can I have my key from your ring?" I asked Ed. "I can't find mine, and I have an appointment with Dr. Hurst."

"No. I don't want you losing all our keys."

"I have to see Dr. Hurst. I'm very sick."

"You misplace everything, Caroline. You need to learn a lesson."

I glanced at Ridly. He didn't move or look up.

"Please. I'm having trouble breathing."

Ed grinned. "How does it feel, sweetheart, not to be able to breathe?"

Horror shot through me. Ridly's shoulders twitched, and the gesture was like a hug from a friend. I knew that Ed hoped I would die from my lung condition. When I was diagnosed with chronic obstructive pulmonary disease, he had purchased a one-million-dollar life-insurance policy, naming himself as beneficiary. I hadn't wanted to sign, but he had placed his hand on his heart and promised to educate and support my children if I should die. "If the children were beneficiaries," he said, "we'd get into guardianship hassles, and it would be hard for me to look after their financial welfare." I signed, though I had chills.

"Please give me the keys, Ed."

"I can tell by your color that you're not sick. It's people like you who drive up healthcare costs."

He turned back to his work.

Coughing severely, I went to the house and phoned my father.

"You sound sick, dear heart."

"I think it's pneumonia. Could you take me to the doctor?"

"Well, uh…"

"Yes?"

"Uh, honey, could you give me directions to your house?"

I got the willies. Dad had been to my house many times. He had been a brilliant professor, but increasingly since he had retired, he acted childlike and confused. I depended on Dad since I couldn't rely on Ed, and if anything happened to him, I'd be lost. I gave him the directions.

Dad got lost and was late. I looked at him in alarm as we drove to the doctor's. His white shirt was soiled, and he smelled faintly of sweat and urine. His hands clutched the wheel tightly. He kept glancing left and right as if looking for something on the sides of the car. Next on my list was to get Dad to his doctor and find out what was wrong with him.

After taking x-rays, Dr. Hurst said I had double pneumonia. "You need to be in the hospital on an IV drip to thin the mucus in your lungs. The way it is, you could strangle." He was puzzled that my lungs looked so diseased. "Are you under stress? I've told you the importance of leading a calm life. If you don't, you'll continue to plunge downhill."

"My life's a mess." I began to cry. "My husband is cruel." I related what Ed had said when I asked for the car key.

"If you'll agree, I'll phone him. Sometimes husbands just don't understand how serious their wives' conditions are until a doctor explains it. Once he realizes how much you need affirmation and a peaceful environment, he'll come around."

Although I felt too sick to cope with a letdown, I nodded okay.

After Dr. Hurst finished speaking to Ed, he said, "He seemed to understand."

My emotions changed course immediately. "That's great. I—uh, just didn't think he would."

"Try and think more positively for your health's sake. I'll see you at the hospital."

When I arrived home, Ed's car was gone. I looked in the kitchen for a note, but found none. I held back my tears, because I had to perform long enough to make arrangements for the children's care. Dad sat in my bedroom while I phoned my mother, who agreed to watch the children. My mother had a three-hour drive, so I phoned a neighbor to fill in. I hurriedly packed, then, my duties finished, I rushed as fast as I could to the car, trying not to think about Ed's cruelty.

In my hospital room, a nurse inserted an IV to supply fluids and antibiotics, inserted a nasal cannula to provide oxygen, and covered me with an extra blanket. Feeling disoriented, I closed my eyes and saw the swampy everglades and felt the hot humidity on my skin. Then I was in a Paris restaurant with Ed, smelling the wine sauce on my veal while Ed blew me kisses from across the table.

When Ed came that evening, I had not moved from that lovely restaurant. I smiled, knowing he had taken Dr. Hurst's advice.

He leaned close to my face and glared.

"Please, Ed," I protested. "I'm so sick."

"Get on that phone, Caroline. Call your mother and tell her to get your kids to clean the house. It's a mess. The breakfast dishes are still in the sink. Trent left the garbage can open, and raccoons scattered garbage in the yard. Kay threw her books all over the living room. She and Trent are fighting over some potato chips. Our perfectly good garbage disposal is stopped up because you crammed god-knows-what in it! Your mother was trying to fix it with a broom handle when I left. And you left the house without putting away the ladder!"

"Please don't do this to me," I said, shielding my eyes.

"Call your mother now!"

Bands of emotions squeezed the air from my chest. Finally, I managed, "You expect the house to be perfect. But you can't control your filthy tongue."

Ed squeezed my forearm, his eyes burning with anger. *Will he hit me here?* I wondered in panic.

"Call! Now!"

"I can't deal with it."

He started out, but turned at the doorway, and the bright light in the hall glittered on his back. He looked dark and evil, and I knew I saw the devil. His dark lips parted, and he said, "Sweetheart, as far as I'm concerned you can rot."

Maybe his hatred hexed me, because that's exactly what I did—rot. I was so anguished it took me a week to recuperate. Ed never phoned, never came. My mother visited me, loved me, and loved Ed, for he acted like an angel in front of her. The day after I returned home, I heard Ed in the family room, coaching the children. My mother had just left for home, so she missed his statement. "Your mother's very sick, and she might die." He explained that chronic obstructive pulmonary disease was the fifth largest killer of people in the United States. "It's very much like cystic fibrosis, which affects children and often makes them die young. You kids will have to keep the house up if your mother becomes bedridden. I don't want a mess like last week. Get it! No filthy little pigs!"

I walked into the family room. The kids' faces were white. "Ed, how could you?" I turned to the children. "I could die, but there's a good chance the disease will stop and I'll live to be ninety. I really expect to see you marry and have children. There's a lot that can be done with medicine and prayer. So don't be afraid, and please pray for me."

I went to the master bath. I despised Ed for frightening the kids. All their lives all they had seen was disarray, abuse, and violence, and it was my fault. *All my fault.* I hated my addictive dependence that had sacrificed my children and health to Ed. I turned toward the wall and banged my head against it, feeling relief as sound drummed in my head. I had to leave Ed tonight! I had to find strength to pack. I hit my head over and over. *I will not cling to him,* I thought. *Ed isn't worth my love.* Then the tragedy of being without him engulfed me, and I felt alone in a dark void with no stars.

I opened the bathroom door as the bedside telephone rang. "How are you, sweetie?" my dad said.

"Great, just great."

"And the kids?"

"Never better. How are you doing?"

"I'm writing a novel about a society that functions compliantly after they all have—what's that operation on your brain?"

"Lobotomy."

"I'll let you know how the book comes out."

Dad had never written a book, and in his fuzzy state he couldn't. It occurred to me that Dad had symptoms of Alzheimer's disease, and I felt bereft. More than ever, I needed my dad. I hung up and curled up on my chaise with *Women Who Love Too Much* by Robin Norwood. I had read it before and turned to her list of characteristics of love-addicted women, noting those that applied to me:

- You will do anything to keep a relationship from dissolving.

- You are willing to take far more than 50 percent of the responsibility, guilt, and blame in any relationship.

- In a relationship, you are much more in touch with your dream of how it could be than with the reality of your situation.[1]

That last item was particularly true of me. I loved a fabrication of my imagination and had injected my entire being into extracting love from it. It sounded crazy. Maybe I was! I had to straighten myself out.

I heard Ed screaming at the children. "You kids get your rooms cleaned now, or I'm calling the health department!"

"Please don't, Dad," I heard Judy wail.

I felt too weak to intervene again. *Maybe one good thing will come out of their living with Ed,* I thought. *They will be organized people; they would never get that skill from me.* I made inner promises to help the kids. *I won't make Ed angry, then he won't lash out at the kids as much. I'll get after the kids to keep their rooms clean so he won't yell at them. We'll all avoid him, except when he is nice.* My head spun sleepily, and I went to bed and slept.

The sun was bright when I woke to a cheerful, "Good morning." Ed carried a tray of orange juice, milk, cereal, scrambled eggs, wheat toast, and even the raspberry jam that I preferred.

"This is so nice!" I said.

"Well, you're a sick baby, and you need a little care."

I filled with joy and love.

"Anything else you need?"

"Well, a hug."

Ed held me and stroked my hair, and I knew that at the depth of Ed's soul dwelt love for me.

Later as I carried my tray downstairs, I heard Ed on the kitchen telephone. I stopped outside the entryway to listen. "Yes, she's doing better. I've really been sick with worry this time. She's such a special person—my whole life. You know she's always been dynamic, an electrifying personality, and the thought of her going downhill with this lung thing scares me."

I had heard enough to live on forever. My heart glowed.

LOVE ADDICTION

CAROLINE'S ADDICTION

Caroline is mixed up, misdirected, and mistaken in love, and as an analytical woman, she knows it. "I know we are not talking about *agape* love [Greek for pure, unselfish love] between Ed and me. My love is filled with lust, jealousy, and bad thoughts. At first, I had such an overwhelming attraction for Ed that whenever he hurt me, I could forgive him just like that when he apologized and be totally in love again." Caroline's love is not grounded in wanting what is best for Ed, even though she would give the best to him; rather, it is grounded in a need for the "high" his attention gives her. By definition, a practice is termed addictive when overuse of it damages your life. Caroline's obsessive pursuit of Ed to get good feelings has ruined her life and qualifies as an addiction. Her hope that he will return her love eventually is fed by a myth that just won't die: A woman's love can turn a beast into a beauty.

The cycle of addictive love that follows describes how Caroline's obsession with Ed causes her to react to his abuse. Look carefully at this cycle to see if Caroline's experience fits yours.

THE CYCLE OF ADDICTIVE LOVE

You withdraw. You are devastated after he has abused you and has shown no remorse. Hurt feelings are too painful, so you flatten your emotions. *I won't talk to him,* you think, or maybe you think, *I'll be civil and reasonably pleasant, but no more than that.* Inside you are angry, but you suppress it. Although you ignore your anger, it does not ignore you, but festers within, damaging you. Essentially, you hope that your relationship will self-heal while you are on emotional hold. Caroline says, "For a few weeks I build a wall and say it isn't worth it. I withdraw and I don't pursue Ed. There is little interaction. If I don't ask him into the house for dinner, he eats out or in his office. If I invite him, he might eat in. If I don't talk, he doesn't talk. I back off, only because I can't take it anymore. I have to protect myself."

You panic. You fear your distance might cause your husband to abandon you. The more you think about losing him (he feels like your lifeline), the more panicky you become. So you pursue him. "I want him so badly," Caroline says. "I say grab the 20 percent. Take it and enjoy it. It's more than most people have; being truly in love with someone you adore. So I take it."

You don't have the chance to panic. Your husband breaks into your withdrawal with sweet talk. This melts you. But for him the interaction is a control measure; he can't dominate and hurt you unless he

can manipulate you, and he can't manipulate you if you are withdrawn.

You strive to be the wife he stipulates. You cook, dress, and act to
please him. You try to ignore any displeasure that he causes. You hope
your devotion will win his permanent love and end the abuse. Or
maybe you have had enough experience to know bad times will return,
but you want to prolong the good times at almost any cost.

You are abused again. Finally, he is violent or verbally vicious again.

This cycle exists only when you obsessively love your
husband/boyfriend and hope your relationship will improve. Once that
hope dies, the cycle dies, and your love dies. According to R. Emerson
Dobash and Russell Dobash, authors of *Violence against Wives: A Case
against the Patriarchy*, "Over time, the increasing frequency and severity
of the violence and the man's hardening position result in the woman's
loss of affection for him. Inwardly she will feel increasingly hopeless."[2]

If you are love addicted, your addictive behaviors can be identified
now, before you sink into hopelessness. Write them down. Keep a list.
If your list convinces you that your love is addictive, you can act to set
up a saner and safer life, either with your abuser or separated from him.
Whatever you do, it is vital to seek advice from wise Christians. Due to
abuse and emotional turmoil, your ability to evaluate choices is diminished. Proverbs 15:22 says, "Plans fail for lack of counsel, but with
many advisers they succeed" (NIV).

*T*hree months after Christmas...

I entered Ed's office as he was repotting a cactus, one of the dozen or so
plants that he tended lovingly. I wanted sympathy. *Ed must have sympathy in his soul,* I thought, watching him love his cactus. I had just had a
triweekly treatment to remove built-up fluid in my lungs, after which I
had visited Dr. Hurst. He said that due to the inefficiency of my lungs,
my organs were increasingly oxygen-deprived. Removal of the two most
diseased lobes of my lungs might improve my lung function, but there
were no guarantees since the COPD was diffused throughout my lungs.
Dr. Hurst concluded I should wait until I had to have the operation—a
kind of last-ditch hope.

While I briefed Ed, he pressed the soil around the cactus then rinsed his hands. "Well, I can't help you. It's between your doctor and you. I've got to get back to work." He sat and spun his chair to face his desk. Ridly typed away at the computer, but there was the now-familiar twitch to signal his disapproval.

I lost my temper. "How can you call yourself a Christian who loves his brother when you absolutely kill your wife with your tongue!"

He didn't give me a glance. I fled, more devastated over his rejection than my lungs.

EYEWITNESS TO THE HOOK

My habit was to interview Caroline in her home on Monday morning between ten o'clock and noon. I typed on my laptop while she talked rapidly. One Monday she left during our interview to answer the telephone; normally she ignored it. Her conversation concerned nursing-home care for her father, who had been diagnosed with Alzheimer's disease and had gone rapidly downhill. I walked around the living room. *Even the decor reflects that the home is troubled,* I thought. Prints of females in groups, stuffed animals, and photographs of her family were interspersed with sculptures in stark alabaster and fine reproductions of classic French furniture—an eclectic mix, that kept the eye darting around the room.

Standing on one table was a photograph of Ed holding Judy in his arms at the wedding: a striking picture—a handsome stepfather, a darling little girl, a deceptively touching bond of love—but a lie in this uneasy room.

Caroline returned for our interview, and later Ed entered, dressed casually in a white shirt with an open neck.

"Baby," he said, "how about lunch?" His eyes were tender as he touched Caroline's shoulder.

She smiled up at him, her eyes bright. "I can't. I have to take Dad to the doctor. He's not doing well."

Ed raised his hand to show a bit of space between his thumb and index finger. "Couldn't you move the appointment up just a tad?"

"It's the only appointment available."

"I wish we could have lunch," he purred. His love appeared genuine.

When he left, Caroline said, "You just saw the hook. He's got me. At this moment I would die for him."

"I saw it."

"If I stay withdrawn, which I have been, he can't hurt me. He needs me close to hurt me. He has a pathological need to inflict pain. It's his way of dealing with his inner pain."

She sighed, "I'm totally hooked. I'll do anything."

God lives forever and is holy. He is high and lifted up.
He says, "I live in a high and holy place, but I also live with
people who are sad and humble. I give new life to those
who are humble and to those whose hearts are broken."

—Isaiah 57:15 NCV

Six

Speaking of the Unspeakable: Marital Rape

Susan's honeymoon...

I didn't expect it. It came from out of the blue, violating me at a gut level as he forced himself on me and used me like a piece of merchandise. I was a virgin and expected the first sexual intercourse might hurt, but I also expected tenderness. I had no idea that my husband would rape me on our wedding night. I'd never heard of marital rape. I thought the voluntary nature of the marital union precluded rape.

Just minutes before, Rich had swung me over the threshold of our hotel in Birmingham. The air that swirled around me had smelled like honey and love. It was the late '50s, and I wore a real pearl necklace and a sheath dress (presents from Rich) and white gloves. I caught a glance of myself flying past the hall mirror and noticed that my mop of brown curls tumbled over my face. I thought, *Oh, there it goes again. Will I ever learn to manage all that hair?*

I jumped from Rich's arms, eager to experience my honeymoon to the fullest in this five-star hotel. I had high hopes for a wonderful future. I had a B.A. in English and planned to teach English until Rich and I had children. He had a B.A. in English as well and would start his M.Div. that fall while pastoring a small church.

I noticed a bedroom on one side of the hall and a sitting room on the other. The beige plush carpet engulfed the spikes of my heels. A suite like this must have cost Rich a mint. I noticed that a long table in the hall held a vase of roses. "Oh, darling," I cried, running to smell them. "From you or the hotel?"

"Me."

I hugged Rich, but I felt sad as I recalled my mother's tears as she waved good-bye. I knew she hated the idea that I had married Rich, though she had never directly said it. Mom loved me dearly, but it wasn't losing me that bothered her, it was Rich's blatant, flashy materialism. I could understand that. It had bothered me at times, particularly since I had grown up in poverty.

I had been the next-to-the-caboose child, the fifth in a line of six, with a ten-year gap between the fourth oldest child and me. Dad worked at whatever work he could find: carpentry, welding, fixing cars—whatever. As he pursued work, we moved all over the state of Alabama from one dilapidated house to another, some without water or inside plumbing, some with splintered wood floors and sheets for curtains, some in the city, some in secluded areas, and one near the tracks where hobos frightened us kids. We never had enough beds, and I doubled up with Lillie (two years younger than me), who was and is my best friend. Our houses were in areas where everyone else struggled to keep food on the table, so I thought everyone lived like us.

Dad was an alcoholic when my older brothers and sisters were growing up, but by the time I came along he was in A.A. His drinking was never discussed, and I thought alcoholism was his other life, belonging to my older siblings, not to me. Though Dad never hugged me or told me he loved me, I thought he considered me a peer, a friend, and a bright person. He was intelligent and discussed issues with me. It impressed me that he read the newspaper line for line every day.

My mama was petite but muscular from the hard work of raising six children in a family that was constantly relocating. Mama was the bedrock of the family. I knew she could accomplish anything. I always knew I would have clothes to wear, food to eat, and would get to school on time. She never said, "You can't achieve," but always, "You can!" She expected each one of us to go to college.

I tried to be as responsible as Mama was when I started first grade. Every school day I walked two miles and crossed a four-lane boulevard, clutching the hand of a neighborhood girl who was physically handicapped. There were no special-education classes at school, so she was my responsibility in the classroom.

I loved church and didn't remember ever *not* being a Christian. I loved to pray, even when I was only five. Mama always said, "Trust in the Lord with all your heart, and lean not on your own understanding." I never thought there was anything else to trust in but Mama and the Lord.

I loved my denominational college in Georgia, attended by students planning to enter Christian work or who wanted a Christian education. To pay expenses, I relied on loans, scholarships, and working half a day at the college bookstore, but I still had time to be a cheerleader and a class officer. I wanted college to continue forever.

As a child, I dreamed the usual hopes of girls in the '50s. I would find Mr. Right. He would be a mix of a movie star, a great father, and a great breadwinner. He would provide the perfect house, which I would decorate with Italian or French provincial furniture. My husband would flip over the gourmet meals I cooked. We would have kids— three would be best. The first would be a girl, an Ivory-soap-ad baby. Here my dream departed from the norm; my husband would be a minister, because I wanted to marry a man who lived for God.

I pinned my dreams on Rich, whom I met through a young man I dated. Rich apparently was strongly attracted to me. I was terribly impressed that Rich planned to become a pastor and devote his life to God, and I easily fell in love with him. Rich was the moneyed man on campus, the only one with a new car and dollars to burn. His first gift to me was an expensive, leather Bible, engraved with my name. He wined me, dined me, and took me to shops where he bought me entire outfits. I had never owned an expensive dress. In fact, my sister and I had always made our own clothes. I thought Rich's extravagant spending signified love. Yet after he bought the clothes, he acted as though he still owned them. "Why did you let Lillie borrow that dress?" he'd say angrily. "It's not hers. You really make me furious."

Another time he said, "You can use my car anytime, honey."

My dad had an old pickup truck, so I was stunned to drive a Pontiac convertible. But whenever I returned, Rich said, "You went pretty far, didn't you? You know how much gas that takes?" It didn't occur to me that he was manipulative. It didn't register that every gift had to have a consequence.

Though I did feel squeamish at times with Rich, on every occasion I put his unpleasant behavior out of my mind because I adored him and knew my love would smooth his rough edges. Usually when I was with Rich, I felt wonderful, bursting with excitement for our life in ministry.

Another event alarmed me, one that Mama never heard about. Rich disappeared from campus without a word for three days.

"Where did you go?" I asked.

"I had business to take care of."

"But you aren't in business, are you?"

"Look, if we're going to get along, you'll have to trust me that there are some things I can't talk about. I don't hound you about what you do—do I?"

"Well yes, you do. You're always checking up on me."

"Cut it, Susan. Leave me alone."

I kept these worries secret, because I loved him and didn't want to lose him, and I was sure he would settle down and become more normal when we married.

My mother's last words to me before the wedding ceremony were, "Susan, he's buying you." I thought she was wrong. I did not view Rich's generosity as down payments on me.

In our hotel room, I stood on my tiptoes to kiss Rich. I loved the security of his strength; he weighed 120 pounds more than I and was a foot taller. I didn't consider Rich handsome, but he had straight white teeth, a clear complexion, and an easygoing manner that attracted young and old alike. I tightened my arms around his neck. I would do everything to make Rich the happiest minister on earth.

I looked around our hotel room. "I love it," I said. My family had once traveled to Chicago to see an aunt, stopping on the way at a cheap motel where you had to pay extra if you wanted TV or ice, the total of my motel exposure. This room had a brocade Italian couch and a round table with two high-backed armchairs. There was a fruit bowl and a bucket of iced champagne on the dresser. In the center was a round bed with a red satin spread.

"All for you, my bunny," Rich said, leading me toward the bed.

I blushed when I noticed the mirror above the bed, not able to imagine exactly what lay ahead under its reflective eye. Looking down at me from the mirror was a wide-eyed girl in a demure dress with a high neckline. I looked as if I were about to attend church, not to enter a round, red bed.

"Oh—uh, a mirror," I said. "Is that automatic in a honeymoon room?"

"I checked a few hotels to make sure we had one."

"Oh." I supposed Rich had read about mirrors. I wondered if Rich had ever gone all the way. I thought he might have because he had pressured me a few times and had become insistent and sullen when I wouldn't.

"Champagne, bunny?"

I gulped down a glass to settle my nerves. There hadn't been any liquor at the reception, held at my parents' church. Rich offered me another. "No thanks." I unclasped my suitcase to unpack.

"No—not yet," Rich said.

"But I need to get my night things."

Rich stripped off his suit coat and threw it on the couch. He was shedding clothes fast, and I felt jittery. *Shouldn't there be kissing first?* I thought.

"I need to change—in the bathroom," I said. I had bought a white ballerina-length gown with sequins on the skirt. With its matching peignoir, the set had cost a week's wages from the bookstore.

I've had nightmares about what happened next. Rich grabbed me and jerked my clothes off so fast he tore my slip. He did not caress or kiss me. In a minute I was flat on the round bed, trapped under his entire weight. I cried out in terror, "Rich—please, wait!"

He pressed his mouth over mine. It wasn't a kiss; his lips felt more like a gag. His skin was hot and feverish. *Oh, dear God,* I thought. *Oh, dear God.* I struggled to be free. His hands pressed down harder in my shoulders. I panicked and scratched his arms.

"Cut it out!" he snapped.

"Please, please stop."

"Don't be an idiot. You'll like it once we get going."

It only took a few minutes, but I felt raw and torn inside, and my legs were slick with blood. He flopped over on his back, and I ran to the bathroom.

I sank to my knees and vomited. Terrified and humiliated, I curled up on the cold floor. I knew I had been terribly violated. The act had contained no love. It had been angry sex by an angry man.

Would it always be like this? I wondered. If it were, I couldn't bear it. Yet I loved Rich. Maybe he had suppressed his sexual urges so long that he kind of exploded, I thought. As I sat up, my legs trembled. I didn't hear a sound from the bedroom. I wanted to go home to Mama. I wanted her to tell me that everything would be all right. But I could never talk to Mama about a thing like this.

Rich called, "Baby doll, what's going on in there?"

"I'm coming out in a minute."

"You're sure you're all right?"

Definitely, I heard contrition in his voice, I decided, and I felt certain now that a lifetime of sexual suppression had carried him away.

I wrapped myself in a towel and returned to the bedroom to find Rich under the covers, peacefully reading *Newsweek.* He smiled and patted the place beside him. "I'm sorry if I was a little rough, bunny. I—I love you so much that I—well, I might have gone too fast and a little too hard. If I scared you, I'm sorry."

"You did scare me." I began to cry. I couldn't describe how terribly it had hurt. I didn't have the words to relate how betrayed I felt.

He pulled me beside him. "I'm sorry, my little bunny. But what you feel is fear. It always hurts the first time. When you're nervous, your muscles tighten up, and it just doesn't go right. Next time you'll be relaxed. You'll see." He continued on, even getting ministerial, calling our first intercourse a symbol of our one-flesh union in God, at which my gaze turned to horror. I felt as if I were in an asylum where everything rewrote itself crazily at the hand of a madman. *What happened was awful*, I thought, *no matter what you say.*

Rich stroked my back gently. "Just settle down, bunny. Be a sport. Don't be so serious."

Maybe I am too serious, I thought. Maybe a feather would have hurt me. I pulled away from Rich, opened my suitcase, and went to the bathroom to put on my gown. When I opened the bathroom door, I was relieved to see Rich asleep.

I lay awake most of the night, trying to reconcile this Rich with the godly one who would enter seminary and pastor a church in Perry, Florida. Yet I should have known he would be rough, I thought, remembering the night we had been kissing in a little forested area, when suddenly Rich had yanked me over his knees and slapped my bottom really hard several times. I had cried out in pain.

"It was just in fun," he had explained. "You've tickled me plenty of times."

"That was different. I didn't hit you."

"It's different but it's similar. Playing around can be fun and uncomfortable at the same time."

"I guess." I loved him so much that I had stretched my belief system to include spanking as playing.

I should have known he'd have some of his father's traits, I thought, turning quietly so I wouldn't wake Rich. Rich had talked at length about his father, Ernie, and not always in flattering terms. Between Rich's comments and my exposure, I thought his dad was a difficult man. He was gruff, fat, and bragged about his Midas gift of turning brass into gold. He owned a car lot, cattle, commercial real estate, and more farming land than anyone else in the county. He was a man who didn't like sitting in church, but he liked leading groups, so he taught Sunday school but skipped the main service. "Got to get back to the farm," he explained. The Taylors had been so influential in the county for so many generations that the high school was named Taylor High.

Those were the public facts. In private, Ernie belittled his wife and made her the butt of his "she can't do anything right" jokes, until her spirits failed, leaving her with only the impossible goal of pleasing

Ernie. He called her "dumb." (Actually she had once taught German and was more educated than he was.) He criticized her cooking yet ate it heartily. If he wasn't demeaning her, he was giving her the silent treatment. Rich said that his dad's silence ruled the house, and his mother tiptoed around like a phantom. Basically, he was the kind of man who did what he wanted and spit tobacco juice when he felt real satisfied.

Whenever I visited the Taylors, Ernie muttered hello and left the room with Rich in tow. That was the sum total of his conversation with me. Rich told me his dad didn't like the fact that I was from Alabama, not northern Florida, and most particularly his county, where pure American blood ran in people's veins. I would taint his grandkids with the down-and-out blood of my impoverished Alabama heritage. I determined to knock myself out for Ernie to prove the worth of my blood, for Mama and Papa's sake.

When I talked with Rich's mother, she was either cooking or in bed with diabetes or low spirits. She had kind eyes and a pointed little chin, almost hidden in pillows of flesh, but sticking out a little, as if it were her last holdout as a person. I liked Priscilla at first sight because she seemed to need to be liked. We had developed a good relationship so far, but we had not discussed anything personal. Despite her having a housekeeper, the house was messy—jammed with doodads from her shopping sprees: pillows, artificial plants, knickknacks, sets of dishes, linens that they would never use, things all over the place. Shopping was her comfort. Ernie probably allowed her to buy lavishly because goods displayed his wealth.

During his childhood, Rich had only heard his mom openly criticize Ernie once. "I do wish that Ernie wouldn't walk through my ladies' circle meetings dressed in filthy overalls and smelling so bad."

Rich had told me that discipline at home had been counterproductive. If his dad denied him a request, his mother filled it, and if his mother denied it, his dad got it for him. Ernie bought him an expensive camera, a Rolex, a car—whatever would make his boy stand out as a Taylor. His mother bought him anything that would make up for the death of Rich's younger brother from polio.

I didn't want to think about his parents anymore. I didn't want to wonder if Rich would turn out like Ernie and if I would end up like Priscilla.

I fell asleep finally.

That morning Rich made love sweetly, and though I was too tense to enjoy it, I felt assured that last night was an aberration.

I now wish I had left Rich that honeymoon night. Things I still find difficult to talk about happened during the next thirty-one years. Things I hate to think about. Things I never told one person during the first thirty-one years of Rich's ministry because he was so respected and loved. All those years I thought it was my fault that I was sexually brutalized. I was so ashamed to be a person treated so despicably. Finally I had to tell. If I hadn't, I would have died. I almost died anyhow.

Rich's new pastorate...

Rich attended seminary in Tallahassee, nearly an hour's drive from our home in Perry, Florida. In addition to his schooling, Rich pastored a little white church on the outskirts of Perry, an area that smelled of the slash pines that were everywhere, spindly pines without the fullness and grace of the trees I knew in Alabama. The downtown area was hardly a downtown area at all, just some buildings slapped around, not even lined up as in a proper downtown. Even the beach outside of town was not a beach exactly, but a dirty spot where one had to compete with the cows for a position and one had to be careful where one walked both in the water and on the sand because the cows had been there first. But the town rang of old southern traditions, black-eyed peas and cornbread, and the echo of the wails of bobcats that the old-timers said once lived in the pinewoods. I loved Perry right away.

The parsonage was not attached to the church, but a mile away—a frame cottage with green shutters, a little garden in back, and a yard full of pine cones. On the second floor was a small room with a view of the pines in back, which Rich claimed as a study. Alongside it was our bedroom, also small with dormers that added charm and faded wallpaper that did not. "I'll redo it," I said shortly after we moved in, anxious to turn the faded house into a showplace.

"Be careful," Rich said. "I don't want you wrecking the walls or making noise while I'm studying."

I planted a kiss on his nose, ignoring his demanding attitude, and focused on having an open house for the church after I decorated.

Rich was quite busy studying, visiting his flock, and preaching— remarkably well. Every week newcomers arrived to hear the wonderful new preacher, and after five weeks I noticed the church was appreciably fuller. Rich expressed his physical love tenderly, and I had almost forgotten the horror of the wedding night until late one Saturday night, six weeks after our arrival. I was reading in bed while Rich finished his sermon. Not wanting to disturb him, I had the door shut and the radio low. Suddenly the door burst open, and Rich's massive frame filled the doorway. He glared at me. His jaws worked angrily. Fright stabbed deep into my body, as I thought, *Somehow this is like the wedding night.*

"Why is this door shut?" he yelled.

"The radio's on. I didn't want to disturb you." I stared at him, frantic to understand why a shut door bothered him.

"Never shut this door again. I want to look over here when I'm working and see your light and know that you're available." He plunged toward the bed in six strides, and I shrank back in fear. He yanked me out of bed, ripped off my nightgown, breaking the straps, and forced himself on me in a brutal manner. He didn't even bother to undress.

When he finished, I ran downstairs to the bathroom and sat on the floor hugging my knees to my chin, rocking and weeping. The house was silent. When I returned, Rich was asleep, his clothes dumped on the floor. I slipped in bed and lay near the edge, afraid to touch him with my body.

At breakfast I was silent. Finally, he said, "Are you mad about last night?"

I pushed my scrambled egg around my plate. "Yes. How could you treat me in such a rough and uncaring manner!"

He continued to shovel in eggs and bacon while I stared in shock. How could he eat when I was obviously upset? Didn't he have any guilt over last night?

He swallowed his last bite, wiped his mouth, and looked at me. His expression became remorseful. Tears erupted from his eyes. "I'm a worm—a snake in the grass. I'm just no good, Suzy. I don't know what got into me. I thought you were shutting me out of your life, and I wanted to be a part of you. It's a need a man has. I can't explain, but honeybun, I love you so much. Please don't be mad. I have the sermon ahead, and God knows, I need your support. It will never happen again. Believe me, baby doll, love caused me to get carried away. You're all the world to me."

As a woman, I couldn't fathom his rationale, but I had to support Rich or he wouldn't preach well. "Do you promise—I mean never—never?"

"Absolutely."

He pulled me up and kissed my face and neck all over. It seemed that he truly adored me and that he was flooded with remorse. I forgave him immediately.

At church I sat in the third row on the right side, now apparently the minister's wife's seat, as no one had claimed the spot since I first sat there. I was next to an open window, which let in the scent of pine, plus insects. Rich preached about how Noah was a righteous man and blameless among his people, his voice reverberating through the church without a microphone. He was transformed before my eyes to a godly man. I felt convicted to lead a more godly life. Guiltily, I wondered if I had shut the bedroom door because I was miffed at being alone on Saturday night. The radio might have been a handy excuse. "Dear God," I prayed silently, "please help me be all that I can be for Rich. I have to understand that he's under great pressure. I'm so sorry that I shut the door on him."

Rich prayed at the end of the service, "May God fill your life so that you serve him and love him as did Noah."

I stood with Rich at the exit to the sanctuary as people filed by and shook his hand.

"Great sermon," said Mrs. Cascade, a wizened woman in a blue suit who leaned heavily on a cane. "You'll do well, son."

Rich smiled genuinely as he shook her hand. "Thank you. Nice to see you."

"I plan to have you to a nice southern dinner—pulled pork, my specialty."

"Great, I love pulled pork!"

He was giving 100 percent to these people, I thought. His goal was to pastor a large church, and I vowed to be the support he needed.

On the drive home, I asked, "Rich, if the piano player ever needs a Sunday off, do you think I could substitute? I love to play." In fact I had learned as a little girl that I could play by ear. If I heard something, I played it.

"Well—I don't know. I don't want them to think I'm pushing you on them—know what I mean?"

"But wouldn't that be helping out?"

"No, it would be pushing. It's saying, 'Look, we plan to run this show.'" He patted my hand. "On this one I'll have to pass."

It crossed my mind that Rich liked to run the whole show. *No*, I thought, *Rich is right; one Taylor up front is enough.*

The next Saturday I read in bed with the radio off, and things went fine. After we returned from church on Sunday, I fixed a fried-chicken dinner because Rich liked to eat heartily after preaching. In fact, he had been eating heartily at every meal since we married. He pushed back his plate. "This is the last big meal," he announced. "I've got to lose weight." He went to his study and returned with a pamphlet. "Here it is, my diet."

I leafed through the pages and found a high-protein, low-carbohydrate diet. Breakfast one day consisted of scrambled eggs, bacon, and kippers. Lunch was a six-ounce hamburger patty on half a bun, a hard-boiled egg, and cottage cheese. Dinner was chicken, cottage cheese, milk, and green beans.

"It seems unbalanced," I said. "Some days there isn't any fruit. There are hardly any vegetables. How will you get your vitamins?"

"I'll take supplements. This is only for short term. I'll drop forty pounds and be done with it."

"Forty pounds is a lot to just drop."

His face burned angrily. "I'll lose it! Please, Suzy, would you mind cooking this food?"

"No, I guess not. But I've always thought a balanced diet was best."

"Not when you're losing weight. If you don't mind, I need you to eat what I eat, so I'm not tempted."

"Okay," I said reluctantly. I was petite in build with slim, long legs, and if I lost any weight, I would look like a scarecrow. As it was, I had lost three pounds since we moved to Perry due to nerves at Rich's unpredictable behavior. But most of my weight loss I attributed to loneliness. I missed my family. The one time I had phoned Mama, Rich had paced the kitchen in a fit of agitation and continually motioned me to hang up. He then forbade me to telephone my family except for an emergency.

"I think I could do better on this diet if I could call Mama once in a while," I said.

"What on God's green earth has losing weight got to do with calling your mother?" His voice rata-tat-tatted like a drum. "You *are not* going to call your mother. I explained all this before. Money is tight, and we can't afford it."

I forced back tears as my world constricted to limits that seemed unendurable. No piano, which I had always played at church; no phone calls home; this ridiculous diet; those times in bed. I ran to the bathroom and had an attack of diarrhea. When I returned, I noticed Rich had polished off the entire chicken.

"Protein," he said.

I nodded, deciding he would blow up if I mentioned the fatty skin he ate. To maintain my health I would have to eat fruit, vegetables, and carbohydrate snacks when he was gone.

"Oh, my little baby. I just love you."

"I love you too, darling."

"Let's read the paper in bed and nap," Rich said. It had become a habit to nap together Sunday afternoon.

"I'm not tired. I'd like to do the dishes and maybe take a walk."

"Honey, you can do the dishes later."

"But I really *am not* tired." I didn't want to be with Rich. I wanted to roam around in a world that was wide open and all my own.

"I need you with me after church. I can't tell you now stressful it is, honey, to keep up with all I do. On Sunday when I can finally relax for a little while, I need you to lie by my side so I can hold you. Then all the stress falls away."

Rich is right that we have little time together, I thought. *I can walk when he is out.* I crawled into bed with him.

Soon, I found a teaching position and my spirits soared. I had always wanted to be a teacher. Furthermore, because I would be busy, I wouldn't focus on Rich's erratic behavior. Best of all, I'd have money to call my family. Surely Rich would allow me to telephone them. Wrong again! On the day I signed the teaching contract, I felt exhausted, short of breath, and I noticed with panic that the whites of my eyes were yellow. Tests revealed that I had pneumonia and hepatitis of the worst kind, the kind that had killed one of my friends in college. The hardest thing I ever did was to cancel that contract.

I was hospitalized for a month, after which I was ordered to remain in bed for two months. My mother came to cook and help, a situation that Rich hated. In bed one night he whispered in the dark. "Tell your mother to go home. I'll take care of you, honey doll."

"You can't—you're not home until dinner."

"I'll get women from the church to come while I'm out."

"Oh, Rich, can't you understand I'd rather have my mama?"

"Okay," he muttered, "whatever you want."

Rich alternated between treating Mama nicely and nastily, until she gave up on him and left after three weeks. A trail of kind women from the congregation checked on me, and I loved getting to know them. Besides helping during the day, they provided dinners, usually loaded with starches and calories. Rich had long since forgotten about the protein diet, and he heartily ate everything that came in.

At times, I'd lie in bed, overcome with anger at Rich. He had stripped me of so many rights, particularly the right to have my mother take care of me. But I had to ignore my feelings because I loved Rich and I had my dream: marriage to a minister.

MARITAL RAPE DEFINED

Susan didn't identify Rich's sexual violence as rape for more than thirty years. She says of their honeymoon night, "I knew that he had violated me and that sex should not be like that." She knew it by instinct, even though the term for Rich's assault was not yet coined. During their marriage Susan told no one about Rich's assaults, "not even my best friends or family." It is agonizing to bear repeated rapes as Susan did, but harder yet to bear it in silence, particularly when you can't name it. Stephen Spender wrote, "In order to live in the world, we must name it. Names are essential for the construction of reality, for without a name it is difficult to accept the existence of an object, an event, a feeling."[1] Before marital rape was named, when a woman found the nerve to describe it, it was as if the deaf spoke to the deaf without the benefit of sign language. No one understood exactly what had happened. Today, even with the term *marital rape* in place, wives hate to specify it. Why? Because sexual intercourse is assumed to be an integral right in marriage, and women naively or charitably may stretch that right to include any type of sexual intercourse.

When a woman is raped, she is forced or coerced to have sex, satisfying the rapist's hunger for power and control. This definition holds whether the rape occurs on the street or on the marriage bed. In each instance the rapist intends to dominate his victim (wife or stranger), render her helpless, and terrorize her.[2] When a man rapes his wife, he performs the same acts as a rapist on the street. He might carry the same weapons into the marital bed that a stranger carries in his jacket: a knife, a gun, a clubbing device, or ropes. A husband, like a street rapist, disregards his victim's protests about his brutality. If a husband has a gun, his wife is just as terrified of being shot as a woman is on the street. If her husband rips off her clothes, she is just as frightened and shamed. If her husband threatens her, she is just as cowed. Eventually, Susan named Rich's and her bedroom "the chamber of horrors." What made this tragedy all the more horrible was that Susan had to sleep with her rapist.

Perpetrators of marital rape feel little or no guilt, and some women report that their husbands want to hug and be near them after brutal sex. If women protest the violence, they may be called frigid. At first Rich expressed contrition (the intent of such apologies is to gain the victim's good graces to control her again), but he eventually titled Susan "the ice queen." Rich maintained that if Susan weren't so frigid, he wouldn't have to be so forceful.

The aftermath of marital rape is nearly as traumatic as the act. A wife may sit alone in the bathroom, apart from her husband, feeling nauseated, scummy—prostituted. She may have suffered injuries that need medical attention. In a survey of victims of marital rape, David Finkelor, Ph.D., and Kersti Yllo, Ph.D., found that all the victims reported some of the following injuries: hemorrhoids, torn muscles, and an injured or sore vagina or rectum. They found that some husbands insisted on intercourse even though their wives had just given birth or had gynecological surgery.[3] Mitch Finley, author of "A Doctor Responds," in *Facets*, says, "Women who are victims of domestic violence are more likely to go to their doctor or a hospital than to a shelter or use a law enforcement agency."[4] As a result, there is a growing movement to teach emergency-room personnel, doctors, plastic surgeons (for they often repair the damage of battering), and nurses how to ask patients questions that will identify domestic violence, including marital rape.

Understandably, women do not easily confide intimate sexual details to friends. Women do not readily *listen* to such marital intimacies either. When a woman finds the courage to specify marital rape, we often draw back in discomfort. A letter printed by etiquette columnist Elizabeth P. Post demonstrates what I mean: "A friend confides the sexual details of her troubled marriage.... Although I've told her I'm uncomfortable hearing her complaints, she continues to ask my advice. How can I shut her off?"

Post's advice: "Just be firm. Tell her you're not an expert...and you'd rather she talk to someone who is."[5] Elizabeth Post sides with the letter writer. Post does not advise the writer to offer compassion, support, or a referral to an appropriate source of help. Rather she suggests a firmness that will likely shame the troubled woman.

In the '80s, when marital rape began to be recognized as a valid form of rape, many states reformed their rape laws. Though there is now a measure of legal recourse for victims of marital rape, in many states it continues to be difficult to prosecute perpetrators. According to the *Harvard Law Review*, "The majority of states continue to accord marital rape a lower level of criminality than 'rape.' In some states a man cannot be prosecuted for rape unless he is separated from his wife. In other states a 'marital rape exemption' exists based in the belief that 'nonconsensual sex in marriage is legally impossible.'"[6]

I found disregard of marital rape in a plastic surgeon. "Some of my patients say they wrestle as foreplay to sex," he said. "It gets pretty violent, but I think they need the stimulation to have orgasms." To the contrary, it is a rare woman who requires violence to enjoy sex. While interviewing marital rape victims, researchers Finkelhor and Yllo found few women who derived any sexual pleasure from brutal sex. They had hated the violence at first, but after repeated assaults they made the best of it. They would have preferred nonviolent sex.[7]

Finkelhor and Yllo believe cultural attitudes promote male violence toward women. "Physical and sexual attacks against women are not isolated events. They are part of the social fabric in which economic and legal inequalities, sexist attitudes, exploitation of women's bodies, and violence are all interwoven. It is important to understand rape by one's husband as part of this fabric."[8]

I don't hear marital rape mentioned in sermons or in seminars connected with church. Yet statistics show that one in seven women experiences marital rape,[9] among them women who go to your church and mine. Since a significant number of Christian women suffer marital rape, we must define it for them and offer them relief. Often at a Sunday service or a church event I feel so cozy and safe. Yet sitting in my pew may be a woman who is raped at home but feels she cannot tell anyone, because rape isn't nice and church people seem so nice—too nice to hear such things. Are we?

Eventually Susan read *License to Rape* by Finkelor and Yllo and realized that Rich's angry sex was rape. She handed me a copy of a chapter littered with stars, exclamation points, and underlines—angry bruises left from Rich's brutality. Here are several sentences with Susan's exclamation marks.[10]

> For most of the women the rape experiences continued to have an emotional impact years, even decades, later. !

> [After the rape] to her amazement, he moved over toward her and wanted to put his arm around her in a caring way. It made her cringe. !

> I felt like a [prostitute]. What I was engaged in was nothing but

prostitution. I was buying another hour of peace and quiet—
that was all it was. !

He appeared to need to be angry with her in order to enjoy sex.
He would hold her in a tight restraint and tear off her clothes. !

She could have coped much better had a stranger raped her. !

Some of the marital-rape victims had lived in terror for years,
never knowing when a physical or sexual assault might come.
[This insecurity lasted after separation.] For it was hard to get
away from the psychological presence of a brutal husband. !!!

The sexual abuse was the worst part. The violence felt like it
was external. But the sex was taken from me. !!!

[The victim] had great difficulty sharing her pain with anyone.
[Susan wrote in the margin]! "Didn't, couldn't, wouldn't."

A wife suffering marital rape may interpret 1 Corinthians 7:4–5 to
mean her body belongs to her husband so she must bear his angry sex.
"The wife does not have authority over her own body, but the husband
does. And likewise the husband does not have authority over his own
body, but the wife does. Do not deprive one another except with consent for a time, that you may give yourselves to fasting and prayer." Yet
the verse defines that a husband's body belongs to his wife equally as
much as hers belongs to him. If she finds a sexual act repulsive or a horror, she can, by right of ownership, forbid his body to abuse her body.
Whether he will listen depends on whether he honors the Bible. The
word *consent* in verse five stresses the harmony that God expects in
decisions regarding sexual intercourse. No way does one partner have
the right to stake a claim on the other partner's body and say, "Sex goes
my way!"

ABUSED MINISTERS' WIVES

A pastor's abused wife is nearly the loneliest person in the church if
she is silent about the abuse, and the most maligned if she tells. It is
assumed that her husband models integrity; therefore, if she reports the
offenses, she often appears vindictive, a liar. It is even hard for the pas-

tor's wife to believe the man admired at church beats her at home. She thinks, *Can I trust my senses?* Generally, a pastor's wife opts to be silent about her miserable home life, as Susan did. Mary Stamp, project director of the Clergy Families in Crisis Project of the Spokane Counsel of Ecumenical Ministries, says, "A pastor's wife wants to believe the public image of who her husband is, so her denial is harder to break through, and she ends up emotionally deceived and disoriented."

How many wives of pastors are abused? Stamp estimates, "Based on a Hartford Seminary study finding that clergy divorce at about the same rate as laity and the rest of society and based on interviews with wives and ex-wives of clergy (anecdotal research), it is safe to assume that ministers abuse their wives at about the same rate as non-ministers."[11]

If a minister molests a member of his congregation, his act often reaches beyond that person's physical and emotional trauma to disrupt the roots of her faith. If he abuses his wife, her trauma is exponentially increased, her faith more disturbed. Even her image of God may bear the imprint of her abuser. Susan says, "As my marriage progressed, my relationship with God was so entwined in Rich that God and he became almost the same. God was good, bad, punitive, ruling, a gift giver, and a butt kicker."

What happens if a minister's wife separates or divorces because of abuse? Eldon Olson, director of Northwest Consolation to Clergy to the Lutheran Church, notes, "Their whole lives have been subsumed under their husband's ministries. The system encourages their enmeshment and then abandons them. As a result, ex-spouses of clergy experience intense pain, anger, and feelings of betrayal and abandonment, not only by their husbands but also by the church. Other women who divorce find comfort, support and strength from the church, but 92 percent of clergy ex-spouses leave the church they were in, and some leave the Church, too. Her husband's job meant relationships, identity, God, sacredness. She loses everything."[12]

Stamp works to aid ex-ministers' wives. She says, "Clergy wives who have suffered from the misconduct of their husbands need to network with other wives who have similarly suffered. The church, rather than shunning these families and keeping wives apart, needs to rally to their support and hear their stories and pain." Stamp points out that, as it is now, if a pastor's wife reports abuse, his superiors may focus on healing the pastor, not his wife and children. Even if wives and children are included in counseling, often counseling may encourage clergy wives to cope, survive, and heal on a personal psychological level with no recognition of the need for spiritual, economic, or emotional restoration or justice as essential to reconciling and healing persons, relationships, and families.

"Church bodies often 'wash their hands' of the uncomfortable situation," Stamp says, "because they don't know what to do." Though voices inside the parsonage may be silent for a long time, when they are heard, painful ripples fall near and far.

Hypocrite! First remove the plank from your own eye,
and then you will see clearly to remove the speck
from your brother's eye.

—Matthew 7:5

Seven

Lamb in the Pulpit; Lion at Home

Six months after Susan's wedding...

I strode down the country road near our house, enjoying the smell of
the pine trees and feeling the past that shrouded them, infusing them
with tales of how it used to be in Perry. I never tired of the old-timers'
stories about the drugstore with a soda fountain where everybody con-
gregated to hear the news. I thought Rich would be happier in a city,
though, where he could enjoy fine dining, his favorite activity when we
dated. He was often in low spirits and had a dual personality, treating
me with utmost love and kindness one moment then raging at me the
next. He kept a gun under his car seat, and when he was in a foul
mood, he sometimes shot rats at the town dump. I told him it scared
me that he killed in anger, but he refused to stop.

I looked at my watch: 5:30 P.M. If dinner was not on the table at six,
Rich had a fit. I would have run home, except I had learned I was pregnant earlier that morning, and I didn't want to jounce my baby. I
doubted Rich would like this pregnancy. He had told me not to get

pregnant until he finished seminary so it would be quiet in the house when he studied.

When I entered the house, there was a note on the table. "Where were you, Susan? I had to fix a snack and get to an early meeting at church. I can't imagine why you would leave without a note. I'll be home at 9:00. You can at least count on me."

When Rich came home right on time, my stomach jumped with nerves. I wore a pretty peignoir to please him. "Darling," I said throwing myself in his arms, "I'm so sorry. I was walking. I didn't remember your meeting. Will you forgive me?"

He raised me to kiss me at his level, carried me to the bedroom, and made love gently. Afterward as we lay together, I put off telling him about my pregnancy, not wishing to ruin the moment. Rich was hungry, so we went to the kitchen, and he ate a cold turkey sandwich. Afterward while we had chocolate cake and milk, I asked him a question about a scripture I had read earlier.

Rich waved me off. "I get enough questions about the Bible at church. This is my time to relax."

I stared at him in shock.

"Don't look so put out. My advice is don't read the Bible so much. Keep a balance. Otherwise you'll get so spiritual [he strung out the a-l] that you'll be of little earthly good."

Included in my dreams about marriage had been talks about God with my minister/husband, but it seemed that couldn't be. "You do love God?" I said tentatively.

"I'm a minister, aren't I?" he snapped.

I nodded. Obviously, as a minister, he loved God. I stood to clear the table.

"Let's go to bed," Rich said. "You can clean up in the morning."

"Okay."

We read in bed. The room was cheerful now. I had stripped off the faded wallpaper and painted the walls light yellow and the baseboards and door a darker yellow. I put down my book, too unnerved about my pregnancy to concentrate. Maybe Rich would hate it, but the congregation would love it, for this would be the first baby born in this parsonage in one hundred years.

Rich looked up from his *Newsweek.* "About ready to sleep, honey pie?"

His "honey pie" convinced me there would be no better moment. "Darling, I know that it's a little earlier than you planned, but I have news."

"Yes?"

"I'm pregnant."

His eyes hardened into gray rocks. "I specifically told you not to get pregnant."

"I didn't do it on purpose."

He slapped down his magazine. "You tricked me! All you think about is baby, baby, baby."

I remembered the nights I had inserted my diaphragm with shaking hands because Rich had manhandled me. I wasn't at all surprised a diaphragm had failed.

"I can't study with a baby crying. You," he jabbed his finger, "will keep the brat quiet, you hear!"

Tears fell down my face. "Honey, it's our baby."

"Just keep *it* quiet." He snapped out the light.

I felt great during the pregnancy except that scents of certain foods nauseated me. My nausea didn't alter Rich's request that dinner be served at 6:00 exactly. If the meal was late, he cursed me. I learned one trick; if I had the table set when he came home, dinner could be a few minutes late without him hitting the ceiling.

One night I had to flee the kitchen several times to escape the scent of pork roast. In between bouts of nausea I peeled potatoes and wondered if Rich (like his parents) had an eating disorder. His weight ranged between 230 and 260 pounds. When he wasn't dieting, he expected huge meals, and when he was dieting, he expected me to cook rigid diets and eat them with him. I had noticed cookie bags in his car during his diets, and that angered me. It made no sense for me to slave over his diets while he secretly consumed high-calorie snacks.

Rich walked in. I had two potatoes left to peel. "What's holding you up!" he yelled. "I'm starved."

"The pork smell is bothering me. I have to keep running from the kitchen."

"Don't be a sissy. You got yourself into this pregnancy, so don't whine about it." He glared at my figure. Rich hated every one of the ten pounds I had gained. "You look like a bloated old cow. That bloat is what's making you feel sick. I hate the look of a pregnant woman. Just get this brat out so you'll look like you used to."[1]

My tears spilled over.

"If you hadn't messed up with your diaphragm, this wouldn't have happened."

My stomach churned. I would throw up any second if I didn't leave. "Excuse me."

Rich grabbed my shoulders. His cheeks puffed in and out like a toad's. He shoved me backward, banging my head into a cabinet door. He slammed his fist into the cabinet, missing my head by inches. "I hit the cabinet, but it could have been your head!" he yelled.

I screamed in terror. Rich had boxed in college, and I knew that he could kill me. As he drew back his fist, his face blanched with fright. "What have I done?" he cried. "Oh God—what have I done to you, my bunny?"

"Just let me leave." I ran to the bathroom, locked the door, and threw up.

He pled with me from the other side of the door to come out. "I don't deserve you to ever look at my face again. I'm so sorry. I didn't mean it. I just wasn't thinking. I wouldn't hurt you for the world. Please come out!"

I threw up again. When I could speak, I said, "I hate you! I'm sorry I ever married you. I can't believe that you can speak about love in your sermons and treat me like this. You're a hypocrite. You don't care anything about our baby. It's like I'm having it alone! And my mama's so far away. I want to go home to Mama."

His voice pled as if he begged for his life before a firing squad. "Please forgive me. Don't leave. I'd kill myself. I mean it, Suzy. I've got tranquilizers for a little depression I'm having. I guess I didn't tell you about it so you wouldn't be upset. I'll take the whole bottle if you leave. I didn't hurt you deliberately. I had a horrible day, a run-in at church, and a bad grade on a test. Believe me, it had nothing to do with my love for you. I love you more than life itself. You're so much better than me, bunny. I—I'm the luckiest man to have you."

He's losing his confidence as a man, I thought with guilt. I shouldn't have come down so hard on him. If he fell apart, he couldn't carry on his work at church. In the future I would start dinner earlier to compensate for my nausea. I had to remember how pressured he was between school and church. I flew out of the bathroom and into his arms. He stroked my hair and carried me to the couch, and for many days he was tender and loving.

Three weeks before my due date, I fell asleep early, and I didn't hear Rich come to bed. Suddenly kicks shoved me off the bed. I grabbed for the covers, but they slipped from my hand.

"Get out of here," Rich yelled.

I managed to break the fall with my hand, but my belly was jarred. Panicky, I ran my hand over my stomach until I felt the baby kicking. I pressed the bed edge for balance and struggled to my feet. *Dear God*, I anguished, *why would Rich kick me out of bed?*

In the dim light from the hall night-light, I saw Rich propped up on his elbow.

"You may have hurt the baby."

He didn't say anything.

"But why?" I cried.

"Because I'm sick of you."

I lay on the couch without a blanket, too frightened to return to the bedroom closet for one. I didn't sleep all night. He had treated me with disdain so often during the pregnancy, but this was the limit. Now he had risked his baby's life. What a horrible father he would be! *I'll go home to Mama and never return*, I thought. But I was a Christian, and I believed our marriage vows were holy. I knew I had to stick by Rich for better or worse.

In the morning, I fixed Rich's breakfast while he whistled in the shower, enjoying every splash. While he ate bacon and eggs, I busied myself at the sink, too angry to look at him. On his way out, he turned me around, kissed my lips, and smiled, as if nothing had happened. Bewildered, I had to conclude that Rich had suffered a violent nightmare. He obviously didn't realize he had kicked me out of bed.

I visited the doctor that day, telling him I had fallen downstairs. He said, "The baby's heartbeat is strong. Don't worry. Babies are hardy. It's not unusual to fall during pregnancy. Due to pregnancy hormones, the joints are lax, which increases the risk of falling or other injury. Be careful and walk slowly."

Colleen was born in November, and when we arrived home with her, Rich held her gingerly for a minute, then handed her back. "She's kind of cute. Be sure she keeps quiet, sweetie pie."

"I'll do my best."

That was his nicest comment about her. Within days Rich was insanely jealous of her, raging when he thought I fussed over her too much. He never did anything for her or our two children who followed Colleen because he said that was the mother's role.

Assault in the parsonage...

Brenda was born two years after Colleen, not long after Rich had earned his M.Div. and had been appointed to a larger church in Jacksonville, Florida. Rich was as successful in Jacksonville as he had been in Perry, adding new members weekly. He was convinced he would go far in his denomination. We lived a block from the church in a brick ranch-style home surrounded by live oaks, dripping with Spanish moss that traced eerie shapes in the moonlight and fed nightmares into my imagination when I was stressed out over Rich.

After Brenda was off the bottle, Rich demanded that the children be fed early so that he could eat in peace. But I still had to jump up for the children, which annoyed him. One evening as I washed dishes, Rich spun me around. "Baby doll, you've got a lot to handle. I'd like to give you an hour a week off, all to yourself. You can go anywhere you want."

"Thanks," I said gratefully. I didn't know it was abnormal for a wife to have only an hour a week free from childcare.

Every Monday night I excitedly hopped in our Chevy to see the sights or shop. The first fifty-five minutes were exhilarating, the last five were nerve-racking because I didn't dare be late. Rich's parting words always applied the screws. "Get back on time. You know how I worry, honey."

One Monday, a long freight train delayed me, and I returned ten minutes late.

Rich flung open the door before I could turn the knob. "It was a freight—" I said.

"Likely story. You met someone, didn't you?"

"No!"

"I want to know the truth!"

I snapped angrily, "One can hardly be unfaithful in one hour per week."

"I'll teach you to sass me."

He hauled me to the bedroom, jammed me down on the bed so hard it bounced, and placed his hands around my neck.

He stared me in the eyes and didn't speak, as if I were a rat whose neck he would snap. I was frantic. Would he kill me? *No,* I thought, *he couldn't take care of the kids. And he'd have to answer to the church. But he might kill me anyway. Should I fight him?* I couldn't; he was more than twice my size. Nearly an hour passed. I didn't see the children and assumed they were asleep. I didn't dare ask. His grip was not tight, but firm. He continued to stare. I was beyond panic. I felt my head dropping into a faint.

Rich released me. As I wobbled from the room, an object smashed into my skull. I turned to see a ceramic bird lying behind me, cracked in pieces. I glanced at it, confused from all that had happened, then continued walking. Rich threw my pillow after me and slammed shut the bedroom door, letting me know he would sleep alone. "Next time, don't be late," he screamed from the room, "or your excursions will be eliminated!"

I huddled on the couch, shaking. How could Rich be so cruel, even if I were unfaithful? But I had never been unfaithful, or thought of it, nor would I ever be. That he would think that of me hurt as much as his trapping me on the bed.

The lump on my head throbbed, and I got up, took two aspirins, and went to the kitchen. As my head cleared, I felt hot rage. I hated Rich! I was so angry that I had the startling experience of seeing everything in red. The countertop was red. The walls. The refrigerator. I paced wildly around the kitchen. I had to leave now—this minute. But where would I go? I'd eventually have to come back for the children, then Rich might choke me again. I couldn't take them now; he'd hear me. My rage grew hotter. It made me wish that Rich would have a car accident tomorrow and be out of my life forever.

I took my journal from its hiding place behind the hutch, and before I wrote, I read some entries from the last few months:

> You kicked me out of bed again. When I left you earlier in the kitchen, you were pleasant. You kissed me good night, then this. I never know when I will be kicked out of bed with objects flung after me: pillows, books, the clock.
>
> Tonight you plummeted and poked me all over in bed while you made love. I swallowed my screams because I didn't want to wake the children. I made it through by assuming an out-of-body-and-mind persona. It is getting so much worse sexually, and you never listen to my feelings of how I would like to be loved. If I touch you, you immediately think it is a sexual advance, and you never allow me to cuddle and just be near you.
>
> I keep rationalizing your irresponsible behavior—try to "smooth over" and make the unacceptable acceptable by giving myself "good reasons" for what you do.
>
> You were charming and lovable all week. Darling, I hope this isn't another one of those fleeting good times, followed by disdainful treatment.
>
> At church whatever counsel you give to individuals in trouble usually works. It makes me wonder, "What's wrong with me?" If only I could tell someone my own problems with you, then maybe I could make some sense out of my life.
>
> I feel so guilty if I rebuff your advances. You're a man, and I know you need sex. But it hurts me when you say, "You're mine. Your body is mine." Is it? Doesn't it belong to me too? It is all that I really own.
>
> You say innumerable times that you would be nice most of the time if only I would stop doing this or change that or be more of this or less of that. It's your behavior that's wrong, and you need to take responsibility for it, past, present, and future. It

seems you are far more concerned with deflecting blame from yourself than with recognizing the pain you have caused me.

You're finally the man I know you can be, and it will be this way forever. Yet, darling, so many times I have hoped it and written it, and by the time the ink dried you had reverted to your abusive behavior.

I started to write, and I wrote for an hour before I released enough anger to lie down.

The next morning while Rich ate his eggs, he cried and ran his hand through his hair so it stood on end like a wild man's. "I'm just no good, Suzy. You are absolutely the most wonderful wife and so extremely beautiful. Really, when we dated I thought you were the classiest girl on campus. You're so far above me. What I did to you last night was unpardonable, but if you will just forgive me this one last time, I'll devote my life to making you happy. You deserve nothing but the best. It's just that I was frantic with worry when you were late, and yes, I thought it might be another man. But, honey, that only means you're so beautiful that I go crazy. Maybe if you didn't wear makeup when you went out, I could relax." He pulled a bottle of tranquilizers from his pocket and rattled them. "If you don't forgive me, I'll kill myself."

"Oh, Rich, please don't. It was all my fault, really. I should've thought about the possibility of a train, especially since I know you worry."

"No, it's my fault," he said glumly. "Will you truly forgive me?"

"If you promise not to kill yourself."

"I promise."

If my forgiving him allows him to go from rage to charm, from attack to apology ad infinitum, I shouldn't forgive him, I thought. But I loved him. I had to hope for the best. "Of course I forgive you, darling."

His tears immediately dried.

Later that day, he brought home three beautiful dresses, which I modeled in the bedroom. *He is a wonderful man,* I thought, as I twirled in a blue dress with a full skirt. "Oh, this is so lovely, darling," I said. "I love them all, but I love the blue one the most."

"Be careful with them. They cost a mint."

"Oh yes!" *The catch, always the catch*, I thought.

Sixteen years of marriage...

We moved to Orlando, where Rich was appointed to a six-hundred-member church, a plum assignment, rightfully earned, for at thirty-eight Rich was a powerful orator. My mind spun during his sermons, as I tried to separate the persuasive speaker who inspired me from the abusive husband who terrified me. The power of his presentation always prevailed, and I squirmed with guilt that I impeded his career, as he insisted I did. "Dear God, I need you!" I would pray. "Am I as awful, inept, unlovable, and scummy as Rich conveys that I am? Help me, Lord, to be a better wife."

Our parsonage was in the hills west of downtown Orlando, not far from Interstate 4, the main route to Walt Disney World. I often thought about driving the children to Disney World for family fun. Our children seldom had fun. Rather, they were the victims of Rich's abuse and my nerves that broke out at times in harsh and punitive remarks. Colleen, fifteen, was overweight, sullen, and a rebel who protested the establishment and fought with Rich, causing her to receive more of Rich's abuse than the other children. Nonetheless, she remained a brilliant student. Brenda, thirteen, carried a chip on her shoulder, was overweight, and, though intelligent, was a terrible student. Her passion was karate, in which she was nearing a black-belt level. She was Rich's favorite child, the one he took on rides, ate late-night snacks with, and confided in—almost like a wife. Nate, eleven, was dark-haired, slim, and quiet around the house. He shared my attitude concerning Rich: appease him, please him, peace at any price. Rich ignored Nate for the most part.

Saturday, sermon-preparation day, was consistently the worst day of the week. One Saturday while I fixed sandwiches, Rich chased Colleen through the living room, fast on her heels. She slammed her bedroom door with a crash that echoed in the kitchen. I dashed to her room, arriving just as Rich smashed his fist through her plasterboard wall before entering through the doorway. "Get out from under the bed, you half-baked ton of manure!" he yelled. His face was so red I thought he would have a stroke. "Get out and take what you have coming."

No sound came from under the bed.

Rich reached for me instead and shook me. "If you don't teach your daughter to be quiet while I work, I'm calling the authorities to remove her from this house."

"You wouldn't!"

"Oh, yes I would!" He stormed off to finish his sermon.

I sat on Colleen's bed. "Honey, what happened?"

As she crawled out, she gazed at her damaged wall. "I hope he broke his fist."

"You know it's better to stay out of his way, especially on Saturday."

"I'll tell you what I did. I had my radio on in the yard under his window. I didn't turn it off immediately because he angered me with his yelling. I hate him!"

She sobbed and I rocked her. "I love you, darling."

The children and I were trapped, I thought. I couldn't tell anyone in Rich's congregation about Rich's violence. No one would believe it. At church Rich was gracious and unassuming and always had flocks of people around him. Mama would believe me, but she had died, leaving a terrible void. My sister Lillie would believe me, but I was ashamed to tell her.

About a year later on a Saturday, I fixed dinner while Colleen and Nate watched a movie in the family room and Brenda practiced karate moves. I saw them clearly, as only a breakfast bar divided the family room from the kitchen. Suddenly Rich plunged into the peaceful scene, rattling his sermon manuscript. "Turn that blasted TV down! I'm trying to concentrate! And stop jumping around, Brenda."

Rich addressed Colleen. "Your garden's full of weeds. Get out and weed it—now!" Rich insisted we all maintain vegetable plots to uphold the Taylor tradition of family gardening. When the harvest was in, I canned and froze the overflow.

"It's hot out there. I'll do it right after dinner when it's cooler."

"Do it now!"

"What's the difference? In an hour or two the weeds won't be any higher."

I stopped mixing a cake batter. "You better go weed, honey," I said.

"It's my garden." She didn't move her eyes from the film. "I'll weed it later."

Rich's face swelled like a melon as he grabbed a cane from the umbrella rack and slammed it on her shoulders. She wore a top with spaghetti straps, and the cane left a red slash on her skin. Rich whacked her a second time, and Colleen fled outside. I stood at the kitchen window crying, wishing I could help her as I watched him beat her all the way to her garden. As she pulled weeds, she wiped off tears, streaking her face with mud. Rich stood over her for a few minutes, then left to finish his sermon. I ran out to her. "I'm so sorry, honey." I always felt so sorry, yet I never knew how to stop Rich. "I'd stay and help you, but you know how Dad is about having dinner on time."

"I hate him," she said.

At 10:00 P.M., I went to her room and found her gone. I called for her in the house and outside. Rich was on the screened porch, reading a book on effective parenting, evidently shaken by his earlier assault on Colleen.

"Your daughter was here at 9:30!" I screamed. "Now she's gone. You've finally driven her away!" My hysteria built as terrible possibilities ran through my mind. "Maybe she went to the expressway and a rapist picked her up. She might be dead. You totally demoralized her. You've ruined her as a person. Oh, I hate you! I'll never forgive you if anything happens to Colleen. What a horrible, evil man you are! How can a man of God attack his daughter with a cane!"

Rich telephoned the police, who said they could do nothing until Colleen was missing for twenty-four hours. They advised us to wait up all night with the lights out; Colleen would likely return if she believed she could slip in unnoticed.

"I have to look for her," I told Rich.

Rich drove slowly along the expressway. There was no moon, and I dimly saw the shoulder, but every darkened spot appeared to be Colleen. Rich glanced around, as alarmed as I. "This is terrifying," Rich said. "Let's go home and wait, as the officer suggested." Rich choked up. "You're right. I'm—I'm a terrible father. I—I love Colleen. I promise you," he sobbed, "that I will never hurt Colleen again."

His words got a cold reception from my heart. "I'll wait and see."

At 5:00 A.M. Colleen entered through the back door, and we followed her to her room. "I spent the night in a ditch by the church," she said. Her face had swelled from an allergic reaction to the weeds. Mosquito bites dotted her face and limbs.

"Oh, honey," I said.

"I didn't intend to come back. Then I realized I'm too young to leave. I have nowhere to go. But the minute I'm eighteen, I'm out."

"Darling, you need a bath to get the allergens and dirt off, then you need to sleep. We were so worried."

Rich said, "I—ah, I'm sorry about the cane thing. You and I need more father/daughter interaction. If we talk things over, we won't get all wrought up. We'll solve our little differences."

Colleen shot him a look of hate. "You make me sick, you alleluia, Bible-pounding hypocrite!" She fled to the bathroom.

Rich never forgave Colleen for rejecting his apology.

Colleen (at age thirty-four) reflects on her childhood...

After the beating with the cane, Mom intervened more on my behalf, and we became close, although Mom got smacked around for it. Dad started seeing us as a constellation of two; I was her shadow and her dog, he said. I think my mom and I developed an unspoken contract that we would protect each other. Up until then I thought no one would help. I now realize what terrible trouble she had in her marriage. Once that transition happened after the cane, we began to talk a lot, and we've had a continuing dialogue about family matters.

But I hated Dad, and I became the quintessential rotten kid. I started to smoke, hang out with tough people, and do drugs. Dad's way of intervening was to find a psychologist to admit me to a psychiatric ward. I was there a week. They had to dismiss me because there was clearly nothing wrong with me. I hated Dad for that more than any other thing. His sending me to the mental hospital was a control thing. Physically he couldn't control me anymore; I fought back and hurt him as much as he hurt me. But my wild behavior was a reaction to the bad stress under which I lived. A big part of it was due to Mom's saying that I couldn't talk to anyone else about family problems, not friends, not adults, not anyone. I am making sure my kids have other adults they can talk to!

I eventually earned a law degree and married a quiet, loving man who is a good father to our two children. Bert's the exact opposite of my father. I refuse to talk to my father on the phone or see him. I'm currently in therapy, working through the trauma of my childhood, a process I expect to continue for some time. My therapist is the first to validate me for not being involved with Dad. I even have tweaks from Mom that I should see Dad for my children's sake. Dad sends me nasty notes; I don't respond. He lies to my receptionist to get through to me, and I hang up. I am so sure he won't reform. I don't want to try to help him reform. I love my family, and I love my job. I simply put up with too much when I was young. I feel the loss of a grandfather for my girls keenly, and yes, it's then that I allow myself to wonder, could he change?

The truth is, Dad will never change. Someone with a conscience could feel another's pain. My dad has none. He thinks of others as objects. It's the same macro-mentality that the Nazis had. If we stop seeing humanity, we can do what Dad does. Why feel sorry about hurting an object? I have seen this in the courtroom in myself when I get so wrapped up in the technicalities of a case that I go to town on witnesses. Then I see them sob. I have forgotten they were people. We all have this in us.

It took so long for me to even be able to ask myself if there might be some Prime Mover in the universe. I didn't step foot in a church from the day I entered college until I married at twenty-three. I won't say I'm in a relationship with God; my feelings are neutral, while before they were hostile. Early on I associated God with Dad, but I have come to realize that God is so much different than that. I'm open to asking questions now. I do think the ministry attracts its fair share of the power hungry, the narcissists, and perverts.

ADULT CHILDREN OF ABUSERS

Currently Colleen's strengths and scars reside within as she continues in therapy to overcome the effects of childhood abuse. Colleen feels that contact with her father would deepen already painful wounds, a stand her therapist supports. In time, Colleen may forgive her father, a goal worth hoping for. Forgiving frees us of anger, an emotion that rips into our peace of mind every time it hits.

There is a population of children, like Colleen, who rise above childhood trauma and stay strong in the face of hardships that may continue into their adult lives. Steven J. Wolin, M.D., and Sybil Wolin, Ph.D., authors of *The Resilient Self*, state, "We are seeing that children can cope with adversity and that, ironically, an increased sense of personal competence can result for successfully meeting the challenges of a troubled family."[2] They interviewed twenty-five survivors of troubled families who didn't mimic their parents' behavior as adults but developed resiliency to battle adversity. The traits they found in these adults were insight, independence, relationships (finding a loving family outside of their own to relate to), initiative, creativity, humor, and morality.

Yet in general, women who have been victimized as children are more likely to be victimized as adults. However, of women who were abused as children, two-thirds do not abuse others.[3] Trauma expert Judith Lewis Herman states, "Many survivors are terribly afraid that their children will suffer a fate similar to their own, and they go to great lengths to prevent this from happening."[4] Colleen fits this picture.

*S*tirrings *of independence after seventeen years...*

I began to substitute teach shortly after Rich beat Colleen, desperate to be distracted from Rich's violence. I hoped the ability to earn a living might give me the courage to leave Rich one day. He agreed to my working part-time, but he hit the ceiling when I said I'd like to update my teaching degree in case I should ever teach full-time.

"No! Dinner will be late. You'll throw it together. The house will be a mess."

"I *promise* dinner will be on time, and everything will get done."

"No wife of mine will ever work full-time!"

"But isn't it good insurance to be prepared should you get sick?" That won his grudging assent.

Rich insisted I endorse my paychecks to him, and he eventually bought a green Chrysler convertible with the proceeds, even though he worried that church people would think the car splashy. During the next several years, I attended college, taught English full-time, and earned an M.A. with a concentration in school administration. Rich hated losing complete control of me, much as he enjoyed my salary, and his violence accelerated. His assaults often left me so enraged that I'd run from the house with no destination in mind. I'd turn the key in the ignition in an absolute panic that the car wouldn't start. I'd spend the night in a parking lot, a hospital waiting room, or a motel. No matter where I was, I couldn't sleep. I'd try to figure out why I felt I had to escape. *He's not all that bad,* I'd decide. *I should be home. He'll be so worried about me. What's he doing now?* I'd think. *The incident was all my fault,* I would decide. *I need to be more understanding of the pressure he's under with my working.* I was that sick in my thinking—that addicted to him.

In the morning, wherever I was, I would phone Rich and apologize for my misconduct. Rich would forgive me. "You overreacted. I'm a nice guy. You've found one in a million, but you just don't realize it." I would go to work, wearing yesterday's clothes, not ready to face Rich yet. I'd smile at everyone at school, telling absolutely no one about my home life. I excelled at work, yet when I walked in the door all that mattered was what Rich thought of me. If that night he called me "a slummy, stupid, scum bag," then I felt as if I was an embarrassment to the world.

Eventually, I was promoted to supervisor of teachers in nine schools, and between my raise and the estate Rich inherited from his parents, he felt well off enough to grant me a checking account and credit card. Yet he badgered me into writing him large monthly checks for "his" budget, which took most of my salary. He expected me to do the housework, including shopping, laundry, and cooking. I often fell behind at home, and Rich said, "My mother had a housekeeper; we'll get one for you." A few months later, he would fire her. "We're throwing our money out the window. If you were more organized, you could get the housework done." For years, I had on-again-off-again housekeepers, depending on his mood.

My achievements continued at school, while the abuse continued at home, and what I didn't realize was that the craziness and contrast was driving me into a depression that would eventually nearly kill me.

T*he crumbling of Susan and Rich's marriage...*

It was a hot, humid July night in Orlando, and it was hard to walk through it or think in it or even get the car air conditioner to cut through it and cool me down. I was driving to Colleen's for dinner. She lived near a six-unit apartment that Rich and I owned, and I decided to stop by and check that the vacant unit was undisturbed. Several weeks ago Rich had snatched my master apartment key without an explanation, so I would have to limit my inspection to peeking in the windows. By now Rich and I had been married for thirty-one years, each one more terrible than the last.

While I parked my car, I saw Rich's car parked farther back in the foliage. Only the green trunk and the license plate showed. I had invited him to Colleen's, but he had said he had to run errands. As I walked toward the door, I was amazed to see curtains hung and lights on, for no one lived there, as far as I knew. I knocked on the door, Rich opened it, and I walked into a living room furnished with pieces from our attic and his parents. A large-screen TV that predominated the living room was tuned to a sports program.

"You had no right to set yourself up like this!" I cried angrily. "This building is half mine. Why did you do this?"

"I need a private place to study."

"You have an office at church and an office at home."

"Our house is overflowing with your paperwork. You can't keep it clean. I need a decent place of my own to relax and work."

"I want a key."

"No."

I spotted his key ring on an end table, grabbed it, and began to twist my key off the ring. Rich sprung at me, fire in his eyes. Frightened, I fled out the door and hid under a second-floor deck. Hunching over, I tried to pull off my key. I heard Rich's heavy footsteps. My heart pounded in fright. In a few moments he ducked under the deck. He pulled me out into the yard, grabbed my arm, and wrenched it behind my back in a hammerlock. I screamed in horrible pain while he then twisted the key ring around my fingers until they were crunched. "Stop it! Rich! Oh God!"

He yanked the key ring from me, and I ran to my car. Unable to lift my right arm to shift my five-speed, I moved my left hand to the gear. Pain stabbed my chest, and only by force of will did I make it to Colleen's. Her face was ashen as I explained what had happened, and when I had finished she quickly kissed her husband and children and drove me to the emergency ward at Princeton Hospital.

I was vaguely aware that the examination cubicle smelled of antiseptic, but very aware of freezing in the air conditioning. The sterile sheet I sat on reminded me of a layer of snow. I asked for a blanket, but I continued to tremble as a young doctor examined my injuries. By now my arm had swollen to twice its size, and three fingers were crooked, mashed, and purple. "What happened?" he asked.

"I—tripped going down the stairs."

"Mom, if you don't tell him what Dad did to you, I will," Colleen said.

Shakily, I told the doctor that Rich had wrestled me for my apartment key. I felt sure the doctor wouldn't believe my story because I had mentioned that Rich was a minister.

"Has this kind of thing happened before?" he said sympathetically.

"Yes."

"Many times," Colleen said firmly.

"After we take x-rays, I want to talk to you further about this."

X-rays revealed torn tendons in my arm and hand and severe sprains in three fingers. The doctor immobilized my arm and fingers in plastic splints and supported my arm and hand in a blue sling that covered the splints. He said that one finger would probably be permanently crooked and two would not be usable for months. "I'm recording on your chart that your husband assaulted you. If you press charges, this documentation will help you. I urge you to file charges. Rarely does an abuser stop his violence unless he's shocked into quitting."

I shook my head. "I would never do that to my husband because he's respected in his church."

The doctor handed me a brochure from a women's crisis center. "At least telephone them. They'll give you advice on how to be safer. You're certainly not alone. Studies show that 30 percent of the women seeking emergency care for injuries have been battered by their partners."[5]

In the car Colleen urged me to sleep at her house, but I wanted to be in my bed with my pillow and my familiar things around me. Rich and I had recently taken separate bedrooms, and mine had a lock. But with or without a lock, I would be safe tonight because a violent episode always calmed Rich down. "No, I'll be okay."

"Then I'll sleep with you. I don't trust him."

We stopped at McDonalds, and Colleen ate a hamburger and fries while she drove. I had no appetite. Just the smell of the hamburger unsettled my stomach. In the garage Colleen picked up a long-handled wrench, just in case. Dressed in pajamas, Rich met us in the kitchen and laughed at my sling. "You're just faking it."

We brushed by him, locked my bedroom door, and Colleen helped me into a nightgown.

In a few minutes Rich tapped at the door. "Please let me in, honey," he pled. "I didn't mean to hurt you. I felt as though you were stealing my key ring, and I just wanted it back. I don't know what got into me. I felt so lonely in the apartment, and I was wishing I had gone to Colleen's. You're right—I shouldn't have set up the apartment for myself. I suppose I was jealous of your job, and I just needed to express myself as a person in a place of my own. I love you so much, and I would never injure you like that purposely. I forgot how strong I am and how little you are. I'll do anything, bunny doll, anything to make it up. I promise to change for good. I vow it on a Bible. You name any terms, anything you want, and I'll do it."

He sounded truly sorry. "Let him in, Colleen."

"No."

"Yes," I said firmly.

Rich entered, straddled my desk chair backward, and placed his hand on his chin, assuming the position of a negotiator. He appeared in control, unlike the pleader outside my door.

Colleen held up the wrench, and I thought back to the time Rich had beaten her back all the way out to her weed garden. That pudgy teenager had grown into a sturdily built woman, but the look in her large, green eyes had not changed. They sparked fury. She wanted revenge. "If you move from that chair, I'll use this on you. You're nothing but an actor."

Rich winced and let tears fall down his cheeks. "Let's make peace, bunny. It's time for a new beginning where our love can grow." He described some of the good times we'd had; there were a few pleasant memories between the violent episodes.

I inwardly pulled to his side. "It was dark in the yard. Your father couldn't see well. He didn't mean to hurt me. I'll be safe, honey, now go."

Colleen left reluctantly, carrying the wrench. Rich kissed me gently on the check and left, closing the door quietly.

In the morning when I heard my door open, I kept my eyes shut. During the night, though I had taken pain relievers, I still throbbed with pain. I was furious that I had fallen for Rich's sweet talk when the fact remained that he had deliberately assaulted me. Later, I phoned Rich at church. "I'm reporting your assault to the police. I don't know if they'll arrest you, but you'll have a record."

He ranted and raved, completely out of control, and I thought of the ludicrousness of his howling in the company of his Bibles and theology texts. I hung up on him and filed a report at the police station.

"Do you want your husband arrested?" the officer asked.

"No. I want to report the incident—that's all."

I walked out slowly, my head hanging down, feeling like a turncoat to our entire church for reporting Rich.

At home, I perched on the edge of my yellow couch—uptight as a caged tiger, ready to spring the moment I released my cage door—and I was ready. I had to get away. I swallowed a pain pill, got in my car, and headed for my sister Lillie's, two hours south of Orlando. Although the pain of shifting was excruciating, I finally pulled up the long drive of Lillie's orange-tree farm, which she had managed since her husband had replaced her with another wife. Healthy orange trees lined the road and ran in three directions to the horizon, neat and orderly, proof that Lillie knew how to farm.

As Lillie ran from around the back of her house to greet me, her brows shot up in amazement. "You look like you fell down a flight of stairs. What is going on?"

"I'll explain inside," I said.

She kissed me, led me into her family room, and settled me on a soft couch. The air smelled like orange juice, which Lillie drank liberally, convinced it boosted her immune system, for she hadn't had a cold in ten years. After placing my injured arm on a pillow, she jammed her hands into her jeans pockets. "Give it to me straight. What happened?"

Lillie was muscular, lanky, and animated, and her skin was perpetually tanned from the sun exposure. She attacked her business problems like a bull, without fear or tears. Touched, I watched my sister weep as I told her how Rich had abused me for thirty-one years.

"You should have told me long ago," Lillie said.

"I couldn't. Rich is so prominent in his church—I couldn't tell anyone. He's so respected that I somehow felt it was my fault."

"I never trusted him, not when I saw how he threw money at you when you dated. But I never suspected he was a batterer." She asked my plans, and I said I had none as yet. "Well, that's enough talking for now," Lillie said. "You need to rest. You can stay here as long as you like, permanently if you wish."

"I didn't bring any clothes."

"You can wear my clothes. What about lunch—did you eat?"

"I'm not hungry."

I took two pain pills and slept in Lillie's guest room. When I woke, I hated myself for reporting Rich to the police. I reached for the telephone by my bed and dialed home. I told Rich about the police report, then said, "I shouldn't have done it. I don't know why I did. I asked them not to arrest you. I—I'm at Lillie's. Please forgive me."

"Now I know for sure that sling is fake. If your arm were as injured as you said, you couldn't have driven there!"

"Rich, listen, please. I know it's all my fault I got hurt. I shouldn't have tried to take the key. I should've realized you needed a hideaway. I know my papers are scattered around and that can be annoying."

"I want you home tonight. We need to talk. You've caused me problems." He hung up.

Lillie entered with a cup of coffee. "I heard you talking."

"I'm going home, Lillie."

She gazed at me in shock. "After what you just told me? Why that's crazy. You can't drive, and I'm not going to take you. I'm not letting you go back to that monster."

I looked helplessly at her, paralyzed by a fear that Rich would discard me. My self-identity appeared to have fled, and the only place where I knew I could find it was with Rich. "Rich wants me home to talk, and I've got to go because he's upset."

She sighed. "Then I'll drive you, honey."

I shook my head. "I have to be alone with Rich. I'll make it all right."

After she fixed me a sandwich and a thermos of coffee for the trip, she filled a bag with oranges and walked me to the car. As I drove off, she hollered, "Call me when you get home."

Pain stabbed my chest while I drove home, and afraid I was having a heart attack, I stopped at Princeton Hospital's emergency ward. After tests, the doctor attributed my pain to strained chest muscles from the hammerlock and driving, which the doctor forbade for two weeks. He also ordered bed rest. I phoned Lillie to tell her I was at the hospital but that I was all right.

When I got home, Rich walked past me with a curt hello, left the house, and didn't return until midnight. I lay in bed, crying and wondering why he had urged me to come home then had left. The next morning (Sunday) Rich entered my bedroom, put his hands on my shoulders, and gave me an "I'd like to do sex on you" look. "Stay in bed today," he said. "Don't come to church."

"What about our talk?"

"When I'm ready."

"Are you very mad—about the police?"

"Just stay put." He brought in a tray of cereal, milk, coffee, and fruit.

I was out of my mind with worry over Rich's odd behavior. I wanted Rich to hold me and tell me that we would work out our problems, as he had done one thousand times. *Even fake promises would do*, I thought.

When Rich returned from church, my daughter Brenda's husband was with him. They started to carry out Rich's clothes and his family's antiques. I paced around in a frenzy. "Rich, please stop moving out! Let's talk!"

"Get out of my way," he snarled. "Get back to bed."

"Why did you ask me to come back?"

"We'll talk tomorrow."

"Rich, please talk now!"

He refused to comment. In six hours he and his things were gone— transported to his hideaway in our six-unit apartment building. I didn't know then that after I informed Rich I had filed a police report, he had hired a lawyer to start divorce proceedings. The "talk" was a ruse to plant me on home territory to receive divorce papers, which arrived in the morning by courier.

I shakily handed the packet back, sensing what it contained.

The courier said, "No, you can't give them back."

I read the papers in the kitchen, having absorbed enough law from Colleen to know there was no way to avoid a divorce. Florida was a "no-fault" divorce state; when one party filed for divorce, it was granted. No grounds were required. *I will die without Rich,* I thought.

The packet also contained a restraining (protection) order against me. It shocked me more than the divorce papers.

Susan M. Taylor is hereby restrained as follows:

1. From harassing or annoying Richard J. Taylor.

2. From expressing to the congregation of Plaintiff's church or person related of or affiliated with the congregation of Plaintiff's church, or to persons in the community of Plaintiff's church, or to the superiors and principals, officials, and employees of the hierarchy of Plaintiff's church, false, misleading, demeaning, harassing, defaming, derogatory, uncomplimentary and/or degrading statements, whether oral, written, or otherwise, about the marital relationship between Plaintiff and Susan M. Taylor or about the Plaintiff.

Within my congregation were my family, most of my friends— people who could support or help me. If I talked to them about Rich's abuse, I would be jailed? A murderous rage overtook me. I phoned Rich. "This restraining order is unconscionable! I—"

"I'm in the middle of a meeting. My lawyer wrote the order, not me." He hung up.

I telephoned Colleen to read her the restraining order. "I believe it's illegal," she said. "Do you want to fight it in court?"

"Yes!" I hired an attorney whom Colleen had recommended. For the court date I dressed in a tailored suit, the only part of me that looked smart. Insomnia and pain had ravaged my face, leaving purple bags and sallow skin. Lillie, who was not affiliated with my church, was with me. Colleen, who was affiliated with my congregation, was not. After my lawyer's remarks about the illegality of the restraining order, Judge Webster called me to testify.

I sobbed to the judge, "I want to live with Rich. I just want him to stop hurting me."

I was on the stand an hour, while Rich's lawyer and Judge Webster questioned me. I cried the entire time and made an awful impression. At Rich's lawyer's request, Rich was exempted from testifying. The judge ruled that the restraining order against me would stand, and he ordered a similar edict be issued to Rich.

Crushed, I asked to speak to Judge Webster. "My husband doesn't care if he's issued a restraining order," I said. "He doesn't want to talk about our marriage to anybody. After all, he's the one who injured me. I'm the one hurt by a restraining order. I can't go forward with my life without the support of my family and friends, who are just about all within my church family."

"Then call a psychiatrist and talk to him," the judge snapped, dismissing court. I did not know at the time that Rich's lawyer and Judge Webster were golf buddies or that Judge Webster often ruled against the interests of abused women.

I phoned Colleen to explain what had happened at court. She blew up, then asked, "What do you want to do?"

"Put him in jail." I wanted an eye for an eye. "Fortunately, I filed that report with the police. I'll have him arrested."

At the police station, I asked that Rich be locked up where his high blood pressure could be monitored. Even while I charged him, I had to protect him.

Rich later told me that the police had arrived at midnight and had shone flashlights in his bedroom window, waking him. He jumped from bed in fright. When they told him he was under arrest, he was so rattled that he grabbed his dirty gardening clothes from the chair. They handcuffed him and drove him to the justice center. He told me, "I felt furious and humiliated. It was so horrible that I wished I could have had you arrested so you could understand what it felt like to be handcuffed and forced into jail."

The morning after his arrest, I was at the courthouse by 9:00. They led Rich out in handcuffs. Even his legs were shackled. He wore a faded yellow plaid shirt and dirty jeans. Stubs of hair fringed his chin. He walked as haltingly as an old man. I sobbed aloud. *I'm killing the father of our children*, I thought. *I've ruined his career.*

Judge Webster did not hear my complaint, but Judge Turner, a tough-looking man with iron gray eyes, leaned far over his bench and glared at Rich. "Preacher, you're as big as a horse, and your wife is a small woman. You obviously tried to break her arm. I'm only surprised that with your strength you didn't. I'm going to put a twenty-five-hundred-dollar bond on you, and if you say one word of protest, I'll make it for two million dollars and you'll never get out of jail."

Rich said nothing. He was released. He had been in jail for a total of twelve hours. From then on I rapidly declined, shedding twenty pounds because I could not eat. Lillie moved in with me, and she and Colleen stuck straws in my mouth to force milkshakes down. I wanted Rich—even with all his rules. Without him, emotional pain and the desire to die ruled me. God, to whom I had prayed all my life, didn't hear my pleas for peace of mind.

THE NARCISSIST: FACE LIKE AN ANGEL, SOUL LIKE A DEVIL

No one can know the true state of Rich's or Ed's heart or any other human's heart or any abuser's heart, except God. But men (and women) who are totally self-absorbed, who think they are superior (despite any contrary evidence), who are driven to gain their will through any tactics (even malevolent or violent tactics), and who resist relating to the feelings and needs of others are considered narcissists.

In Greek mythology Narcissus became so transfixed with the

beauty of his reflection in a pool that he stared at it until he starved to death. From this one act sprang the concept of the narcissist, the man (or woman) who loves himself to the exclusion of all other beings, including God. The narcissist positions others to revolve around him, as planets around a sun. Chillingly, God is one of the planets.

Not all abusers are narcissists. Certainly abusers are selfish and verbally and/or physically brutal, but some retain a greater ability to love and to respond to needs of others than the narcissist. It is not certain if Rich is narcissistic, for he has not, to Susan's knowledge, received that diagnosis. Caroline's husband, Ed, has been diagnosed with narcissistic personality disorder.

Dr. James F. Masterson, director of the Masterson Institute, says the "narcissist is motivated by the continuous need for 'supplies' to feed his grandiose conception of himself. 'Supplies' here means quite specifically those activities, [possessions], and relationships that reinforce his grandiosity."[6] If the narcissist is physically violent, he is highly dangerous and volatile whenever he perceives his wife has crossed him. After all, she has injured a being whom he feels is perfect, and she must pay.

Masterson notes that though the person who is successful in the narcissistic role appears invulnerable to troubled spirits, underneath this veneer of excellence is a great deal of depression and anger. A narcissist often gravitates to a profession that attracts plaudits: politics, ministry, modeling, or an executive position, to name a few. He tackles living fiercely, working hard for praise and approval, and is often a workaholic.[7] He has an obsessive need to control others in order to maintain a good frame of mind. To control others is not a bad thing in itself; parents need to control the behavior of their children. But a narcissist's control is the vicelike grip of a despot.

Narcissists who profess Christ are dangerous, for they also claim the right to interpret Scripture to serve their purposes. Their pride is the same type that filled Satan's mind when he abandoned God to run the world. Dr. Gary Sweeten, director of Life Way Counseling Center in Cincinnati, says, "Narcissists are like black holes. They pull apart the personalities of others and destroy them. I've rarely treated a narcissist with any success. The problem is that they are fragile within, and any external disharmony can upset them: a messy house, noisy kids."

However, the self that the narcissist inflates has no more substance than jelly, only a fragility that requires vigilant maintenance to uphold. Caroline has futilely poured herself into Ed for several years. "Everything I do is for him, yet he destroys it all," she says. "It is never nearly enough. Ed's a total narcissist. He loves himself and his image. He can never be dirty; he is always perfection to the tee! He would never kiss me if I had lipstick on."

Susan feels Rich exhibits some narcissistic tendencies. She said, "Rich is an egocentric person, the *I* that is the center of everything. He loves how the Sunday service moves toward the sermon, and who preaches that? The minister. He loves that all church meetings revolve around the minister. I believe the ministry can attract the narcissistic personality, the showman type whose ego craves applause."

The narcissist knows how to exploit, which endangers others. The narcissist cannot be intimate. He expertly hides his frailties so that we do not discover any imperfection in him—unable even to tolerate any self-discovery of this vulnerability. If you are married to a man who appears to be narcissistic, it is doubtful he can ever be emotionally intimate. You will need to develop intimate relationships with female friends and relatives, and most importantly with Christ.

No one can know where Rich or Ed began downward slides into violence. But today they are violent men, grotesque caricatures, men with outward faces of faith and apparently the inward guts of Satan. It is comforting to remember that no abuser is beyond redemption; the most evil heart can be regenerated by the grace of God.

Eight

Give Me Liberty

Thirty-one years of marriage for Susan…

I slipped into a blue sleeveless dress, thankful that it was summer and I could wear a dress that easily slid on over my splints. I clumsily buttoned the dress with my left hand and applied powder and lipstick, which I had become proficient at doing left-handed. I had visited a couple of churches in my denomination. This week I would visit church number three. I sank to the edge of my bed. I hated to look for a new church. For thirty-one years Rich had been my pastor, and I couldn't see myself in any other church but his. I had so many friends there. He was the one who had assaulted me, yet I was the one who had to leave my church! It wasn't fair!

Recently Rich's area supervisor had telephoned to urge me to drop criminal charges against Rich. "You'll ruin his career if you allow a misdemeanor or felony on his record. Let's pull together for the sake of everyone. You're a good woman, and he's a good man." I hung up the phone infuriated that Wes Jordan was more interested in covering a

151

crime than in exposing the truth, more concerned about Rich's image than my agony. But it did no good to be angry, when all that I wanted was Rich. Living with Rich was horrible, but living without him was unbearable.

I telephoned Rich at his church office. "Rich, I'm so sorry. I'll do anything to get you off. I don't want a divorce. I want a happy marriage."

"Well, I'm glad to hear that. Let's get together tonight."

Rich arranged for dinner at Bergamo's, an Italian restaurant with singing waiters and homemade pasta, which we both loved. We talked for hours, ignoring that our restraining orders forbade contact. I was submissive, loving.

"My attorney will write step-by-step instructions on exactly how you can get me off this charge," Rich said. "Your compliance is crucial. If you change your mind, I'll spend every penny we've got to avoid a criminal record. I'll borrow. I'll do anything."

"I won't change my mind." I reached for his hand.

At the trial I followed Rich's attorney's written instructions, and as a result Rich's record was expunged of his felony charge. To reward me, Rich dropped his divorce suit, canceled the restraining order against me, and allowed me to spend a few nights a week at his apartment. He wrote to his church, "Sadly, we are separated but we are working on our relationship and need your prayers." At his request, I continued to attend my new church. "Your presence here will confuse my congregation," Rich said.

Believing that if I were a perfect wife Rich would return to our parsonage, I devoted myself to pleasing him. In exchange, he showed scant tenderness and usually treated me with verbal contempt: "You're an embarrassment. You're a wrinkled up old woman. You're a trespasser in my place. You give me no peace. The more often I let you spend the night, the more often you ask to visit." He also called me "a religious fanatic, just as your mother was."

"Won't you ever forgive me?" I asked one night while we ate a meat loaf that he had prepared. Although he had not cooked during our marriage, lately he had become interested in cooking and did well at it.

"Spend one night in jail, Susan, then ask me the question. I will never forgive you for that!"

After four months he decided we must reconcile for the sake of our children and the church, and he wrote the church members the news:

> Susan and I have prayed for God's guidance during this time of painful separation and are convinced that it is God's will that we reunite. We have deeply appreciated your expressions of care and your prayers. God has led us and given us His strength as we have worked through problems.
>
> Susan and I have shared thirty-one years of loving times, marred by some difficult valleys. We do not want a few difficulties to be a barrier to what we see as our happy future.
>
> We both thank you all for your support, and we hope that we can be a strength to you should you need us. "Many are the afflictions of the righteous: but the Lord delivers him out of them all" (Psalm 34:19).

The man who had expressed the gospel so gracefully by letter raped me brutally a few days after he moved back into our home. I held back my tears. I didn't scream. I knew I would never let him do it again. I'd kill myself first. I waited for him to fall asleep. I slipped from bed. I gathered up my clothes that he had yanked from me. I couldn't find my shoes. He mumbled in his sleep. Terrified he might awake, I tiptoed from the room barefoot and drove to a motel.

In the morning I phoned Colleen to pack some clothes for me then left my motel to look at apartments. I felt so low, so alone, so utterly defeated that I couldn't remember which apartment had what features. As I parked at yet another apartment, I knew I was incapable of looking at it or even functioning, with or without Rich. I had nothing to live for. I had vicariously lived through Rich so long that I felt utter torment at facing life alone. I turned around in the apartment's parking lot and drove to the psychiatric ward of Princeton Hospital. "Please help me," I told my admitting psychiatrist. "I'm addicted to my husband."

I remained in the behavioral-care center for three weeks. I was not admitted as "addicted to her husband" but as "clinically depressed." I had been right about myself; I was bad off. Clinical depression is the most serious form of depression.

DEPRESSION IN ABUSED WOMEN

Depression is an illness characterized by a marked lowering of mood, self-image, and world-view, as if everything walking and talking and everything thought or planned were coated in black. Depression can range from short-term and mild to long-term and severe, even taking the form of suicide. In fact, 15 percent of people suffering depression eventually do attempt suicide.[2] Depression can stem from traumatic circumstances (as in Susan's case), biological factors (as manic-depressive illness), debilitation (as in the elderly), medication, or thyroid trouble.

Anger resulting from traumatic circumstances is both a significant initiator and a component of depression. Mortimer Ostow, in *The Psychology of Melancholy*, states, "Depression, at every phase of its development, includes a component of anger, whether visible or invisible, whether conscious or unconscious. The anger is directed against the individual who is expected to provide love but who disappoints. At different phases, the anger may arouse a wish to irritate, to hurt, or to destroy, depending upon the degree of pain which the patient suffers."[3] The anger element of depression sets abused women up as prey, as they absorb wave after wave of anger over their mistreatment.

Each year more than eleven million people suffer from clinical depression.[4] A typical clinical depressive episode lasts from nine months to a year if there is no intervention. As to symptoms, some people report that a heavy weight seems to press upon their chest. Others say they ache all over. They tend to feel their bluest in the morning, with a slight lifting of mood as the day progresses. They may have great difficulty sleeping or sleep too much; eat too little or too much; lack interest in work; lack interest in sex; walk and talk at a hare-paced rate; make elaborate suicide plans.[5] They feel that God is far off and find it difficult to pray and read Scripture.

Treatments for clinical depression usually include psychotherapy, antidepressants, or a combination of the two. Antidepressant drugs are not habit-forming, but they must be monitored because there can be unpleasant side effects.

Another type of depression, dysthymic depression, is less severe than clinical depression, but it can be highly debilitating and last for years, robbing the victim of the joy of living. A few primary symptoms include feeling tired all the time, having trouble concentrating, and sleeping too much or too little. Unlike clinical depression, patients are not routinely referred for psychotherapy, unless they need help in dealing with specific problems. Patients are usually treated with antidepressants. It is important that dysthymic depression is treated, for it can become severe and a major depressive period can occur. (Caroline suffered dysthymic depression during her two marriages.) Cure is probable. "The National Institute of Mental Health estimates that 80 percent of people with depression can be treated successfully."[6]

POSTTRAUMATIC STRESS DISORDER: THE AFTERMATH OF ABUSE

When Susan finally left Rich, she suffered posttraumatic stress disorder as well as clinical depression, and she was, in effect, psychologically paralyzed. Posttraumatic stress disorder was initially identified with the traumatized state of Vietnam War veterans, but the diagnosis is now applied to victims of life-shattering traumas, including domestic violence. Common symptoms of posttraumatic stress disorder are nightmares about the traumas, sudden panic, exaggerated startle reflexes, difficulty in concentrating, guilt, self-blame, repressed anger, preoccupation with the abusive incidents, attribution of total power to the abuser, acceptance of his belief system, withdrawal from former friends, doubts about God's presence, and a sense of hopelessness and despair.[7]

Judith Lewis Herman, author of *Trauma and Recovery*, notes that people suffering posttraumatic stress disorder "have an elevated baseline of arousal: their bodies are always on alert for danger. Traumatic events appear to recondition the human nervous system."[8] It doesn't take too much to trigger a posttraumatic stress reaction, anything that signals the former trauma. A domestic-violence victim may freeze when a coworker raises his hand or gets a certain look in his eyes. She may panic when she hears noise in the yard, fearing her abuser is coming after her.

Due to chronic trauma, a victim's entire personality may be eroded. Herman states, "While the victim of a single acute trauma may feel after the event that she is 'not herself,' the victim of chronic trauma may feel herself to be changed irrevocably, or she may lose the sense that she has any self at all." That is what happened to Susan. She felt that she was Rich's appendage and possession, defined by him, to be used by him, a perception that remained intact despite her success in her profession. She belonged to herself at work, but when she arrived home, she belonged to Rich.

Posttraumatic stress symptoms will abate through dependence on God, the passage of time, and therapy, but they may not entirely disappear if the trauma has been severe and lengthy. Susan says, "The pain Rich caused will be there for a lifetime—in flashbacks, sudden fears, and terrible dreams. Sometimes an everyday event will trigger a trauma, and I'll shake all over or start to sob. But the pain has lessened greatly with time and therapy, and I believe it will continue to lessen."

It is, of course, impossible to heal from posttraumatic stress disorder if the one who caused your disorder still traumatizes you.

Susan now speaks about her difficult road to recovery.

*L*iving alone...

When I remember my stay in the psychiatric ward, I remember the color gray, even though the walls were yellow and the curtains printed with daisies in an attempt to cheer up the patients. I couldn't get a sense of God in all that grayness. All I could pray was, "Oh, God, oh, God."

Daily Rich phoned either to vow eternal fidelity or to curse me because Colleen and Nate didn't phone him. Somehow, despite Rich's badgering, I improved enough under the care of three psychiatrists to be discharged, although I was still clinically depressed. I left the hospital knowing three things:

1. Rich and I had to divorce whenever he or I had the courage to file for one. I could never live with him, because it would kill me, and I wanted to be alive for my children and grandchildren.

2. I would return to my job as a supervisor of teachers. I had no doubt I would function well because I always had, even at the worst times.

3. God was indifferent to me, though I wished that he were not.

I found an apartment with one bedroom, one-and-a-half baths, and a dining alcove—enough room to be comfortable, but not so much that I had to spread out and feel lonelier than I already was. I hated returning to a silent house after work. I left the radio on so that I wouldn't be greeted by stark silence.

Rich phoned one night just as I was about to turn off my bedside lamp. "I've listed the parsonage," he said. "You need to stop by Daniel and Wohlwender Realty and sign the contract."

"Okay," I said.

"Suzy, I'll jump right into this. Is there any chance of our reconciling?"

"No—not any."

"You felt differently when you spent a few nights a week with me at my apartment. You were an ideal wife. I had always wanted to be treated like that—with kindness and tenderness."

"You certainly didn't reciprocate very often."

"I admit I was mean at times—but it was because I felt you had robbed me of tenderness for thirty-one years."

"That's preposterous. You abused me for thirty-one years."

He suddenly changed subjects. "I hate being on Prozac. I don't feel any emotion intensely: anger, love—nothing." He sniffled. "I have the worst regrets that I failed you, honey."

I sighed. "Let's cut this out. All three psychiatrists at the hospital said I must leave you or die. Can't you accept that? Isn't love actively wanting the best for the other person?"

"I feel absolute regret. I wasn't mature enough to change in time to prevent our separation. I want you back."

"Really!" I cried angrily. "Just last week you told me I wasn't going to get a penny out of you if we divorced. You said, 'I'll get my attorney and go for your jugular.' Does that sound like love?"

"Then I guess there's no chance for us whatsoever?"

"No!" I screamed, feeling crazy because he was manipulating me. "The caring 10 percent of you is everything I could want. I hate the mean-spirited, controlling 90 percent. The children and I covered for you for years to preserve your image. We almost wrecked the children with our hypocrisy."

His voice turned cool. "Then let's meet tomorrow to talk about division of property."

"All right." We agreed to meet for breakfast at a busy restaurant to allay my fears that Rich would cause a scene. I was there first, tapping my nails on the booth's table to the tune of rattling dishes. At 8:00, Rich arrived with a briefcase and sat. After we ordered, he removed his glasses and pulled a handkerchief from his pocket. He wiped his entire face with it while blubbering something about his ring.

"What ring?" I said.

He laid his hand flat out and sobbed. "I tried to squeeze my wedding ring on for our meeting, but I couldn't. Oh—oh—I'm so sorry!"

"You promised an impersonal meeting. I'm not wearing my wedding ring. Why would you want yours on?"

"Because I know how it hurts you when I don't wear my ring."

"This marriage is over. We can put wedding rings away forever."

Rich sobbed audibly, while mopping his face nonstop. People around us stared. I squirmed.

"I can't stand the thought of losing you, Suzy."

"Shhh. Everyone's looking."

"I think there's something wrong." He placed his hands over his heart.

My heart thumped. "Your face is beet red. Could your blood pressure be up?"

He dropped his head on the table, as if it had just been struck. "Maybe it's my heart."

"What should I do, Rich?" I began to cry. "Should I call 911?"

"No," he whispered.

"I don't know what to do for you," I sobbed. I dashed to the rest room to wipe my eyes and collect my thoughts. I decided I would call 911 if Rich still could not lift his head. When I returned three minutes later, his tears were gone, he sat erect—glasses on, papers out, and fork in hand—eating heartily.

I was furious. "You actor! You do it all the time. You want to control everything!"

"Your food will get cold."

"You scared me to death!"

"Since this is a business meeting, let's get on with it. I've brought a list of our personal property."

I stared at him, tears spilling. For the next two-and-one-half hours, I cried through business details while Rich coolly directed the proceedings. I determined I would die before I subjected myself to his cruelty again. The next day I filed for divorce. I then had a restraining order issued against Rich, forbidding him to harass me or come within sight of me. Colleen had advised that I get the restraining order. "He'll do you in without it. In addition, at the divorce the judge will be more inclined to award you better economic terms if he knows you've had a restraining order out for domestic violence."

Cancer...

For six months Rich phoned daily, either to berate me or argue an issue related to our divorce, directly disobeying the restraining order, yet I couldn't bear the guilt of having him arrested. As it happened, a problem occurred that was far more difficult to cope with than Rich. I had started my summer leave from school, and though I was still depressed, my health was excellent. I had gone through menopause four years earlier, so I was alarmed to find blood spots on my panties. My mind jumped to the disquieting memory that my mother and grandmother had died of ovarian cancer, but I comforted myself that I had undergone a gynecological checkup in October and everything was fine. Nonetheless, due to my family history, I saw my gynecologist the next day.

After examining me, he said, "There's a large mass on the right ovary."

Tears flowed. I felt so alone with no husband to turn to, and the stark sheet I sat on and instruments in the room made me feel like a specimen—isolated from humanity. My doctor did a sonogram, which confirmed the mass he had felt, plus he discovered a mass on the left ovary. "Is it cancer?" I asked.

"We don't know at this point, but I'm concerned, and I'd like to arrange for a hysterectomy immediately."

"I—have to think about it. I'd like a second opinion."

He arranged for a second examination the next day. At home I phoned Colleen with the disturbing news, then Rich. My conscious mind told me he would hear anyhow, and I might as well be the one to tell him. But inwardly I knew I needed him to say, "It'll be okay, Suzy." I had considered him an all-powerful person too long to yet stop needing his reassurance.

"It's me, Susan."

"What?" he said. "Speak more clearly."

"I have a large mass on each of my ovaries. It's probably cancer. I'm getting a second opinion, but I'm sure I'll need surgery."

He said, "Have you called your attorney yet? The divorce is coming up soon, you know."

I hung up then folded my arms around my body, rocked on the sofa like an abandoned child, and sobbed. Rich had given me less caring than he'd give a dying dog on the street.

My surgeon found cancer on both ovaries, but fortunately the growths were encapsulated in benign masses so that my cancer was rated 1C, the most curable stage of ovarian cancer. The spotting was incidental, from an unknown origin, and later when I developed a happier perspective, I believed it was providential. Ovarian cancer usually spreads silently, not signaling its presence with spotting or bloating until it is too advanced to cure. Though the cancer had not metastasized to other organs, cancer cells were found in my abdominal fluid. To kill these cells I underwent a severe course of chemotherapy. The first five treatments ravaged my body to the point of death, causing my family to urge me to skip the sixth and final treatment. Initially, I refused it. Then I thought, *I'll take it. I'll die and be finished with this miserable life. It will be an easy way out.*

After I had been admitted to the hospital and an IV fluid had prepared my system for chemotherapy, a nurse injected cisplatin and cytoxin into the IV tube. Cisplatin is liquid platinum, a lethal metal that kills cancer and everything living that is susceptible. Cytoxin is a weaker chemical that damages the body less. I was critically ill for days. I threw up so often that my weight dropped from 120 to less than 100 pounds. Fearing the cisplatin would damage my heart, my oncologist ordered continual fluid by IV to dilute its effect. My heart was left undamaged, due to my oncologist's vigilance, but I permanently lost most of the feeling in my hands, wrists, and feet. My hearing was impaired and my corneas scratched, leaving me with blurry vision for months. I lost all my hair. I had tinnitus, a ringing in my ears. I later read that one's brain swells during severe chemotherapy, but I didn't appear to have brain damage.

After all that hell, my one hope escaped me; I didn't die.

While I was hospitalized, Rich's supervisor behaved as if I had been admitted for a tonsillectomy. Wes Jordan patted my arm and described my wonderful future at school, or for that matter, at a church if I wished, "or anywhere—you're so capable." *You would think my sickbed was a launching pad to success,* I thought angrily. I knew my health would not permit work. Wes knew it. His real purpose was to enlist my aid in protecting Rich's reputation. During our separation, Rich had been dating a well-to-do woman with a wide circle of friends. The relationship, I had heard, had gotten very serious. But it would look despicable for Rich to divorce a nearly dead woman to marry a wealthy one. My role, for the good of the church, was to act as if I were doing great. I heard later that Wes told church officials, "Susan's fine. She'll be back to work soon. Her cancer proved to be nothing overly serious."

The pecking order was quite clear. First came "The Denomination," then came "The Minister," then came "The Interests of the Congregation," then finally "The Minister's Wife." By the time I was completely pecked on by all levels of the church hierarchy, I knew how the lowest bird in its social hierarchy felt after the bird brass had pecked all over him. He usually died. So would I.

My depression deepened after I returned home from the hospital. I shuffled around. I turned on the TV and stared, absorbing nothing. Often I let the phone ring. I usually huddled under the bedcovers, hiding from Rich and the church. Colleen urged me to stay with her, but I said, "No, I have to do it this way."

My health improved enough to tolerate "second-look surgery," a common practice in ovarian cancer victims to examine organs susceptible to metastasis. The night before the operation, I panicked and sped to the doorstep of Rich's apartment, my thoughts as wild as a crazy woman's. I wanted Rich to take me in after the surgery and nurse me to health. It was a reflexive need. I determined to beg for his help if I had to. Rich opened the door, wearing a terry robe. His hair was wet. "I guess you were in the shower?" I said.

He nodded. "Come in."

He didn't invite me beyond the foyer. "I—Rich—we've been married almost thirty-two years. Could you give me just a few more weeks? I'm going to be very sick after the operation. Could I just stay with you until I'm well? Please!"

"It's not possible."

"I've never asked much of you. I've given you so much."

"My life has changed," he said. "I can't take care of you. I'm quite serious about someone else. Call Colleen. She's always been your little mascot."

My knees wobbled. I had no husband, no house, no hair, no hope. "Please! Please!"

He said, "Buck up. Don't be a pity-pot." His gray eyes were cool. "You've got that restraining order out on me anyhow!"

"I'll cancel it right now!"

"No, it won't work out."

As I drove off, I decided to overdose on pain pills and die that night. *No, I couldn't,* I thought; *the kids would feel guilty, thinking they should have saved me.* Instead I willed myself to die in the operation. *Then I'll be in heaven, a far better place,* I thought. If God didn't cooperate, but rather spared my life, I hoped they found me riddled with cancer. Then I'd request massive doses of morphine that would knock me out until I died.

When I woke in the recovery room, my surgeon said, "Good news! You're completely cancer free."

I wept. God had locked the door to heaven, leaving me to rot on earth.

My doctor looked at my face a long time then touched my hand and quietly walked away. Before I left the hospital to stay with Colleen, he handed me the name of a psychiatrist and urged me to contact her. "You're very depressed, but I believe Dr. Roth can help you."

"Thanks," I said, but inwardly I doubted I would contact Dr. Roth.

*In what darkness of life, in what great dangers
ye spend this little span of years!*

—Titus Lucretius Carus

9
Nine

*T*he Dangerous Departure

Sometimes getting away from an abusive husband is a matter of life and death. Sometimes a husband's abuse is so extensive that a woman's life—and the lives of her children—are at stake. If she doesn't escape, she may be killed.

Kelly, a heavy, blue-eyed blond who came to the shelter where I volunteer, fled from her home with only the clothes on her back. She told me, "I dropped my children to the ground, climbed out of a window, and ran for my life." When she arrived at the shelter, an advocate took her and her children to our clothes closet, where we maintain an inventory of outfits. She also received her complimentary bag of essentials: toothbrush, toothpaste, hairbrush, deodorant, and soap. I wanted to cry out, "Unfair, unfair! Where is the justice in your husband's getting the use of your house, furniture, and all his belongings, whereas you get a few toiletries and used clothes? Why are you here, and why is he there?"

Dee called the shelter's hotline from a women's crisis center. She and her husband had inadvertently walked by the center, and when she saw the crisis center's name on a placard, she broke from her husband and ran inside in a panic. She was afraid her husband was going to kill her. This had been her chance to escape. Her voice was hysterical. "He never lets me out of his sight." She needed shelter immediately and was wise enough to know it. But we didn't have any beds. All that we could offer her were other shelters' telephone numbers. What an awful feeling! Would she call them? Would they have room? Would she be safe?

Subsequently, through generous gifts, the shelter now has fifty-five beds and five cribs. We don't have to turn down so many women in crisis. But we need seventy more beds because our waiting list ranges between forty and seventy women a month. What is the situation in your area? Has your city so little shelter space available that many women like Dee are turned away?

One woman didn't realize how severe her danger was when she phoned her father to say that her former fiancé had threatened to kill her. "I can handle it, Daddy," she said. "I just wanted you to know." But the tremor in her voice alarmed her father.

A few days later her former fiancé walked into the restaurant where she worked and shot her to death. My husband and I passed the restaurant on our way home from biking. I saw the yellow tape that roped off the restaurant. I read about the woman's death the next day in the newspaper. Her father's alarm was well founded. His daughter couldn't handle her abuser.

When "Jane" runs away, "Dick" is furious. He has lost control of the item he prizes above all else. He'll show her. So he paints a picture of what perfect control looks like through a violent man's eyes. It is a canvas of a dead body. From one angle it looks as if Jane is killed by a gunshot, from another angle a knife, fists, or kicks. Now Jane won't run. She won't leave the salt on the stove so it's not on the table when he eats. She won't insist she's late because she got delayed in a traffic jam, when he knows she is monkeying around. Never again will Jane plague him as she once loved to do. He's shown her who is boss. He actually does not mean boss; he means God.

A study shows that possessiveness—the desire to control and dominate—is the primary reason males kill their partners. That is why Jane died.

The question you need to ask yourself is, "Am I safe?" If you are not, the next question is, "How can I be safe?" This chapter and the Safety Plan in Appendix A will provide you with this information.

OBTAINING A RESTRAINING ORDER

Laws in communities can differ, and the information that follows applies generally. To learn how the court and law-enforcement agencies help battered women in your area, contact an expert, such as an attorney or a staff member at a women's crisis center. (Crisis numbers are listed in the telephone book and with the local police.) If you are to be protected, you cannot keep "the family secret" any longer. You will be in contact with professionals and agents of the law who will probe for facts, so it's best to be straightforward about your husband's violence. It will do you no good to minimize your situation to protect him. In fact, that attitude may permit him to abuse you in the future.

You can receive orders that protect you from violence or threats of violence either through the civil court or the criminal court. The orders to protect you have various names, depending upon your locale. To avoid confusion all protective orders will be called restraining orders. They are issued against your husband and given to him, but you can receive a copy. During the period a restraining order is issued against your husband, you can request that the police arrest him if he harms you or threatens you. Here are the differences (which are important to know) between restraining orders issued in criminal court and civil court.

CIVIL COURT

A civil court can issue a restraining order against your husband for either harming you or a family member, threatening to harm you, or attempting to harm you. A civil restraining order doesn't punish your husband for an abusive incident, but serves as a threat to arrest him for any further violence or threats of violence. It is generally valid for one year. You may decide to go to civil court as a first step because you have no desire to file criminal charges, or you may simply want a document to stop the violence. You do not need an attorney to petition for a civil restraining order.

You can include a variety of terms in a civil restraining order: forbid your husband to menace, harass, hit, stalk, or threaten you, either in person or over the telephone; forbid contact with you for any reason; order him to pay child support; and grant or forbid child visitation rights. If visitation rights are granted, you will likely use an intermediary to transport the children to your husband.

In some communities when a wife files for a civil restraining order, the police automatically escort her husband from his home. If your community issues restraining orders without a police escort, go to the district station, show them your restraining order, and request they accompany you to inform your husband of the order. He will likely be in a dangerous mood.

If your restraining order calls for "no contact" with your husband, you must not see him, ever! If he should stop by to see the children, don't let him in! If he telephones you, hang up! If you communicate with him, the court is apt to conclude you don't mean business. Also keep your restraining order on your person and give a copy to your district police. It is far easier for the police to arrest your husband if the restraining order is in hand, not filed away in your house or perhaps misplaced. In addition, call your police department and ask what they will do if you alert them to a violation of the restraining order. It is reassuring to know they will respond quickly.

Should your husband think the restraining order is unfair, he will be assigned a civil court date when he can contest it. He can bring an attorney, as can you.

CRIMINAL COURT

The usual sequence for obtaining a restraining order in criminal court is to phone the police after your husband injures or menaces you. He will then likely be arrested. The restraining order is not issued at the time of your husband's arrest but at your husband's arraignment,[1] which is usually the next day. The purpose of the arraignment is to determine if he will go to trial. If a judge decides your husband is to be tried, a restraining order is issued against him at that time. You will receive a copy of the restraining order from the clerk of courts, who is usually present at the arraignment. (In some localities a victim does not automatically receive a copy of the restraining order unless she is present at the arraignment. If the victim didn't attend the arraignment and later wants a copy of the restraining order, she must take a photo ID to the clerk of courts. The restraining order will forbid your husband (or boyfriend or partner) to threaten, menace, stalk, or contact you, but it will not include any terms concerning your children. It is simply an order (hopefully) to safeguard you until his trial. Restraining orders with specifications about children are obtained from a civil court, as described above.

It shakes up many husbands when they are issued restraining orders, and they obey them to preserve their jobs, reputations, or marriages. Some men disregard restraining orders entirely, despite the threat of arrest. If at any point you feel unsafe, I strongly suggest that you go to a safe place or a shelter.

POLICE RESPONSE TO DOMESTIC VIOLENCE

Until the last several years, police officers often disregarded domestic-violence calls, considering them family disputes, and they often counseled the husband to cool off then left. They generally helped the wife if she were seriously injured, but not always. In 1984, Tracy Thurman won a landmark award of $2.3 million from the Torrington, Connecticut police department for their failure to protect her. When she called them for help, they watched while her husband stabbed her thirteen times and broke her neck, leaving her partially paralyzed. It was not the first time she had called the police for help and had been ignored.

Thurman's nightmare is not likely to be repeated. Increasingly, police departments take domestic violence more seriously due to tougher arrest laws, stiffer penalties for perpetrators, and police training on how to respond to domestic-violence calls. More often than not in domestic-violence cases, police at least take a formal report. And many police departments have units to deal specifically with domestic violence. The Metro Nashville police department not only has a designated domestic-violence section but also an Internet page that informs about domestic violence and encourages battered women to seek help.

The law in your state may specify either "preferred arrest" or "mandatory arrest," meaning that if it looks like domestic violence occurred, the officers must arrest the party or parties involved. In my home state of Ohio, there is a preferred arrest policy, which means it's up to the police officer's discretion whether to arrest. If the officer does not arrest, he must submit a written report stating his reason. If it looks like domestic violence, normally, officers arrest.

If you wish to know whether your local government has a mandatory or preferred arrest policy and how that policy is practiced, call your local women's crisis center for information. Ask a lot of questions. It is wise to know in advance what to expect when you call 911. That way, if you aren't treated right, you will recognize it and can object.

Unfortunately, there are still police officers who brush off wife abuse with a "Call me if it happens again" to you, and a "Settle down, buddy" to your abuser.

WHEN TO CALL 911

You may wonder when it is appropriate to call 911. Here are occasions when it is vital that you do.

Call if your husband violates a restraining order.

Call if your husband injures you, even if you think, *Well, this is just a black eye, and this is not that bad.* Here is why. You may need police intervention, despite your doubts, for the situation may turn increasingly violent. Your call will record the incident should you need proof in a future legal action against your husband. Calling may protect you from future assault; annual reports by the U. S. Bureau of Justice indicate that women who report abuse to authorities are less likely to be attacked again for at least six months. (However, studies also indicate that an unemployed man may batter his mate even more following an arrest for domestic violence.)

When the police arrive, specify exactly what happened: "He punched me in the chest and left a two-inch–diameter bruise." "He choked me, and I passed out." Don't vaguely say, "He got into it again." The more detailed the information you give, the better the prosecutor can later defend you, should the police arrest your husband.

If the police decide to arrest your husband, they will probably photograph the scene, including your injuries, and gather evidence. If police officers neglect to photograph your injury, request that they do.

Many communities instruct police officers to inform you of the availability of restraining orders, shelters, and other emergency facilities as well as offer to transport you to these places of safety.[2]

Before police officers leave your house, write down their names and badge numbers in the event you need to refer to them later.

Call if your husband stalks you. Stalking is usually defined as a pattern of more than one menacing incident. But one incident is considered sufficient to start criminal or civil proceedings if the stalker prowls where you live, work, or visit. Examples of stalking are threatening phone calls, persistent phone calls, following you, threatening notes, trespassing, damaging your property, and leaving items like dead flowers or animals on your porch that signal what could happen to you.

What frightens a battered woman would not necessarily frighten a woman who has not been abused. Courts use a *reasonable person standard* to judge if a stalker's actions would terrify a woman who has suffered under his hand.

To prove your case at court, gather as much evidence as you can. Tape phone calls, keep threatening notes, take a photograph of your husband on your property. Treat stalking as serious business. Studies show that half of the women who leave abusers are later stalked.[3] In fact, as many as "75 percent of visits to medical emergency rooms by battered women occur after they have separated from the violent partner."[4]

All states have enacted antistalking laws, enabling you to file criminal charges against your husband if he stalks you. In some states you can file civil charges, should you prefer. A conviction of stalking carries a fine or incarceration (or both) and orders to stay away from you.

In addition, the Violence against Women Act of 1994 creates federal crime penalties for anyone who travels across state lines and commits a crime of violence against a spouse or intimate partner or who violates any item in a restraining order. Therefore, if you have a restraining order against your husband and he stalks you across state lines to harm or harass you, you can have him immediately arrested. You don't have to file for a restraining order. States must enforce restraining orders from all other states. This greatly helps women with very obsessive or violent husbands. If your stalker is convicted of stalking across a state line, he is guilty of a felony and is liable for a jail term of between five and twenty years, or longer if he disfigured you or inflicted life-threatening injuries.

WHEN NOT TO TELEPHONE 911

Don't telephone 911 if your husband is attacking you and saying, "If you pick up that phone, I'll kill you." Try to survive his assault with as little injury as possible. You know from past experience how long his rage usually lasts and what triggers his anger to the highest levels. Do what you can to minimize his rage. Certainly do not argue with him. When the incident is over, leave the house as soon as it is safe to do so and contact the police.

At the shelter where I volunteer, when we receive hotline calls from women in extreme danger, we ask for permission to telephone the police. If a woman says no, we respect that she knows best how to be the safest. It is wrenching, though, to end a call in that manner.

THE ARREST

You'll be involved with the court once your husband is arrested, an event that can be terrifying. Joan Juhkne, crisis intervention team facilitator of Women Helping Women and advocate for domestic-violence victims in Cincinnati, says, "Imagine what it's like for a victim survivor coming in the courthouse and fearing her abuser will harm her or kill her for having him arrested. She's scared. But I've seen other women go firmly, ready to prosecute and do what it takes."[5]

Do not go to court alone. Contact a women's crisis agency. Many of these agencies run court advocacy programs, so they can explain the court experience and attend court sessions with you. Court advocates charge no fees. They can be located either in the telephone directory, through your local police, or through the National Domestic Violence toll-free hotline: (800) 799-SAFE (7233), which accepts calls twenty-four hours a day. Make use of this valuable support.

THE ARRAIGNMENT

The arraignment is the court hearing at which your husband's plea is entered and his charges are either dismissed or officially defined. The arraignment usually takes place a day or two after your husband is arrested. Once you file a criminal charge, it becomes the state versus your husband, not you versus your husband. Ask the arresting officer how to find out the arraignment date, for you will not automatically be notified. Though you are not required to attend the arraignment, it is strongly recommended that you do. Here is why:

- When the complainant does not show up, prosecution tends to be weak and often the case is dismissed.

- The judge or prosecutor can question you about the incident, should they wish. You can then portray the seriousness of what happened, which is taken into account when setting a bond amount.

- You can receive a copy of the temporary restraining order. If you weren't there, you would have to go to the courthouse and get your copy later.

- You have the right to ask the prosecutor to drop charges at the arraignment, and he will then decide upon your request. Keep in mind that many states have a "no drop" policy, meaning charges are rarely dropped.[6]

If the judge officially charges your husband with a misdemeanor or felony, then he will generally take the following actions:

- Set bond, which can either be a dollar amount or on one's own recognizance—meaning no bail is posted because he is considered trustworthy enough to return for the trial.

- Ask the defendant if he wishes a jury trial.

- Grant a restraining order, valid until the trial is held. If your husband tries to contact you, his bond will be revoked, and he will be jailed until the trial.

- Refer the case to the Assignment Commission for a trial date.

Before I became a court advocate, I observed the following courtroom arraignment scene.

Sharon was poised on a concrete window seat outside the courtroom.

She wore a smart, teal pantsuit and a fully made-up face. She clutched her purse and looked ready to jump out of her skin.

"Where's the prosecutor?" Sharon called out as Ginger, a volunteer court advocate, approached the courtroom.

"Inside—come on with me," Ginger said.

They entered courtroom B, a large room filled with people, most of them women abused by their partners. Terror filled Sharon's eyes as she sat with Ginger. "I've got to stop this proceeding. My husband will hate me for putting him in jail. It's all a mistake. We love each other! It's all my fault. We were having a fight, I was screaming, and he had to stop me. I got mad and went to the police station and filed charges, but I didn't mean to have him put in jail!"

"What did he do?" Ginger asked.

"He pushed me into a chair and tried to choke me, but it was my fault!"

Ginger asked, "Are you saying that he had to choke you to stop you from screaming?"

"Well, no," Sharon said hesitantly then suddenly jumped up. "I'm going to be sick."

Sharon and Ginger ran to the rest room. When they returned, Sharon was more determined than ever to drop the charges. Ginger said, "I can't promise that the prosecutor will allow you to, but of course you can ask. We'll let the prosecutor know your intention."

Charges were not dropped.

When the judge called Sharon's case, Ginger was allowed to join her at the stand. A police officer escorted Sharon's husband in, a boyishly handsome man, who shot Sharon a look of pure hatred. At Sharon's opportunity to speak to the judge, she said, "This has gotten way out of hand. I begged them to let me drop the charges last night, but they wouldn't let me. They said it was out of my hands." Sharon kept glancing at her husband, her eyes full of hope that he understood.

The judge warned Sharon, "If you back off with a report now that is 180 degrees different than the alleged facts, you may end up being charged with perjury. I advise you to stick to the truth. Don't perjure yourself to protect him."

"But we love each other and he loves our baby, and I didn't mean it and I don't want this! It's all my fault."

A trial date was set. An OR (one's own recognizance) bond was issued as well as a temporary restraining order.

As she left, Sharon said she intended to visit her husband that afternoon, violating the restraining order. At least Sharon has the one incident documented, a record that will help her case should she be battered again.

THE TRIAL

Most trials for domestic violence take place a month or two after the arraignment and last between fifteen and ninety minutes, depending on how many witnesses are called. You, as the prosecuting witness, are issued a subpoena, informing you of the trial date, time, and location. Be sure to have a court advocate from a women's crisis center with you for reassurance and for the information she can provide.

At court, the prosecutor will brief you, which takes only a few minutes. Prosecutors are busy and don't have time to spend with victims of misdemeanors, the usual charge for domestic violence. This brevity of communication can be nerve-racking, and you may wonder, *Does he understand my case at all?* For this reason Women Helping Women suggests you telephone the prosecutor before your husband's trial to familiarize him with your case.

During the trial, the prosecutor will ask questions to lead you through your story. Here are tips from Women Helping Women to help you testify competently.

THE EXAMINATION

1. Before testifying, picture the violent incident from beginning to end (the objects in the room, the distances between you and your husband) so that you can clearly describe what happened.

2. Dress neatly and conservatively.

3. Tell your story accurately and honestly, recalling important particulars.

4. Speak up clearly and never nod for yes or no.

5. Answer only the questions asked of you. Unless questioned, never volunteer information, give conclusions, or provide opinions.

6. Give no snap answers, but think questions through. If you don't know the answer to a question, say "I don't remember."

THE CROSS-EXAMINATION

1. The cross-examination is the most difficult time of the testimony, and you might become angry or confused. The attorney cross-examining you may be trying to discredit you. If you answer incorrectly or unclearly, correct your statement at once.

2. No matter how you feel, don't lose your temper. This is vital, as the attorney for the defense might be trying to get you to do just that and damage your testimony.

3. Never argue with the defense attorney. Always be courteous and serious.[7]

If your husband is convicted of a felony, meaning a weapon was involved in his assault or he is a repeat offender, he will generally be sentenced to a jail term and fined. If he is convicted of a misdemeanor (the usual domestic-violence charge), the judge will usually suspend his jail sentence, contingent upon his attending a therapy group for batterers or doing community service or both. Many experts support diverting batterers to therapy, reasoning that diversion is a quick action, one that can capture the batterer's feelings of guilt, whereas a criminal procedure is long, and by the end of it, his guilt may be long gone.

THE WOMEN'S SHELTER

A shelter is usually a basic, no-frills residence with a mission of providing battered women a safe haven. If a woman can't stay with a relative or friend because her husband has threatened to kill her and/or them, a concealed shelter may be her only option. It's vital that its whereabouts remain a secret. If an angry batterer enters a shelter, not only is his victim in danger, but the entire shelter population. Revealing a shelter's location often results in dismissal.

Public shelters house women of all races, but the higher a woman's economic status the less likely she is to use one. Dana Gilbert, Women's Program Coordinator at a shelter, says, "Upper middle class women have access to monetary resources and credit cards, and it is easier for them to fly to another state or check into a hotel. Also for some women there is a stigma about staying in a shelter, a place that is free and locally funded. Many times women don't want their situations to be public information."[8]

The National Coalition against Domestic Violence says that for every woman who is admitted into a shelter, two are turned away, a number that more than doubles in some urban areas. Shelters keep long waiting lists and employ a triage system. Many shelters, if they have no beds available but have extra funds, will put a desperate woman up in a hotel or squeeze her into the shelter somewhere. At the shelter where I work, most of the women stay an average of three weeks.

To enter a shelter, typically you will be picked up at an anonymous rendezvous point, where your luggage (often hastily filled plastic bags) is loaded into a taxi or an advocate's car.

At the shelter you meet an advocate who enters personal information on a form: vital statistics; information about your children; a description of your husband, boyfriend, or stranger-stalker; a description of the abusive incident; your short- and long-term goals.

The advocate reads the rules of the house, which help assure your safety from your abuser and promote good relationships among the residents. There is also a list of rules to manage children, should you have them with you. One rule is that children cannot be hit or yelled at. Many mothers do, we know, take out their anger at the abuser on their children, and we want to break this pattern of violence.

"You will be assigned chores," the advocate says, "and cooking dinner is rotated among the residents. Tonight there is spaghetti."

You are taken to a linen closet, where you receive a set of towels, sheets, and a blanket. You make your bed, and since you have just the clothes you grabbed, an advocate takes you to the clothes closet. Choosing outfits eases your nervousness, a lighter moment in a dark day.

Another resident tells you her story. She's hopeful that she can find subsidized housing, receive aid to attend school, and make a future for herself. She says, "Nobody deserves to be beaten." You think, *Maybe I can find a future for myself too. Maybe I'll try it here.*

The next day an advocate commits herself and the rest of the staff to helping you achieve your short- and long-term goals. Her support and kindness spark resolve in you to create a new life.

I lead an upper-middle-class life, where I have it pretty easy. The women at the shelter show me another side of life—the raw courage of women starting out on their own, fashioning a new life out of the same hard-rock soil of determination and courage as the pioneer women.

The effects of shelter life can be wonderful to behold. Susan Schechter, author of *Women and Male Violence*, states, "Temporarily freed from threats of retaliation and danger, battered women in shelters [can] display their long-ignored energy, rage, and coping abilities and reveal their similarity to all women." She cites the "extraordinary personal transformations" that can occur in a shelter.[9]

At the shelter, 70 percent of our women eventually (many come and go a few times) live independently of their abusers. Residents are not pushed to separate from their abusers but are given information and assistance that will help them construct new lives should they wish. Importantly, this assistance includes how to apply for welfare should they meet the income standards. Welfare recipients receive a monthly check, a medical card (very valuable with children), and food stamps. To apply for welfare, women must provide their children's birth certificates, their marriage licenses (if married), and their Social Security cards. If their husbands have destroyed these documents, it can be laborious to refile, but it has to be done. The first welfare checks arrive one month after women apply for them.

The shelter also helps women locate housing, schooling, homemaking programs, parenting classes, day care, and job training programs. We run a support group where shelter residents relate to their peers.

If you are calling to find a shelter in a crisis, all you need to ask is,

"Will you take me?" Following are a few more questions to ask if you are not in immediate peril:

1. What is the maximum length of stay?

2. What items can I bring with me? (You might have photographs or other precious mementos that you are afraid your husband will destroy.)

3. Can my teenage boys be sheltered? (There is an age limit in some shelters for young men, due to many residents' fear of men.)

4. Will you help me relocate?

5. Is there any charge?

6. Is your location secret so my husband won't find me?

7. How will my children get to school?

8. Can I bring my car?[10]

SEPARATION

The day may come when you feel you must leave your husband to save your life or sanity, either due to physical, emotional, verbal, or sexual abuse. A Christian woman often fears that if she leaves she will disobey Mark 10:9: "Therefore what God has joined together, let man not separate" (NIV).

Separation, though, need not signify the end of marriage but rather an exit from an unendurable situation until the abuser reforms. If anything motivates an abuser to change, it is the crisis of his wife's departure. But if the abuser demands the wife return or begs her on bent knee, promising roses, and she complies, she presents herself as a weak, dependent woman, one deserving punishment for abandoning him. If anything, he may believe she needs more monitoring, regulating, and corporeal punishment than before. And she is in more danger than ever.

Paul, and other believers in Scripture, fled from danger. "Now after many days were past, the Jews plotted to kill him. But their plot became known to Saul. And they watched the gates day and night, to kill him. Then the disciples took him by night and let him down through the wall in a large basket" (Acts 9:23–25). Similarly when Jezebel vowed to kill Elijah, he "ran for his life, and went to Beersheba" (1 Kings 19:3). In addition, when Saul sent men to David's house to kill him, David's wife Michal lowered him out through a window. "And he went and fled and escaped" (1 Samuel 19:12).

Pastor Daniel Keller, who counsels abusive males, says that he never told an abused woman in his congregation to leave her husband. But he did say, "clearly and pointedly—that no one in the church and nothing in Scripture commanded her to stay with a man who jeopardized her life."

But you can't, shouldn't, mustn't follow a course of action that doesn't fit your biblical views and personal beliefs. God's Word is true, but we do have various interpretations of it. Some women choose to live with their abusive husbands; others divorce them. Others remain separated for a lifetime, doubting that their husbands will reform, but praying for it, rather than seeking a divorce.

WOMEN WHO KILL IN SELF-DEFENSE

A battered woman living with a physically violent, erratic, menacing, cursing husband does not know from day to day if she will see tomorrow. In her terror, she may seize upon the only way to be sure of safety—to kill her batterer.

Up until twenty years ago, courts refused to include expert testimony concerning the effects of battering as part of a battered woman's self-defense plea. Killing in self-defense was recognized only when it could be clearly seen that the victim was actively defending his/her life. This definition excluded a battered woman who, believing her husband would soon kill her, killed him when it was expedient, when he was asleep or drunk or off guard. She knew that she couldn't match her husband's physical strength, and to take him on when he assaulted her would be committing suicide.

The Francine Hughes murder case alerted the legal system to the need to expand the definition of self-defense to include the circumstances of battered women. Francine married her husband, Mickey, when she was sixteen, and they had four children. For seven years

Mickey physically and psychologically tortured Francine, until finally she escaped through a divorce. Six months later she returned to help care for Mickey after he had a near-fatal car crash. She lived next-door to his parents, and Mickey, who spent time at both houses, was soon strong enough to resume his violence. Finally Francine killed Mickey one night when he was asleep in bed, satiated with the pleasures of food, sex, and beating up Francine.

Earlier that evening, one of Francine's four children had called the police to stop a beating their mother underwent. The officers disregarded Mickey Hughes's comment that he would kill Francine later as just empty words. After advising Mickey to cool down, they left. Mickey burned more intensely, determined to force Francine to quit business college. She had enrolled in school to learn a job skill so that she could escape Mickey and support her children. That hope was all she had. Before the police arrived, Mickey had torn up her schoolbooks and notebooks, forced her to burn the books, and ordered her to turn in her car to the dealer. After the police left, he insisted she say she would quit school. She just couldn't speak the words.

Furious with her, Mickey swept the entire contents of the dinner table on the floor and forced her to clean it up. After she had cleaned up the mess, he dumped the contents of the garbage can on the floor, rubbed the food into her hair, and pounded his fists on her, yelling at her to say she was not going to attend school. Finally she said it. "I'm not gonna…" She was crying too hard to finish. Then Mickey ordered her to fix dinner. After he ate, he ordered sex and fell asleep.

Fearing Mickey would ruin the children's lives, as he had hers, Francine hurried her children into the car then doused Mickey's bed with gasoline and lit a match. Crying hysterically, she drove directly to the gate of the Ingham County Jail and told the police officers, "I did it!" She was charged with first-degree murder. The year was 1977.

Francine's lawyer did not argue self-defense, for there was scant legal precedent to support the plea. He argued that she was temporarily insane, a plea that had won some battered women freedom in the past. It won Francine's. Presiding Judge Ray C. Hotchkiss later expressed distress over the defense plea of temporary insanity. "All of a sudden, we realize that we have thousands of people who have had no recourse under the law. Where are we when these people are crying out for help? Self-defense is a real issue, but it was never really covered in this trial."[11]

Advocates for battered women began to fight for a definition of self-defense that would include acts such as Francine's. Ann Jones, an expert on violence against women, states, "To acknowledge that a 110-pound woman might need a weapon against her 255-pound husband or that she might try to catch him off guard is not special pleading but facing facts."[12] Eventually the facts were faced. In State vs. Wanrow, the Washington State Supreme Court ruled that a battered woman's perceptions of what constituted imminent danger were key to court verdicts. Her perceptions differed from a woman's who did not live in terror. It became increasingly common for courts to allow battered women to claim self-defense and support their claims with expert testimony on the effects of battering. This special self-defense of the terrorized mind came to be known as the battered women's syndrome.

Betsy is a beneficiary of these legal understandings. Her sad, dark eyes in her color photograph in a newspaper caught my attention, as well as the sad eyes of the serious little girl on her lap. She described her marriage as one long and terrifying nightmare where she never knew if she would live or die. One day, when her husband raised his arm to hit her, she ran for his gun and shot him to death. She was charged with involuntary manslaughter, but her attorney argued that she suffered from the battered women's syndrome, and she was acquitted.

Each year about eight hundred women kill their husbands or boyfriends, in most cases to escape abuse. We could reduce the number of final solutions if we had more shelter beds for desperate women, coupled with increased free counseling for domestic-abuse victims. At the shelter some women arrive frightened to death because they almost "did it." Our staff considers these women emergency entries, and they spend time counseling them that killing is not the answer; staying away from *him* is.

Before turning to chapter 10, see Appendix A—The Safety Plan—a vital document for women in peril that will provide practical, immediate help.

> One must never, for whatever reason, turn his back on life.
>
> —Eleanor Roosevelt

10 | Ten

Sentencing Yourself to Life

Susan's addiction to Rich...

I sat on my apartment couch several months after my second-look surgery, staring at a spot where Rich's recliner could be if he lived here. I wept. He had read me theology passages for his sermons from that chair in happier times. I let my knees flop out like a rag doll's. I knew that angry people kicked or raged or pulled their knees in, but I lacked that spirit. I was deeply depressed, despite therapy with Dr. Roth. I was ready to die. I knew if I died I would go to heaven, but I sensed an ugly trip ahead, through grief that would tear me apart before I got there.

My mood was too dark to tolerate the sunlight coming through a crack in the draperies. I pushed up from the sofa, went to my bedroom, gathered up safety pins, and fastened the draperies shut.

If only Rich would phone and say, "It's off with Rita. Let's try again."

Last week Rich had dropped in from out of the blue with a box of candy. He sat at my side, pouring out his everyday problems, just as he used to. I felt he sought me rather than Rita because only I could comfort him in the right way. When he left, I telephoned this message to his answering machine:

> I'm so glad you came by tonight. It makes me feel important to you when you ask my opinions about finances. You seemed tired, and I want to help—to be there for you and do the helpful, loving things that make you feel good. How can I help with the finances in general and check-writing in particular? Will you talk with me about this tomorrow? Also, are there things I can do to lighten your load as you head into the weekend? One more thing, will you please give me your sermon tapes?

He hadn't returned my message.

I slumped against the sofa and planned my death. *I'll drive to the parsonage,* I thought. (It was sold but vacant pending closing, and I still had a key.) *I'll pull in the garage and turn on the motor. I'll fill up the car with gas to be sure I have enough, and I'll bring towels and stuff them in the doors to make the garage airtight. I'll bring my Bible and read Revelation 21 and 22 until I die.* I hoped that Rich would be the one to find me. Odds were he would; he usually checked the house daily. I'd love to show him how he had brutally ruined my life!

I stood, satisfied that I had chosen a painless and fail-proof way to die. I stuffed towels into a paper bag then paused and dialed Colleen. Confused, I didn't understand why I hesitated. Then I glanced at Colleen's list of thirty activities to prevent suicide attached to the refrigerator; number one was to phone her.

"I don't want to hurt you," I said when Colleen answered, "but I just can't go on."

"Mom, you have to for me and the kids. It would be selfish to kill yourself and deprive us of you forever."

"I've thought of that. But I can't make it."

"What are you planning to do?"

"I'd rather not say."

"Mom! Think of me! I love you."

I started to cry. I loved her, too, so much.

"Can you hang on until I get there?"

I didn't know where the transition had occurred in which she became the mother and I the child, but I needed her to hold me and say that better times lay ahead. Yet it wasn't fair. Sunday was her family day because she and her husband had busy careers. "Honey, I'll be okay. Otherwise I wouldn't have called."

"I'm coming."

After she arrived, she packed my suitcase and drove me to the same psychiatric ward I had been in before; only this time I met Dr. Phillips, who saved my life.

Dr. Phillips entered my room, wearing a tan, crumpled suit and a smile that nearly spanned his narrow face. I guessed him to be about forty-two, though his graying hair would have indicated he was older. He studied me with alert eyes, but his eyes quickly softened, indicating he noted my deep despair. I immediately liked him.

He said, "I'll be your main psychiatric doctor, if that will be all right."

"It's fine."

"If ever it isn't, let me know, and I'll find someone that fits better. But I hope it works out between us."

He led me to a small room with white walls and a print of water lilies on a pond, which I knew to be a Monet. I had grabbed my notebook as I left my room, and after we sat at a round table, I opened it.

"I studied mental disorders at the medical library," I said. "I know I've got dependent personality disorder. I did the same kind of research when I had ovarian cancer. The more I know about what's wrong, the better I can handle it." I started to cry. "But I can't handle this. Counseling won't help me. According to the medical books, people with dependent personality disorder can't ever live alone."

"Let's talk about what you've studied."

He patiently listened while I read each symptom of dependent personality disorder and compared it to my unyielding dependence on a man who had abused me half a lifetime. Three hours passed; I cried the entire time. It sank in that this man took me far more seriously than Dr. Roth, who had advised me to date, enforcing my theory that I was hopelessly dependent.

When I finished, he said, "I don't tag people with a particular disorder without being very sure. However, I don't think you have dependent personality disorder."

I stared at him. I had been certain.

"You've suffered more than most people do in a lifetime. I want you to know that I believe every word you've told me."

Dr. Roth had never said that.

He said with certainty, "You are going to be like the phoenix rising from the ashes."

I wondered, *Could I rise?*

"We'll meet every day. I'm going to prescribe an antidepressant and vitamin therapy. You're very thin."

The staff would not let me stay in bed. I did artwork, made a stool, did carpentry, and carved a black swan, of which I was proud. Buoyed by Dr. Phillips's validation, I gradually improved. He often cried with me. You couldn't pay a doctor to care that much.

When I left the hospital four weeks later, we arranged to meet twice weekly and talk by phone twice weekly. Dr. Phillips continued to gently pull my story out of me. It took many sessions before I could share in depth the more painful events of my marriage. I had blocked out many horrors or retained only the faintest impressions of them. Everything hurt. Thinking hurt. Touching myself hurt. Even my skin hurt. Only sleep relieved hurt. I hated to wake up. I'd take sleeping pills and maybe get eight hours of sleep, then I'd hurt.

Dr. Phillips carefully stated the bits of improvement he saw. He knew that I was not sure I wanted to get better. Thoughts of dying still haunted me. He knew he couldn't say to me, "Oh, you look so good! You're getting better!" That wouldn't have done a thing for my clinical depression. I would have felt rushed and anxious. I needed to feel the process was *slow.*

Dr. Phillips asked me to write about my marriage to Rich and read it to him. I saw in black and white how Rich had robbed me of a happy experience as a mother, a sense of joy within myself, the ability to love God without hindrance, and the ability to love a husband who loved me back. I felt so bitter, so angry. But getting out the anger and rage began my healing process. That scared me. "I'm so afraid I'll fall back," I told Dr. Phillips.

"If that happens, we'll deal with it." I believed him because I trusted his treatment.

Throughout my therapy, I clung to Scripture. I marked special Scriptures with red and blue colors and dates, sometimes two or three dates for one Scripture. I could sit down in the worst state of mind, open my Bible to a psalm, and I would feel better. I memorized Psalm 23.

> The LORD is my shepherd; I shall not want. He makes me to lie down in green pastures; He leads me beside the still waters. He restores my soul; He leads me in the paths of righteousness for His name's sake. Yea, though I walk through the valley of the shadow of death, I will fear no evil; for You are with me; Your rod and Your staff, they comfort me. You prepare a table before me in the presence of my enemies; You anoint my head with oil; my cup runs over. Surely goodness and mercy shall follow me all the days of my life; and I will dwell in the house of the LORD forever.

The ravages of chemotherapy had left me unable to return to my supervisory position, but I was able to work part-time as a secretary. I felt proud that I was accomplishing the big task, living without Rich. I remembered that Dr. Phillips said that one day I would rise from the ashes like a phoenix, and I walked into a jewelry store and said, "I want a piece of jewelry with a phoenix on it."

The saleswoman showed me a phoenix charm and a gold bracelet. I thought of how the phoenix could not be defeated by destruction or torment. "Perfect," I said. I clasped the phoenix on the bracelet and wore it out of the store. I did not remove it from my wrist for over a year.

DEALING WITH SEPARATION

HEALING AFTER SEPARATING

Susan explains why it was particularly hard for her to leave a minister. "Rich was the symbol of God to me, and since his congregation admired him as a powerful and wonderful man, I believed he must be. Yet I had the fearful thought that I would never truly know God as long as I remained with Rich. It didn't come often, but when it hit me, it scared me."

That Susan finally emerged from thirty-two years of domestic violence, a major depressive episode, and cancer with her mind, courage, and faith in God intact gives us hope regardless of our circumstances. Susan's story poignantly tells abused women: Don't keep quiet about abuse, but seek help—early, far earlier than she did. Susan's story also shows us how difficult it is to separate from an abusive relationship, even though we feel it's imperative to leave. And her story reveals the decimation of abused women who leave their husbands, women who are not only shattered from abuse and indignities but also grieved at the loss of a marriage they had cherished. Yet deep inside, these women know they can't change their husbands.

This chapter is addressed to you who have separated from your spouse and wish to heal from anger, depression, and grief. It is also for you who are considering separation. (I will not suggest that any of you separate from your spouse, for clearly that is a decision only you can make.) You may wonder how to live independently when your emotional reserves are low. There are therapeutic resources in your community, church, the power of Scripture, within yourself, but most of all in God's power that can return you to mental and spiritual health.

THERAPY FOR SEPARATION

You can consider using any of the following aids to heal from abuse. You know how you feel inside. You can probably judge which therapies will help you. If you feel too confused to know, ask someone you trust to help you evaluate your needs. Help is available from several sources.

Hospitalization

If you are deeply depressed, particularly if you are suicidal, seriously consider admittance to a psychiatric ward. Depression diminishes your ability to think at a time when it is crucial to plan rationally, and suicidal thoughts drag you from life, not toward it. Psychiatric doctors can provide therapy and medications that can clear your mind and enable you to establish goals for your future. Many Christian counseling organizations maintain psychiatric wards in hospitals or have their own private clinics. Call a Christian psychologist or psychiatrist in your area for a referral. Or ask your doctor to choose a psychiatric ward.

Support Groups

A support group run by a women's crisis center connects you with women who are struggling with problems like yours. During meetings, members share what it was (or is) like to suffer domestic abuse and what it is like (if that is the case) to live independently. Secular groups are usually led by social workers or therapists, who validate the members' experience, provide domestic-violence information, and help members express anger and set goals. Groups also encourage new members to develop support systems so that they are not alone as they heal from trauma. Everything discussed is held confidential, except when a member is in danger of hurting herself, others, or committing a crime.

Joan Juhkne of Women Helping Women has seen many abused women from her support group recover. "It's the support from other group members and our agency, for this may be the first place they were treated in a nonjudgmental way and listened to. They know they aren't alone. They are validated. They focus on their strengths and skills and call themselves survivors." Juhkne explains why she likes to lead support groups. "It's a motivator to me. I see women taking control of their lives and themselves. I hope to be a benefit for them."

A *Woman's Day* survey of one thousand battered women reports that "women's groups" were the most effective help sources.[1] You can find a community support group through the YWCA or women's crisis agencies.

A Professional Therapist

A professional therapist can be a psychologist, psychiatrist, or a social worker with a master's degree who is licensed to do therapy. How do you know you have found the right therapist? You click with the therapist on the first visit, as Susan did with Dr. Phillips. You feel that the therapist is empathetic, interested in helping you, and well-informed about domestic violence and the cycle of violence. You may be more comfortable with a woman, for often abused women distrust men and tense up around them.

How do you know the therapist is wrong for you? Psychologist Rich Meyer advises, "If a woman feels what is being said is wrong, she should trust her intuition. If she asks for clarification, and does not get it, she should be wary; she is justified in asking for clarification. If there is blanket blaming of her, she should beware and go elsewhere."[2]

Your medical insurance policy will probably pay 50 percent of your therapist's fee. If your funds are limited or you don't have insurance, ask your therapist if she can reduce the rate. Some medical plans pay the entire fee, with the exception of a minimal copayment.

Your Pastor

If you decide to ask for his help, be sure he is empathetic, values women, and rejects the idea of submission to an abusive husband. These viewpoints are not necessarily overtly stated but are revealed in sermons, conversations with your pastor, or comments others have made. If you know women who have sought advice from your pastor, ask them how they were treated. Your pastor probably can't counsel you individually, for most pastors lack the time or the expertise in domestic violence, but if he can validate you, refer you to help sources, and keep tabs on your progress, he will be an invaluable link in your healing process.

DEALING WITH ANGER

ANGER DEFINED

Anger is an emotion that God placed in the limbic system of the brain, which is the center of emotion, and also in the neocortex, the center of reason. Therefore anger has two components: emotion and reason. When you are angry, adrenaline pumps through your system, causing your heart and thoughts to race, priming your body to act. Your center of reason is alerted, and you choose how to express your anger. We feel anger intensely because God meant us to be provoked enough to address mistreatment and brutality. But as females we often don't react at all. Instead we may suppress our anger because we have absorbed from our culture, upbringings, and churches that expressions of anger are not appropriate for the female. Joan Juhkne with Women Helping Women says, "In our support groups some members are not in touch with anger. When a facilitator says, 'Let's do a feeling word,' some members say, 'I'm just fine.' They can't even say a word to express their trauma." After years of psychological or physical abuse, no one is "just fine."

Suppressed anger at your abuser does not disappear but erupts in a variety of emotional events: vivid flashbacks to abusive situations, nightmares, preoccupation with the abusive relationship (including fantasies of revenge), sieges of self-blame, and bouts of shame. The tension that suppressed anger generates can erupt in physical problems as well: weakened circulatory and immune systems, gastrointestinal disturbances, tension headaches, pelvic pain, and sleep disruptions. Author Candace A. Hennekens, survivor of two abusive marriages, describes how suppressed anger attacked her. "At first my nose twitched, then half my face, and finally painful neuralgia shot through the left side of my face. Fearful that I was suffering from post-polio syndrome from the illness I had had as a child, I went to see a neurologist. The doctor found no illness, but prescribed advice that helped me recover. 'Deal with your feelings or you will continue to feel this pain.'"[3]

In its finality, suppressed anger, particularly in women, devolves into depression. "Experts find in depression a strong component of anger against a loved one with whom the sufferer identifies. 'Depression is rage against someone else turned inside against yourself,' said Theodore Reik, a colleague of Freud."[4] Reik's statement applies to Susan. "I needed to deal with anger turned inward," she says, "and when it started to turn outward, I started to get better."

Ephesians 4:26 states, "'In your anger do not sin': Do not let the sun go down while you are still angry" (NIV). Though it is likely that many suns have set on your anger at your abuser, it is never too late to deal with it. It is imperative to learn effective methods to eliminate long-term anger.

Healing from Anger

The following five actions will help you identify your anger at your abuser and release it. Do them as often as necessary, remembering that healing from anger is not a one-time event but a process that will take time and repeated efforts.

1. Admit Your Anger

As a first step, admit to yourself that you are angry and that your anger is justified. When I was in A.A. I had to take the first step, admit I was an alcoholic and that my life was unmanageable, before I could move through the other eleven steps of recovery. Similarly, you can't recover from anger until you know you are angry. You don't have to necessarily feel your anger, just take it on faith it is within you.

2. Tell Your Story

Telling your story connects you with the abusive incidents you endured, allowing you an opportunity to feel anger and to release it as you describe the incidents. Tell your story often, for eventually, repeated confession normalizes your experience, reducing your anger and pain.

You can tell your story to a women's crisis advocate, support group members, your pastor (if he supports abused women), your therapist (if you have one), friends, and relatives. Choose people with whom you feel safe. You will be revealing personal information that you neither understand well nor yet know how to cope with. You will need validation, love, and empathy, for as you talk you'll feel danger, pain, fear, and trauma along with your anger. Snatches of events may flash in your mind that you can't quite see, but you can feel the horror.

Careful as you are, you might tell a person about your abuse who disbelieves your story, doesn't want to talk about such unpleasantness, underestimates your pain, blames you for leaving your husband, or blames you for not yet forgiving him. She may insist on prayer to fix you up right now. It is impossible not to be hurt and angry at such reactions. You might be tempted to withdraw from everyone. This would be a tragic misstep. If someone demoralizes you, tell your therapist, pastor, support group, or trusted friends and work through your pain. Keep in mind that one person's comments do not define you, your past horrors, or your current courage in overcoming adversity.

You can also tell your story through writing, a technique that Susan used extensively. "I wrote on computer paper that was still hooked together. One whole stack was titled 'Things That Were Good in the Marriage.' Another was 'Things That Were bad in the Marriage.' I cried as I wrote. The stacks of good and bad were about equal. It was a baby step, the beginning of getting better."

Not only does writing help you release anger, it provides a document that records your growth.

It has been faddish for therapists to encourage clients to vent their anger through pounding objects and yelling. Venting anger is much like stoking a furnace to red-hot. The more you stoke, the hotter the furnace, and similarly, the hotter a person you are inwardly and outwardly.

3. Tell God about Your Anger

For a time King David lived like an outlaw, stalked by King Saul. Psalms record how David poured out his anger, anguish, and terror to God in those dark times. Similarly you can tell God about the abuse you suffered and your anger over it, and He will comfort you. David was so sure of receiving God's comfort that he cried out, "Show me a sign for good, that those who hate me may see it and be ashamed, because You, LORD, have helped me and comforted me" (Psalm 86:17). Like David, you can pray for a sign for good that can shame your abuser, reduce your anguish, and manifest God's love and care for you.

An effective way to release your anger to God is to read aloud psalms that express David's anguish, reacting to David's words with those that describe how you feel. The italicized words are my examples.

> LORD, how they have increased who trouble me! Many are they who rise up against me. Many are they who say of me, "There is no help for him in God" (Psalm 3:1–2).
>
> *Oh, Lord, I'm so angry with my husband; please help me. No one understands. They all say I should read my Bible and I'll be*

okay. I'm not okay. My mind is even too cluttered with confusion and fear to worship you. All I do is dwell on what he's done to me.

But You, O LORD, are a shield for me, My glory and the One who lifts up my head. I cried to the LORD with my voice, and He heard me from His holy hill (Psalm 3:3–4).

I hate him so much, Lord, and I know that is wrong. Help me at least stop hating him. Be a shield between me and my hatred. Hear me, like you heard David.

I lay down and slept; I awoke, for the LORD sustained me. I will not be afraid of ten thousands of people who have set themselves against me all around. Arise, O LORD; save me, O my God! For You have struck all my enemies on the cheekbone; You have broken the teeth of the ungodly. Salvation belongs to the LORD. Your blessing is upon Your people (Psalm 3:5–8).

How could he do what he did to me? Where were you, God? Why did you let it happen? But you say you have broken the teeth of the ungodly. I know that retribution is yours, Lord. It's strange though. Part of me wants him all better, so I can love him and he can love me. I know I'm confused. Just let me be in your will.

4. Correct the Loss Abuse Caused

An effective way to eliminate anger over abuse is to correct the losses and problems the abuse has caused. You do so through combating negative conditions, situations, or attitudes that are attributable to your abuse with positive actions. I like to list things. Then I know what I have to do. I suggest you develop an Anger Correction Worksheet, which is really a list that spells out improvements you plan to make in your life to reduce and eventually eliminate your anger.

Take a sheet of paper and draw a line down the center dividing it into two columns. Title one side "Losses Due to Abuse." Title the other side "Substitutions for Losses." As you think of ways to compensate for your losses and difficulties, your anger will likely subside and your faith and confidence will rise. Then as you carry out your plans to correct problems your abuse caused, your anger will continue to recede. Here is a sample worksheet:

Anger Correction Worksheet

Losses Due to Abuse	Substitutions for Losses
I don't like myself and feel ashamed to be among normal people. There must be something wrong with me that I took all that abuse.	I will find a support group that affirms me as a person. I will read scriptures that tell me how precious I am to God. I will keep telling myself that God's opinion of me is more important than my husband's.
I don't trust men.	I realize trust will take time, but I will try to see the good points in men whom others consider trustworthy. I will read biographies of godly men.
I feel sorry for myself because I have missed so much of life.	I will volunteer to help battered women. I know that others have lost more than I.
I feel so inferior that I have lost confidence in my ability to hold down a job.	I will attend school to learn job skills.
I lost my hearing in my left ear when my husband pounded it. I can still hear with my right ear, and I want to be grateful for that, but I'm not.	I'll visit with a deaf person who can't hear at all. Maybe I will learn from this person how to handle my hearing loss.
My children are angry with me for not defending them when their father abused them.	I will write them each a letter, asking their forgiveness. I will list specific instances when I didn't defend them. I will share what I feel I should have done so that they know I am truly sorry. I will offer to support them fully now. I will outline how I intend to do that.

I feel unworthy before God because of the vile sexual things my husband did to me and made me do.

I will study the subject of victimization in the Bible. I will volunteer at a center that helps sexually abused children. I realize our situations are similar.

I'm mad at God for letting me go through so many horrors, and I doubt God cares much about me.

I will find other abused believers and learn how they came to trust God again. I will study scriptures that talk about how God brings good from evil to those who love him.

I have lost many friends through the abuse. They either got disgusted with me for staying with my husband so long, or they got mad at me for breaking up my marriage.

I will be a friend to other victims who need friends.

I have little money, and the children are often hungry.

I will check out social welfare programs and ask my church to help me financially.

I'm mad at my pastor because he never responded to my pleas for help when I was abused.

I will write him a letter describing how his rejection devastated me, and if he doesn't respond in a helpful way, I will find another church.

My husband tore up all my photographs, and I have no pictures of our children.

I'll write relatives to see if they have pictures I can have duplicated.

I hate my husband.

I will work hard through Scripture and prayer to see him as a sinner, just like me, in need of God's grace. I will pray for his salvation, even if I don't really mean the words.

I am depressed.	I will see a therapist and/or join a support group. I will read Christian books that will uplift and instruct me. I will study the Bible one half-hour a day.
My mind dwells on the abuse, the terror I felt.	I will try to think pure thoughts, according to Philippians 4:8.
I am a people-pleaser, maybe due to trying to please my husband so long.	When I feel like pleasing someone to make her like me, I will stop and think, *What would be the honest thing to do? What would be the godly thing to do for that person?* I will think, *Isn't it selfish to center on myself?*
I am still addicted to my husband. I feel so abandoned since we separated.	I know that I made my husband my god. I will study Scripture on how God is my only God.
I fantasize about how I will take revenge on my husband.	I will replace these thoughts with pure thoughts, described in Philippians 4:8. I will meditate on the story of Cain's sin of anger.
I have trouble saying no to anyone. People easily intimidate me.	Moses had these same problems. I will study his story and learn how he delegated authority and depended on God. I can take a class in assertiveness training to learn how to be confident.

5. Exercise and Eat a Low-Fat Diet

Exercise is one of the best anger reducers. In fact, many Christians who pray while they exercise find their anger dissipates as they concentrate on worshiping God, enjoying the scenery, and pushing their bodies to perform. Susan Forward and Joan Torres say, "Anger is a biological response to frustration or insult, and when it is physicalized much of it can be diminished."[5]

Other benefits from exercise are increased muscle mass (more muscles = more calories burned), a toned heart muscle that can pump oxygen around your system more effectively, and reduced weight. These benefits add up to a body that is healthier and feels better, giving you a mental lift. Importantly, you control your body during exercise (how fast, how long, how hard you work out). Many of you have been so controlled in the past that your body didn't seem to be your own. Reclaiming it gives you satisfaction and reduces your anger.

Exercise three to six times a week, giving your body at least one day off. And try to exercise for thirty to sixty minutes to get the aerobic effect that will improve your heart and health. Pick exercises that you like and vary them. You will be very bored if every day you ride a stationary bike in the same room looking at the same wall.

The food you eat can reduce your anger level. Researchers find that people on low-fat diets are less depressed and angry than those who are not. In addition, "scientists speculate that eating a healthy diet...helps people feel more in control of their lives, which leads to greater self-esteem and well-being."[6] To maintain a low-fat diet, 70 percent or more of your calories should come from carbohydrates and protein and 30 percent or less from fat.

Forgiving

Eventually in your quest to recover from abuse, these questions will likely prick you: Shall I forgive my husband? Can I forgive him? Must I?

These are hard questions in the light of what you have suffered, and certainly your husband does not deserve forgiveness based on the facts of your case. Unfortunately, if you don't forgive him, you will live with bitterness, which destroys peace of mind and harms your relationship with

Christ. But why allow bitterness to consume your mind? Why not allow God to help you forgive your abuser, freeing you for happier thoughts?

After Corrie Ten Boom, author of *The Hiding Place*, finished a speech, a man from the audience approached her. With horror she rec- ognized him as a Nazi SS guard from the concentration camp where she was imprisoned and her beloved sister died. He apparently did not remember her from those days. She boiled with outrage and thoughts of revenge. She couldn't raise her hand to shake his. Then she saw the sin of her thoughts. "Jesus Christ had died for this man; was I going to ask for more? *Lord Jesus*, I prayed, *forgive me and help me forgive him.*"

As she clasped the ex-guard's hand, she felt an incredible current passing through her arm. "Into my heart sprang a love for this stranger that almost overwhelmed me. And so I discovered that it isn't on our forgiveness any more than on our goodness that the world's healing hinges, but on His. When He tells us to love our enemies, He gives along with the command, the love itself."[7]

Corrie's story shows us that forgiving is an act of the will, not an innate ability that arises for the occasion. Corrie exercised her will when she prayed for strength to forgive the guard then reached for his hand. When we supply the willingness to forgive, God supplies the ability to forgive. Our forgiveness of an abuser excuses his vile words, rapes, blows—everything sinful that he did against us. We assume the position that retribution is not in our hands but in God's. Forgiving, I think, is one of the hardest, if not *the* hardest, part of following Christ, and it causes me great trouble. But it also gives me great joy to receive such a remarkable ability from God. Your experience with forgiving your abuser might be similar to this:

You suffer years of marital abuse.

You separate from your husband. (You may be able to forgive your husband while you still undergo abuse, for I do believe that through God a woman can do absolutely anything. But be forewarned that forgiving a person who constantly re-angers you, setting you back to step zero, is nearly impossible. Yet we are commanded to forgive. This is why separa- tion is often necessary in order to initiate the process of forgiveness. You are not, keep in mind, commanded to "*live* with your husband.")

You find a safe place to live, develop a good support team, perhaps undergo therapy.

You cling to God and read the Bible.

You begin to release your anger.

Your conscience reveals it is time to forgive. You realize God commands it: "Then Peter came to Him and said, 'Lord, how often shall my brother sin against me, and I forgive him? Up to seven times?' Jesus said to him, 'I do not say to you, up to seven times, but up to seventy times seven'" (Matthew 18:21–22).

You pray for the ability to forgive.

God provides the ability, maybe through an encounter, maybe through something you read. Whatever the mode, the ability is just there.

Maybe later, angry thoughts come, and you suddenly hate your abusive husband. You haven't failed to forgive, but you have been waylaid. So you determine to forgive again, and God gives the ability again. The important thing to always remember about forgiveness is that it is a process. And that God is in the process, giving the ability all the way.

Whatever path you take to forgiveness, know that it takes courage. Laurence Sterne, an eighteenth-century author and priest in the Church of England, said, "Only the brave know how to forgive.... A coward never forgave; it is not in his nature."

How true. Only a brave woman will say, "Okay, I won't hate you, though I have every right to. I won't seek an eye for an eye. I won't let the past harm your life in Christ, or mine. I hope to make a positive future out of my painful past. I know that retribution is not my responsibility but God's. I know God commands me to forgive, and I will!"

> Carry each other's burdens, and in this way you will fulfill the law
> of Christ.... Let us do good to all people, especially to those who
> belong to the family of believers.
>
> —Galatians 6:2, 10 NIV

Eleven

*L*et's Be There for Her

Caroline's fifth wedding anniversary...

A few weeks before Ed's and my fifth wedding anniversary, I fished
through a shoebox full of pens, searching for a black marker. What I
was about to do horrified me. It made me think that I was mentally ill.
But I felt so overcome with self-hatred that I had to do something or die
inside. The kids were asleep, and Ed was in his office, either working or
watching pornography on TV. Lately he usually fixed his breakfast in
his office, ate lunch there, ate dinner out, and returned to his bedroom
next to mine about midnight. We lived almost completely separate
lives, except for painful moments of conflict. A tugboat sounded, long
and lonely, heading off into the night down the dark river.

I found the black marker I wanted. I slipped my nightgown to my
waist and applied the marker to my nipples until they were jet black. I
examined the finished product in the bathroom mirror. Yes, they would
do. They were just right. Perfect! They were so black that no skin
showed, and the sight was as gruesome as I had hoped. Last night Ed had

invited me to dinner, a rare event, and on the way he pointed out a salmon-colored car. "What a putrid color. It reminds me of those socks I got as a gift." He grinned. "They're the same putrid color as your nipples."

I had gasped and felt as if he had stabbed me in the heart. I knew that he was comparing me to his TV women, and I felt degraded and ugly. I put the marker down. *If you hate my breasts, then I hate them too!* I thought. *If you hate me, then I hate myself. If you don't want me, I don't want myself either. If you say I'm crazy and you're going to put me in a mental ward, well, maybe you should!* Floods of tears fell, running toward the black color.

I pulled up my nightgown without washing my breasts. I couldn't explain why to myself, but I had to keep the black color on all night.

I longed to talk to Kitty, my friend who had broken our relationship because I refused to sell Mary Kay and earn enough money to leave Ed. It had pained her too much to stand by while Ed tormented and battered me. Her parting words had been, "When you're ready to leave Ed, I'll be here for you." That had been a year ago. I wasn't ready to leave Ed, but I had to telephone Kitty.

"Hi, Kitty."

"Caroline."

"I haven't left Ed. It's not quite in my plans, but it's coming, I think. Can you come over for coffee in the morning?"

"Yes, of course," she said in a pleased voice.

In the morning, I sat in my kitchen with Kitty. I served raspberry-flavored coffee and homemade muffins. She had put on weight and was now a little beyond sturdy and definitely pleasingly plump. Kitty hated all forms of exercise, except turning the steering wheel on her pink Mary Kay car and disembarking to sell products. Her husband loved her just as she was, which I thought was wonderful because he was a gynecologist and had some beautiful patients. *If only Ed could be like Bob*, I thought. "How's Mary Kay going?" I asked.

"Great. I've built a good business. It's not that Bob and I need the money, because we don't. But I love helping women look their best. I've had chances to share the Lord. It's great!" Kitty sipped her coffee. "How's it going with Ed?"

"Terrible. I don't communicate with him unless I have to. It takes too much energy, and I end up sick and coughing—from the COPD. He's had his office locks changed five times to keep me out, and I've had the locksmith out five times to redo them. That's how obsessed I still am with him. I write every week on my prayer card at church, 'Please pray that Ed's heart of stone turns to a heart of love.' My pastor can't understand how I can love Ed and hate him at the same time."

"I was hard on you before. All that I thought about was getting you out of here. I put more importance on your leaving than I did on you as a person. I'm so sorry. Please tell me more about Ed. I want to really understand."

I took a deep breath and told her about my black nipples and Ed's comments on their putrid color.

Kitty's eyes filled with pain. "He's an absolute monster."

"Why did I do it, Kitty? Why do I do such things?"

"Because you're heartbroken."

"Would you have done something like this in my place?"

"Absolutely, and more probably."

"Oh, Kitty," I said, tears in my eyes, "I've missed you so much."

"I've missed you every day."

I refilled our cups. "I've had so many people at church tell me to forgive Ed that I'm filled with guilt. Could they forgive their husbands if they were treated like this?"

"I don't think you can forgive him while he's still hurting you. You need some distance from him to start to forgive." Kitty leaned on her elbows. "Obviously, I still think you should leave Ed. I haven't changed my thinking about that. But I won't push you. I'll be here for you no matter what. If you ever leave, and you find you can't make it financially, I'll give you the money to make it. I mean that. I won't let you slip through the cracks."

I stared at her. I had never felt such relief. I had heard a lot of lip service, "Oh, I'll help you if you ever need it," but what did that mean? Kitty had addressed my worst fear, living in poverty with my children. I started to cry. "Nobody's ever said anything so loving."

Kitty got a matter-of-fact look in her eyes. "You need a different color lipstick. That red color is bright enough, but it needs a blue tint to match your eyes." She pulled out a catalogue. "It's on me."

I felt hopeful, bolstered by the love of a friend. Maybe I could leave Ed one day—and if I did, Kitty would be there for me.

A GOOD SAMARITAN

Though Caroline considers coloring her nipples black one of the ugliest acts of her life, she tells us about it because she believes her outer disfigurement represents the inner ruin of many abused women. She hopes her honesty will help us understand what abused wives really endure. It is never nice. It is worse than we think. When an abused woman portrays her life to us, we just see the tip of the iceberg.

We can't all offer the financial support that Kitty did, but we do have the capacity to raise a battered wife's hopes with just eleven words: "I care. I believe you. I will be here for you." Our empathy may give her courage to begin to better her life.

Kitty's offer to help Caroline financially resembles what the Good Samaritan did for the stranger.

> Then Jesus answered and said: "A certain man went down from Jerusalem to Jericho, and fell among thieves, who stripped him of his clothing, wounded him, and departed, leaving him half dead. Now by chance a certain priest came down that road. And when he saw him, he passed by on the other side. Likewise a Levite, when he arrived at the place, came and looked, and passed by on the other side. But a certain Samaritan, as he journeyed, came where he was. And when he saw him, he had compassion. So he went to him and bandaged his wounds, pouring on oil and wine; and he set him on his own animal, brought him to an inn, and took care of him. On the next day, when he departed, he took out two denarii, gave them to the innkeeper, and said to him, 'Take care of him; and whatever more you spend, when I come again, I will repay you.'" (Luke 10:30–35)

A perpetrator of domestic violence represents the thief as he wounds his wife, robs her of dignity, confidence, trust in men, trust in the church, and perhaps trust in God. She, like the stranger on the roadside, may be left half-dead, either physically, emotionally, or both. Many people pass her by, not wishing to be involved because they have enough problems of their own. Some people pass because they think the woman behaved recklessly in taking that road, the reason Kitty once left Caroline. Others walk by because they can't believe any of the good people in the area would harm a woman to that degree, so they decide she's faking. Others are in a hurry and hope the next guy stops.

Finally, Kitty retraced her steps, and feeling intense compassion, she helped her injured friend.

After Jesus told the story of the Good Samaritan, he said, "Go and do likewise" (v. 37). And so must we. Whereas the church has not done its share to help domestic-violence victims, secular organizations have counseled them, sheltered them, and funded them, standing in as Good Samaritans.

Granted, it is frustrating to befriend abused women, for often they refuse to leave extremely dangerous conditions. Shirley, a children's advocate at the shelter where I volunteer, says, "Before I became involved in this work, I saw my neighbor and her teenage daughter running down the street at about 2:00 A.M. The mother was yelling, 'Help, he's going to kill me!' Her husband was following with a gun. I called the police, who later came to give us feedback. They said the woman denied that there was any problem. I was, of course, very upset. *How could she deny it? I had seen it!* I didn't know anything then about the dynamics of domestic violence, so that was my reaction."

Battered women's advocate Dana Gilbert says, "Even though we have an agenda that we feel is best for an abused woman, we cannot impose that on her. If her goal is to reunite with the abuser, it is our role to empower her to do it. We don't say necessarily that it is a great idea, and we can present other options, but we cannot impose our agenda. That would be controlling her, just like the abuser. We are not here to run her life but to empower her to make choices, then out of her own needs she can make the most informed choices possible."

It is vital to accept the reasons your abused friend stays (love, financial worries, and fears he will kill her—described in chapter 2). It is not easy to watch her suffer, especially if you think you know exactly what she should do. But if you can explore options with her without directing her, one day she may gain the courage to separate from her abuser or learn how to live more safely with him.

IDENTIFYING ABUSED WOMEN

There are signs of abuse to help identify victims, since they can be too ashamed to reveal their mistreatment. Anne L. Horton, advocate for battered women and author, says of abused women, "Don't ever assume the victim will offer information. In fact, most victims will not identify themselves."[1]

Signs of Domestic Violence

- She doesn't return telephone messages that you give her husband. She probably doesn't receive them. Abusers tend to isolate their mates to rigidly control them. A key sign!

- She wears unsuitable clothes for the weather conditions: long sleeves or scarves in hot weather. She wears sunglasses inside.

- Her makeup is obviously covering up bruises.

- She wears a cast.

- She limps.

- She acts subdued or nervous around her husband.

- She is distant or troubled during church meetings.

- She often skips Bible study group or church, or is late and teary-eyed.

- She may never talk about her husband, or she may complain, but never specifies abuse.

- She may appear to admire her husband as if he were a god. She talks about his interests and his plans, seldom hers.

- There is something about her husband's manner that bothers you, though you may not put your finger on it. It might be that he is overly charming or slick.

- Her husband has made crude or prejudicial remarks about women.

- She often appears low in spirits.

If you suspect a woman is being abused, you can ask her, "What is it like at home for you?" recognizing that she might wish to hide her secret. If she confides wife abuse and indicates she wants to talk further, let your face show that you care about her and your tone of voice show that you are not prying. If she is reluctant to describe her home life, drop the subject. Tell her, "I care about you, and I've been concerned." She knows of your interest, and she may open up later.

QUESTIONS TO ASK IF YOU SUSPECT ABUSE

If she is open to talking, ask any of the following questions that seem appropriate. These questions are designed to help her define her experience, a vital part of her acceptance of victimization. Often abused women are in denial or do not know what acts constitute abuse.

- What is it like at home for you?
- What happens when you and your husband argue?
- Are you ever afraid of your husband?
- Does your husband ever threaten you?
- Does your husband ever prevent you from doing things you want to do?
- Does your husband ever follow you when you leave the house?
- Do you have to account for your time away from home?
- Does he often neglect to give you phone messages?
- Is your husband jealous?
- Is he hard to please, irritable, demanding, and critical?
- Does your husband put you down, call you names, and yell a lot?
- Does he punish you, such as locking you out of the house?
- Does your husband ever push you around or hit you?
- Are you forced to have sex or do sexual acts that you dislike?
- Have you ever needed medical treatment because your husband

injured you?[2] (Emergency-ward staffs are increasingly asking questions to identify abuse when women arrive with injuries, vague complaints, digestive upsets, or damage from suicide attempts. Dr. Kevin J. Fullin, M.D., says, "It's more appropriate to ask the right questions and get the woman the proper help than to end up doing more scans that don't need to be done and don't show anything."[3])

Sharon, a Bible study leader, heard a speech on domestic violence at her church and later noted that Joyce, a member of her Bible study group, often looked depressed and distracted. When Sharon left phone messages with Joyce's husband, Joyce seldom returned the calls.

After a Bible study, Sharon took Joyce aside and asked, "Is it okay for you at home?" Joyce wept and shared that her husband beat her. He had thrown so many objects against the wall that she had run out of decorations to cover the holes. With Sharon's help, Joyce worked through the Safety Plan in Appendix A. Joyce still lives with abuse, but she has taken steps to seek safety. She has joined an abused women's support group and is attending school to update her job skills should she decide to leave.

HELPING AN ABUSED WIFE

The woman who confides that she is a domestic-violence victim may be your neighbor, the woman who sits beside you at Bible study, or a friend who has never talked much about her home life. How can you help?[4]

- Listen to her story, at times asking questions that will help her define her situation. Robert Hicks, author of *Failure to Scream*, cites a study that found, "Even the perception that social support and help are available has been proved to diminish initial catastrophic stress."[5] At the shelter where I work, as I have listened to the stories of residents, I have seen faces soften, and I have been hugged or thanked for listening.

- Keep what you hear confidential, for the information is highly personal, and you may be the only one she trusted enough to tell. Furthermore, you risk her safety should you tell and her husband hear through the grapevine.

- Validate her. Maybe no one has in years. Say, "I believe what you have suffered is wrong. No one has to take that." Keep in mind that she may not realize she has been emotionally or physically abused. She may also think suffering at her husband's hand is her lot in life.

- Be supportive, but not directive. You want to be like the excellent teacher who asks questions that make her students think, but who doesn't tell them what to think. Advocate Joan Juhkne says, "The last thing that a woman needs to hear is that she should do this and that. She is dealing with a controller at home all the time. When we direct women, they really click into it and withdraw."

- Don't blame her for not leaving her husband. Ann MacDonald, executive director of Women Helping Women, says, "Women are actively working to end the violence every day even though they are not responsible for the violence. Sometimes they are asking themselves, 'How can I stop it?' Sometimes they tell their abusers there will be consequences to their behavior. Sometimes they are thinking about leaving. But we as individuals wonder why women stay because we're not aware of what they are thinking about. We don't have an understanding or a deep empathy of what they are experiencing."[6]

- Express concern for her safety if she is battered, for usually she minimizes her danger. Your concern will help her focus on this issue. Give her a copy of the Safety Plan in Appendix A and offer to work through it with her should she need help.

- Inform her that physical abuse is a criminal act. The best way to end physical abuse is to charge her husband with his crime, holding him accountable to the law. If she has just been beaten, ask her, "Do you want to report this to the police?" Offer to go to the police station with her.

- Assure her that God loves her, and discuss her spiritual concerns. She may fear God has deserted her. She may wonder why God allows her to suffer. She may be trying to forgive her abuser, but because she finds it impossible, she is riddled with guilt. She may fear she can never leave her husband because she believes that divorce or separation is against God's will. These are sticky-wicket issues. Advise her to talk, not only to you, but to your pastor and other wise Christians about what the Bible has to say about the issues that concern her.

- Offer to discuss her situation with her whenever she wishes. Give her the number of a women's crisis agency, telling her they can give her information on domestic violence over the tele-phone or in person. You can offer to visit this agency with her.

A Pastor's Response to Domestic Violence

When a wife reports spousal abuse, her pastor's response can make or break her. If he suggests how she can improve her marriage, he iden-tifies her as a guilty party and crushes her. If he validates her and helps her explore options, the weight of the world falls from her shoulders.

The following fictional meetings feature Pastor Adams, who is well informed about domestic violence. They show the correct way to respond to wife abuse.

Marty

Marty entered Pastor Adams's office, frightened that he wouldn't believe what she was about to tell him. Her husband, Kent, an elder in the church, was considered a good leader and had a likable manner that attracted people. Marty taught a fourth-grade Sunday-school class, but generally kept to herself. People thought of her as quiet but sweet. She nervously twisted a Kleenex as Pastor Adams asked, "Is something wrong, Marty?"

Marty cried as she revealed that her husband was physically and emotionally abusive. "He hits me where it won't show. Last night he kicked me in the ribs, and I'm sore and bruised."

Inwardly, Pastor Adams had difficulty reconciling the sincere elder with the abuser that Marty described, but he knew enough about wife abuse to realize that women minimize their experience. He nodded to encourage her to continue.

"He rips the telephone cord out of the wall after he hits me so I can't call for help. He accuses me of sleeping with other men if I'm home five minutes late from shopping." She wept bitterly. "I have never even thought of such a thing. He terrorizes the children, threatening to call the police when they are bad, but he hasn't hit them yet. He locked me in the closet for six hours when I was a half-hour late one day. I heard the children screaming at him to please let me out." She bent her head. "There's a little voice in me that says I can't be so bad as to deserve all this."

Pastor Adams reached for her hand. "Of course you aren't. What you've been through is horrible. What Kent has done to you is criminal and should be reported to the police. Have you ever done that?"

"No—I can't. He said he'd make me pay if I did."

"What do you think he meant?"

"He said he'd divorce me if our personal life were ever known. He blames me for what he does and says he can prove in court that I'm a bad mother. He says he'll get custody of the children. I won't get a penny. I've been home with the kids since I married. I couldn't get anything more than a minimum-wage job," she sobs. "I couldn't live without them. I've been a good mother. How could he prove I wasn't?"

"I don't believe he can."

Pastor Adams then told Marty that she could file charges against Kent and have him arrested. The court would give her a restraining order that forbade him to contact her. The pastor offered to go to the police station with her.

"I don't want him arrested," Marty said. "I just want him to treat me better."

He offered to shelter her and her children with a couple from the congregation. The location would be kept secret from her husband, the congregation, and her friends. He said that the church would support her financially until she found decent-paying work, should she decide to separate for a time. He stressed that, even though the children had not been hit, they had severe stress from witnessing domestic violence and might benefit from therapy. "Kent's behavior is very damaging to the children and to you. I want you to think about that."

Marty shook her head. "I—guess I'm not ready to leave Kent. I still hope it can work out somehow. I'd like the children to see a counselor, if Kent will agree."

Pastor Adams gave Marty a copy of the Safety Plan (Appendix A in this book), stressing that she make her safety a priority. He warned her to hide it from Kent. He offered to help her work through any part that puzzled her. He referred her to a counselor for her and the children and a women's crisis center, which had a support group, knowing that she needed information and interaction with other abused women to realize her danger.

"Marty, has there been forced sex? Often husbands who batter also rape their wives."

"No," she replied.

"Do you want me to talk to Kent?"

Marty looked scared. "Not yet."

"When you're ready for me to talk to him, I plan to tell him that the church holds him accountable to stop his abuse. I'll recommend a counselor and batterers' treatment program to help him."

"That would be good, but I'm still too afraid of what he'd do if he knew I told."

"I'm behind you, whatever you decide. I'll pray for you, and I want you to call anytime, even if it's in the middle of the night. Let's meet next week, after you work through the Safety Plan. I'd like to see how you're coming along."

Pastor Adams didn't suggest joint marital counseling. He knew marriage counseling assumes that the parties have relatively equal power and potential for change, which was not the case here. It would be like putting a lion in the ring with a rabbit.

"You won't tell Kent I've been here?"

"No. Everything you've told me is confidential. Marty, one last thing. Will you allow my secretary to photograph your bruises? It'll be a valuable record, should you ever need it in court. And she'll keep your situation confidential too."

"Okay."

Pastor Adams did not press Marty to leave her husband but offered her the option and the means. He knew that she had been controlled long enough, and one more directive voice would not help her. He privately prayed that she would find the strength to separate from Kent, until he repented.

JUNE AND TED

June and Ted visited Pastor Adams together. June arranged the appointment, explaining that they had marital problems, but she didn't specify abuse. She served as the choir director, a vivacious woman, except when her husband was around. Ted had never been active in church, but he attended Sunday services.

June looked nervously at Ted while he said, "I have no idea why June dragged me in here. But you know how emotional women can be." He gave June a menacing look.

"What do you mean?" Pastor Adams asked.

"Well, I love June and I like to know where she is. She gets angry when I call her at work a few times a day or ask her who she's talking to on the phone. I love her, and I like to be involved in her life."

"How do you feel about that, June?"

"If I'm late getting home from work, Ted thinks I've seen another man. When I got pregnant, he wouldn't accept that the baby was his, and even now, he has doubts. He even went so far as to have our telephone bugged to see if I was cheating. I do everything to please Ted because I really want him happy, but I can't seem to convince him I'm faithful to him."

June began to cry. Ted said, "You're exaggerating things way out of proportion."

"You don't act like you trust me. That's what love is. If you just once in a while would say something nice to me instead of always accusing me of not giving you what you need—I—I could be so much happier. I feel depressed most of the time. It's just like when I was a kid. My dad blamed me for everything that went wrong in the house."

Pastor Adams didn't know if Ted physically abused June, but he was certain Ted emotionally abused her. He told the couple he would like to meet with each of them in a private session to understand their points of view. "Then I'll recommend some options to you both."

June

During Pastor Adams's session with June, he asked, "Does Ted hit you?"

"No, but he talks about my cheating on him in front of his parents and tells everybody I'm stupid and gives embarrassing examples. It humiliates me. I've even seen him following me to the grocery store."

"Do you think he might harm you?"

"I don't know. He drives like a maniac when he's mad at me. He throws things and has shoved the door in my face a few times, but he hasn't actually hit me with it. But I think being the object of his jealousy and ridicule is worse than getting harmed. I can't get things he says off my mind. I don't know what to do."

Pastor Adams nodded. "I'm sure you're very angry, and you have every right to be."

"I do?" She looked amazed. "I kept thinking I must walk or talk a certain way that gives Ted the idea I'm unfaithful. I was sure it was my fault. I even bought plainer clothes to wear to work. I hate it when things at home are all upset and no one is happy. All that I ever wanted was to love Ted and make him happy."

"Would you be willing to see a Christian therapist to learn to be more assertive and to set limits on what behavior you'll accept from Ted? It may be that Ted won't go along with any limits you set. He may not admit he has a jealousy problem, and then you'll have to decide if it's possible for you to survive emotionally in the relationship. But that's down the road. Ted very well may admit he's acting abusively toward you. If he does, there's hope for a much better relationship. I'm glad you came. It took courage, and you've been through more hurt than you probably realize."

Pastor Adams gave June the telephone number of a women's crisis center, which had a support group. He also referred her to a Christian psychologist. "If you need me, call anytime. I don't intend to let Ted coast. I have an appointment with him, and I expect him to deal with his jealousy and need to control you."

Ted

During Pastor Adams's appointment with Ted, he explained about emotional, physical, and sexual abuse, and handed Ted a booklet about domestic violence. "Are you emotionally abusing June?"

Ted looked amazed that he could be classified as abusive. "I love June. I realize that I monitor her and worry about her maybe a bit too much, but I certainly don't consider that abuse."

"June is very uncomfortable. She worries that she will do something to cause your jealousy to flare up. She says you're critical and demanding as well."

"If she didn't dress so provocatively and flirt all the time, I wouldn't be upset with her."

"I don't see that in June. She told me she loves you and wants to please you. Ted," Pastor Adams said firmly, "we are all responsible for our actions. People don't make us be jealous; we choose to be jealous. People don't make us critical or make us humiliate them in front of others, which June said you've done. The way you treat June is unacceptable in this church, and I expect you to change your behavior toward her."

"Well, I guess I have to do something. I don't want to lose June."

Pastor Adams referred Ted to a Christian psychologist and offered to pray for him and be available when Ted needed support. "I'll be checking up to see how you progress."

DIFFERENT RESPONSES FOR DIFFERENT SITUATIONS

Pastor Adams did everything just right. He addressed Marty's safety issues and referred Marty and June to appropriate information sources, support groups, and therapy. He did not override Marty and contact Kent, which would have jeopardized her safety.

He didn't refer June and Ted to joint marriage counseling, since he knew the problem was not the marriage relationship but Ted's anger and obsession to control June. He informed Ted that his behavior was unacceptable and referred him to a therapist. He also held Ted accountable, saying he would get back with him.

PASTORS REACHING OUT TO ABUSED WOMEN

If I were a pastor I would be concerned about time constraints as I considered addressing domestic violence in my church. I would know I could only stretch so far. It is important that pastors realize they cannot fight wife abuse alone but need the involvement of committed leaders and laity. The following items are suggested methods to motivate domestic-violence victims to report their plights and to provide help for them once they have asked for it.

SPEAK OUT ABOUT DOMESTIC VIOLENCE

October is Domestic Violence Awareness month. Pastors can use the occasion to feature domestic violence in sermons and to sponsor workshops by guest experts or talks by domestic-violence advocates from shelters or crisis centers. The advocates for battered women whom I have heard have done excellent jobs of informing and educating. Don't drop the issue of domestic violence after October; rather, keep it active throughout the year. It is vital to do so. A priest who runs marriage workshops polled participants in a confidential survey and found that their greatest need was help with alcoholic and abusive spouses.[7] Yet I have heard wife abuse mentioned only once in a sermon in twenty-five years of church attendance, and then only briefly.

Important Items for Sermons on Domestic Violence

- Define wife abuse. Women may not realize that hair pulling, degradation, forced sex, and threats qualify as abuse.

- Stress that no one deserves to be physically or emotionally violated. Physical violence is a criminal act, while verbal and emotional violence damage a woman's psyche. The Bible likens the wicked tongue to a raging fire (see James 3:6) and a poison more venomous than a viper's (see Psalm 58:4). This is why abused women tell me they fear verbal abuse more than physical violence. At least the pain from a blow subsides and stops. Poisonous words injected into a mind can linger in full strength.

- Apologize for your church's lack of attention to wife abuse, if that has been the case.

- Assure abused women that their confidentiality will be maintained if they speak up about abuse.

- Explain why women stay in destructive relationships (see chapter 2). I often meet people who tell me, "I wouldn't take that. I'd leave." Or, "She'd leave if it were really that bad." Patiently explain why abused women do stay (and why you might stay if you were in their shoes), for it is a difficult concept for people who have not been abused to understand.

- Clarify submission. Ephesians 5:21–33 specifies that a wife submits to a husband who will defend her, whereas an abuser has quite the opposite goal. Some even have murder on their minds. The Bureau of Justice Statistics reported that during a one-year period, 30 percent of all murdered women died at the hand of a husband, former husband, or boyfriend.[8]

- Assure women they do not provoke abuse, though virtually all abusers sell their victims on this idea.

- Offer to (separately) help both victims and perpetrators who confide in you, assuring them of confidentiality. Mention community organizations that help victims and perpetrators. State that you have information about domestic violence on hand. (Keep copies of the Safety Plan on file.)

PROVIDE SAFE SHELTERS FOR BATTERED WOMEN

For every woman who is admitted to a shelter two are turned away, a number that is higher in urban areas. Michelle Wodtdke, director of the Family Violence Project in Cincinnati, says, "One of my dilemmas is that we urge law officials, health care providers, and hospitals to identify battered women, but when they do, we often say, 'We haven't a bed available in our shelter.' It's so frustrating. If we turn a woman away and she is later shot, we have failed her."

One possibility to help alleviate the shortage of shelter beds is to offer your members' private homes to abused women and their children. These homes must be kept secret to protect the residents, just as public shelters are. The hosts should be well informed about wife abuse and trained to be supportive and empathetic but not directive. Kenneth W. Petersen, managing editor at Tyndale House, suggests that "churches could consider the needs of abused women a kind of mission field, allotting part of their missionary budget to the establishing of abuse shelters and homes."[9]

The idea of sheltering abused women might meet with resistance at your church. Some members may not want the congregation involved in what is considered a family problem, while others won't accept that the church has battered women in need of such shelters. But with education, I believe, resistance to shelters can be abolished. You have, through making shelters available, an opportunity to minister the gospel and Christ's love to women and children in your church and in the community as well. Let's then "go out into the highways and hedges, and compel them to come in, that my house may be filled" (Luke 14:23).

WRITE ABOUT WIFE ABUSE IN NEWSLETTERS AND BULLETINS

Material and statistics to provide content for newsletters and bulletins can be found at women's crisis centers, in "Domestic Violence Fact Sheets" (look at the list of resources in Appendix B), and on the Internet. You can also interview a domestic-violence victim, a reformed abuser, or a person who has helped a victim of violence for your newsletter. I wrote a story about domestic violence for my church's newsletter, which a woman kept for seven months. Finally, she called me for help.

OTHER IDEAS FOR PASTORS

- If possible, provide names of attorneys, nurses, counselors, and physicians who will volunteer their services if an abused woman is without funds.

- Advertise your ability to help domestic-violence victims in letters to other churches and on radio and television.

- Attend seminars on domestic violence, located through contacting a women's crisis center or the YWCA. In some communities clergy and domestic-violence advocates work together to help abused wives. Check out this possibility.

  Dana Gilbert is a facilitator of workshops for religious leaders. She says, "There is a tremendous amount of energy, interest, and willingness from the participants. At workshops, I teach about the dynamics of violence, the resources available, and how to intervene safely when working with victims or perpetrators. It is important that pastors or lay leaders be helpful to all parties concerned, including children, in ways that do not put anyone's safety at risk. It is dangerous to believe that helping abused women is safe work.

"I'd like to see at least one person in each church or synagogue who is trained to do effective interventions in domestic-abuse situations. I'd also like to see support groups in more churches for both abused women and abusers."

- Start a support group led by a trained leader who knows the resources for abused women available in the community. I have co-facilitated a support group for abused women and was impressed at the wisdom that abused women shared, gained from bitter experience. The emphasis should be positive: What can I do to take control of my life?

- Work on an interdenominational level to fight domestic violence, meeting regularly to find out what is working in other churches.

- Teach against violent behavior in Sunday school. Darcus Anderson, family-violence specialist, says, "The earlier we teach children how to deal with anger, the better chance they have of not developing abusive relationships." Anderson notes that young children's minds are quite receptive. Anderson also says that younger children are more inclined to tell if domestic violence exists at home than older children, a point for Sunday-school teachers to note. If a child reveals domestic violence, follow up, but be cautious, for intervention can risk the family's safety as well as your own. Call a women's crisis center and ask how to do a safe intervention.

A Sunday-school teacher can tell her students that if a child confides information to them that makes them feel something is wrong at that child's house, take the child to an adult whom they trust. Trusted people can be parents, ministers, and

Sunday-school teachers. A Sunday-school teacher can give her phone number to her class and say, "I will believe you if you ever have something to tell me. I will always be here for you if you can't find someone to believe you."

RURAL ABUSED WOMEN

As a church, we must be sensitive to the special difficulties abused women in rural areas face. An abused woman in a rural area is far more isolated, and therefore trapped, than her suburban or city counterpart. She may not have a phone, or her phone may be a party line, which means her conversations could be repeated to her abuser. She may not have a car or public transportation to help her escape. Her home usually contains lethal weapons that can be used against her: hunting rifles, axes, saws, and shotguns. If she lives in a northern state, long sieges of cold weather may confine her at home with her abuser, exposing her to increased violence. In rural communities there are few protective agencies and fewer courts. The dogma often runs thick in families that a woman sticks by her man, even if he hits her, a viewpoint that further ensnares her. Finally, a rural woman may endure violence because she is afraid to venture into the unfamiliar environs of the city to locate a crisis center.[10]

Be very understanding of her special fears and needs, especially her fear that she would be "bad" if she didn't stay with her husband. She, more than most abused women, needs to hear that "Nobody deserves to be abused." Give her a copy of the Safety Plan, encourage her to call 911 in a crisis, and offer to drive her to a shelter should she wish to escape.

OLDER ABUSED WOMEN

The church must try to identify older women who are abused and minister to them. In more than half of these abuse cases, the perpetrator is the woman's mate. The domestic abuse may have continued for decades, or it may have started when age-related problems set in. Impotence, for instance, may cause some men to feel emasculated, and to reestablish their power they abuse their wives. Illnesses such as diabetes and strokes can alter a man's personality and diminish his ability to judge, opening the door to abusive behavior. Certain prescription drugs can remove inhibitions, resulting in abuse. Advocates for older abused women find that the death of a relative often precipitates an increase in an abuser's vicious behavior.

The older woman who has lived with long-term abuse finds it hard to leave her mate. Anna Marcel de Hermanas, advocate for older women who are battered, says, "She is like a neoplasm, bent so long until she doesn't know who she is." She may think, *It would be more frightening to live in a new environment than a violent one.* She may even have lost sight of her right to live in peace. She may also hold the attitude, *Why try? I've tried it all and it didn't work. I'll just wait for heaven to be free of misery.* She was brought up in times when a woman was expected to stay married. (You were lucky if you had a good husband, unlucky if you didn't.) Any of these attitudes can make an older woman suffering abuse difficult to help.

Yet even if she wishes to leave the violence, often she can't. She may have never worked and feels too old to be trained. If she is physically or emotionally unable to work, her Social Security may be too minimal to live on alone. She may not be able to take refuge in a child's home because the child is against his parents separating: "Mom put up with Dad all these years. He can't be so bad. What's wrong with Mom?"

If she needs immediate public shelter, more problems loom because most public shelters have programs that cater to mothers with children. One study of shelters shows that 72 percent of the residents brought children. The older woman thinks, "This isn't for me. What am I doing here?"

Not only is it hard for her to find help at a shelter; it is also hard to find social-service help in the community. A check in your community will likely find there is very little, if any, public help targeted for older abused women. Certainly churches have an opportunity to minister to this injured population through sheltering them, providing funds, locating jobs, helping them tap into social programs—and giving them a lot of love and understanding.

Let's not fail any woman. Rather, let's allow our churches be refuges.

> If it is possible, as much as depends on you,
> live peaceably with all men. Beloved, do not avenge yourselves,
> but rather give place to wrath; for it is written,
> "Vengeance is Mine, I will repay," says the Lord.
>
> —Romans 12:18–19

Twelve

*L*egal Medicine That Helps

*S*usan's divorce…

The morning my divorce would be granted, I huddled under the bed-covers, wishing I'd never have to leave their security and go to court. Almost two years had passed between Rich's jail term and today, two years of misery, longing to live with him and hating what he had done to me. I heard Lillie, who had driven in the night before to be at divorce court, snoring in the guest room. She was a heavy sleeper and had a habit of setting two alarm clocks to be sure she woke up. I hadn't slept at all last night, and I envied her.

I reached for the remote and turned on the TV to catch the news. Even after all the horror with Rich, I struggled with the possibility that if Rich phoned and asked me to try it again, I just might. This last year I had told several friends that Rich abused me, and now I wished that I hadn't. *I had no right to hurt Rich like that*, I thought, overwhelmed with guilt.

I eased one leg to the floor, then the other. I reminded myself of an old woman, pushing the last ounce of juice from her body to get it going. I made coffee, sat at the table, and wrote an apology to the people I should not have confided in.

Dear _____

I write this letter to ask for your forgiveness. I am sorry for the hurt and grief that my words about Rich may have caused you, as I know that you care for him.

Without a doubt, the two past years have been the most stress-filled ever for our family. I take responsibility for the pain that my behavior has caused, especially to Rich. I pray that he will forgive me, and I know that God has.

Thank you so much for caring. I pray that your tenderness and forgiveness will help to heal some of Rich's hurts.

I copied the letter four times, put a coat over my robe, and mailed the letters in the apartment foyer. I felt less guilty, but mentally sicker, as I climbed up the stairs. Why did I always fail to remember that Rich had abused me and that he should feel guilt over that? I should not feel guilt for releasing my anguish to a few friends. Why didn't Rich ever feel much, if any, real guilt? Probably because he had lost the ability to see me as anything more than an object, like a hammer. You used it; you put it down. It was useful when you needed it; otherwise, it was in the way. Yes, I thought, I had always felt like his object, his tool.

As I hung my coat, I heard Lillie's first alarm, then the second. She soon entered the kitchen, rubbing her eyes. "You doing okay, kiddo?" she asked.

"I'm uptight. I wish the day were over."

Lillie poured a cup of coffee and got a bowl for cereal. She started bacon sizzling and set out two eggs. In Lillie's line of work, she felt she had to start the day with a good deal of food under her belt. "You gotta hold up. You gotta look like you're altogether, or Rich will get the best of you."

"Lillie, think about it. It was only Rich who ever exploited me. The guys that I dated never did. I know that I tend to give in rather than argue, but I'm not the kind to be exploited. It was love addiction with Rich, but I didn't know it until the end of the marriage. If anything, I thought Rich had love addiction, that he would fall apart quicker than I would if we split up. He might have, except he had Rita. He used to say, 'If you leave me, I'll just get me an old dog and fade off into the sunset. I can't make it without you.'" Tears pooled in my eyes. "Well, obviously he can!"

"Forget Rich. The past is past."

"I can't. I keep thinking crazy things. My depression is worse. I think I might need to go back to the hospital."

Lillie turned the bacon. "That might be good. But for today put your mind and everything else on hold and hang in there." Lillie hugged me and prayed, "Dear Lord, give my sister strength to get through a very hard day. Let her know in special moments that you are with her."

"Thanks," I said. My sister was not only a hard worker but also a hard "pray-er," and I knew she would pray at court.

After Lillie ate (I couldn't), I dressed in a navy suit, white and navy shoes, pearls, and I applied a full face of makeup, fabricating an air of confidence that I hoped would prevent an emotional collapse.

Colleen arrived and drove us to the divorce court. We entered a small room with four rows of benches on the right and four on the left. Rich's party was on the left side, just like at our wedding. With him were his lawyer, my daughter Brenda, and Brenda's baby in a stroller. Four male executives from Rich's church sat behind Rich, their dark suits and conservative ties attaching just the right air of respect to Rich. I reached into the aisle and touched my grandchild's hand. *You know nothing will ever be the same when you have to reach to the others' side to touch your grandchild*, I thought.

Rich greeted Lillie and Colleen but looked beyond me, and I looked beyond him. I clasped my hands tightly to keep myself together. My insides were in such knots that my intestines felt tangled. My suit and makeup failed to boost me.

Today the judge would enter his final judgment concerning economic terms. Since I had filed for the divorce, the law required me to state that my marriage was irrevocably broken and that I had been a resident of Florida more than six months. When called to the bench, I mouthed the words, but I felt dissociated from my body, as if it hovered over my statements.

My lawyer had informed me that Rich's domestic violence was irrelevant to the economic terms of the divorce. To win compensation for domestic violence, I must prove that abuse had robbed me of wages or the ability to work, which was not my case. My lawyer hoped to win me fifteen hundred dollars a month in alimony for the seventeen years I stayed home and kept house. He would argue that during that time I couldn't develop my career.

As it turned out, he argued weakly, and the judge awarded me only five hundred dollars in alimony a month. On the other hand, Rich's lawyer had hammered away that I would earn more money than Rich once I returned to my career. Yet I doubted my health would permit me to return to my supervisory position. I wanted economic parity with Rich. Five hundred dollars, added to my disability payment, left me far lower than Rich in total income. To make matters worse, the judge awarded Rich four of our five properties. Rich had devised false proof that his inheritance from his parents had purchased them, not our joint income.

Later when I had the capacity to analyze it, I decided my lawyer hadn't battled on my behalf because he was irritated with women. He had just been through a divorce, costing him forty thousand dollars in alimony a year for life.

Though I came out badly in court, I was too distraught then to care. I only wanted to flee from Rich's overwhelming presence. As we drove from the courthouse, I felt my life history skid to a stop. I could not imagine a future. I eyed the door handle, longing to pull it open, jump, and die. "I'm in pretty bad shape mentally," I said.

"I can see that, kiddo," Lillie said.

At my apartment, Lillie and Colleen packed my suitcase, then they drove me to the psychiatric ward, where I was admitted as clinically depressed. "Am I hallucinating?" I asked Lillie. "Or is this really happening all over again?"

She hugged me. "Baby, you're right smack in reality, and you're going to be fine."

I stayed in the hospital several weeks under Dr. Phillips's care. When I returned to my apartment, I hated it. I saw visions of past traumas in every corner. I hated the place next to my stuffed chair where the IV stand had stood as nurses administered blood during my siege with cancer. I hated the bathroom where I often had lain on the floor because I was so nauseated. I hated the couch where I had cried over Rich. I hated the bed where I had often wept all night. I phoned Colleen. "I have to move immediately."

Colleen found an apartment on the eighth floor of a high-rise. "You'll love it! You'll love looking down on the grounds. They're partially wooded with several gardens. It's near the expressway and not far from me."

"Fine." I didn't care if I loved it or not, so I didn't look at the place. I sent a deposit, and a week later my family and friends moved me into the high-rise in one day.

I continued to meet with Dr. Phillips twice a week, and as the days passed, I felt hope that I could be well again. *I've had so many expressions of love and help that I have to get well*, I thought. *And really*, I thought, *with the divorce over, the worst is past.*

Several months after Rich married Rita, he phoned to say, "You've wrecked my life, but God is giving me another chance with a wonderful woman. She's everything that you weren't. Thank God, I'm done with you."

"Congratulations."

"Is that all you have to say after thirty-three years of marriage?"

"Good luck," I said. I didn't mean it. I wasn't that well yet. I had a lot of forgiving yet to do. I had talked to Dr. Phillips often about forgiving and had dragged in many books on the subject. I had believed, based on the Bible, that I wouldn't have peace until I forgave Rich, but Dr. Phillips always said, "There will be a time for that. First, let's deal with your anger."

"I received one of the largest churches in Florida [his goal in life]," Rich said.

"Congratulations."

"You could be more enthusiastic."

"Look, Rich, I don't want to talk to you unless I have to. Our lives are separate now, except in matters concerning the children."

"Well, I like to talk to you. I would like to think we could keep up a friendship."

"Rich, please." Even now he wanted to manipulate me into feelings of guilt because I wouldn't be his friend. "Good-bye." I hung up quickly, wrung out. *And this won't be the last time he'll play with my mind,* I thought.

DIVORCE DEFINED

When Susan peeled the layers of what her divorce was to its bare-bones legal terms and stripped away all the agony that had occurred to reach that point, she found that it was simply a legal instrument meant to accomplish two goals: dissolve her marriage, freeing her and Rich to remarry; and settle economic issues. It angered Susan that domestic violence was irrelevant to the economic settlement in her divorce. Since that factor had emotionally destroyed her, she felt Rich should have been punished financially.

In Florida, a "no-fault" divorce state, a divorce is automatically granted when one party petitions for it, regardless of who files. "No-fault" means that neither party has to prove the other party committed misconduct, such as mental cruelty or adultery. Sidney M. De Angelis, lawyer and author of *You're Entitled!* says that if your husband files for divorce and you refuse "to sign an affidavit of consent to a 'no-fault' divorce, your husband can simply wait eighteen months, two years, or whatever the state divorce law says, and get his freedom."[1]

Nothing can remove the trauma of the divorce process, but the following suggestions can help a parent gain custody of her children and receive fairer economic terms. Certainly fear overwhelms you at the slightest prospect of losing custody of your children. Your husband has been so manipulative. You know his tricks. You have every reason to fear him. So you need to be well-prepared legally.

FINDING A QUALIFIED ATTORNEY

Your first step after divorce papers are filed is to find an attorney who is experienced in domestic-violence cases. It is hard to search for a competent lawyer when you are bottomed-out emotionally. If the task is overwhelming, ask a friend to research lawyers and help you choose one. You can, if you wish, bring your friend to appointments with a lawyer. She can note points you miss and ask questions you overlook.

Proverbs 15:22 says, "Without counsel, plans go awry, but in the multitude of counselors they are established." Remember this advice as you work through your divorce.

Following are some ideas on how to find a competent attorney.

ASK A WOMEN'S CRISIS CENTER FOR REFERENCES

Ask specifically for an attorney who specializes in domestic-violence cases. If the agency hasn't a list of attorneys, ask them to refer you to a social agency that does. Women Helping Women in Cincinnati keeps a list of twenty-five attorneys who work hard for battered women. If this agency discovers something negative about an attorney, they remove his or her name from the Rolodex.

ASK ACQUAINTANCES FOR REFERENCES

Ask your pastor (if he is sympathetic), relatives, doctors, and friends to refer a lawyer whom they trust. If the lawyer happens to be their good friend, you will likely get special attention.

DON'T PHONE THE BAR ASSOCIATION

The bar association will provide a random list, not a list of experts in domestic violence. Don't count on getting a Christian lawyer. Many specialize in other fields and do not become involved in divorce cases. There is a great need for Christian lawyers to take on cases where spousal abuse has been an issue.

CALL A LEGAL AID SOCIETY

If you haven't the funds for legal services, a Legal Aid Society may be able to help. You may qualify for free legal service if you are under a certain income level, determined by the Legal Aid Society in your area. Unfortunately, even if your low income qualifies you for free legal aid, you may be turned away because Legal Aid Societies have a limited number of attorneys.

It is not unusual for mothers without funds to go through a divorce without a lawyer. This is a terrible situation, one often leading to visitation and child-custody arrangements that endanger the wife and the children and to inequitable economic terms. If the Legal Aid Society can't help you, ask them how you can better seek free legal services. You can also ask your pastor, friends, and doctors if they know of a good lawyer whom they might persuade to represent you as a service to a victim of domestic abuse.

TRY TO FIND A FEMALE ATTORNEY

Christine Kennedy, crisis team coordinator with Women Helping Women, says, "There are good women attorneys and bad, of course, but most abused women I ask would feel better with a woman and do request one."

INTERVIEW TWO OR THREE LAWYERS

If possible, interview more than one lawyer to determine which one you feel the most comfortable with. If an attorney's firm is large, you will probably be charged for the interview, and if the firm is small, you probably won't be. Ask in advance if a fee is charged for an interview. Colleen, Susan's daughter, says, "My first half-hour is free. I tell my clients, 'For the next half-hour you can pick my brain, and if at the end of a half-hour you want me for a lawyer, and I feel as if I can work with you as a client, fine.'"

You can interview attorneys over the telephone. Some lawyers will charge you for this time, but most will not. Any of the following questions are applicable, whether the interview is in person or by telephone.

1. *What is your experience in handling domestic-violence divorce cases?* Ask for specific cases and results.

2. *What is your experience in child-custody cases?*
   Kennedy says, "Most mothers get custody and fathers get visitation rights. Fifty or more percent of the time when the mother is abused, the children are also. Women, of course, do not want their children subjected to abuse. Yet often the court is not hearing them, and the abusers are getting unsupervised visitation." In Massachusetts, for instance, an abuser left jail, was awarded visitation of his baby, and used the opportunity to kill his wife.[2]

Choose a lawyer who will fight for no visitation or supervised visitation if your husband is actively abusive.

3. *What is your fee?*

A lawyer can estimate her fee and put it in writing. The fee will depend on the complications of the case, the locality, whether child custody is involved, and how large the firm is (smaller firms usually charge less). Hourly rates can range from one hundred to three hundred dollars, depending on a lawyer's experience and your locality. If you cannot arrange in the divorce settlement that your husband pays court costs, you will have to pay court costs you incur in the divorce suit.

4. *Do you require a retainer?*

The retainer is money you pay in advance toward the cost of the divorce. Usually lawyers require anywhere from one thousand to twenty thousand dollars.

5. *Will you send monthly statements of charges so that I can track the divorce costs?*

You will want to keep your own estimates of your attorney's time spent on your case and compare them to her records. If fees appear to be unreasonable, ask for an explanation.

6. *Will you lower your fee?*

If your finances are limited, some lawyers will reduce their fees for abused women. But attorneys usually limit how many divorce cases involving domestic violence they will handle. These divorces are generally complicated and time-consuming. One lawyer says, "I have three divorce cases of battered women now, and I won't take another for a while. I have long since exceeded my estimated fee on these cases and am working for free."

7. *What can I expect in child support, alimony, or property division?*

As to property division, at this writing there are forty-two states and the District of Columbia with equitable distribution of property laws; you may get more or less than half of the property, depending on what the judge feels is fair. Seven states are community-property states, meaning property is split fifty-fifty if it is common property. (Some property might be solely in his name or yours.) The community-property states are Arkansas, California, Idaho, Louisiana, New Mexico, North Carolina, and Texas.

Concerning child support, states have mathematical guidelines that govern how much child support should be awarded to the custodial parent, based on the incomes of the two parties. But a judge can award more or less than the guidelines state. Be aware, though, that it is often difficult or impossible to enforce child-support orders. More often than not, the parent owing child support will not pay the full amount due. An abuser, who is generally bent on retaliation, is even less likely to pay all, or even any, child support.

Of course, some battered women will not file for child support at all; they so dread having any contact with their former husbands that the money is not worth it.

Whether or not you will get alimony is a big question. Divorce lawyer Sidney M. De Angelis says, "The trend seems to run in favor of granting temporary or permanent alimony where there is a disparity in the economic situation of the husband and wife, not merely to award alimony for the purpose of 'rehabilitation' [learning a job skill, going to school]." De Angelis adds that the disparity appears to need to be significant.[3]

If during your interview with a lawyer, she is brusque, intimidates you, or hedges questions, she is not for you. You want someone you instinctively trust, as you will work together on tough issues in a frightening situation. You want someone who exudes warmth, displays intelligence, questions you thoroughly, and understands your dangers. Your lawyer can't be your psychologist or hold your hand throughout the proceedings, but she can be competent and caring.

DIVORCE DAY

Divorce day, Susan discovered, is the day when you divorce the father of your children, the man you loved and still love in some ways.

Remember, he is also the man who abused you. Many women have mixed emotions about their former mates and suffer some degree of guilt and regret. To add to the difficulties, your husband may sling mud and lie in court to manipulate you into giving up alimony, property, or child support. Inform your attorney in advance of potential problems regarding joint property and your husband's character so that preparations can be made. If you fear your husband will kill you if you contest him in court, you may decide to relinquish your rightful claims. You know instinctively what is safest for you and your children.

Try to hold up emotionally in court, which is difficult; you appear more competent to the judge if you can. Many battered women look bad in court because they are understandably petrified, intimidated, and exhausted. Hold on to the Lord for strength and courage. "But those who wait on the LORD shall renew their strength; they shall mount up with wings like eagles, they shall run and not be weary, they shall walk and not faint" (Isaiah 40:31).

CHILD-CUSTODY ISSUES

Ninety percent of child-custody arrangements are decided amicably,[4] but when you deal with an abuser, you may be in the 10 percent of cases that aren't. A main reason women separate from or divorce abusive husbands is to protect their children. Your husband and his lawyer may attempt to force you to forgo financial claims through threatening to fight you for child custody. This is generally a ploy, not a desire for custody. Your husband knows that you will probably agree to anything to keep your children, even raising them in poverty. The stress that you feel can be overwhelming.

You may fear that your husband will kidnap your children. In many states if no court order exists naming the custodial parent, your husband can legally transport the children wherever he wants. But if legal custody is established, it is a federal offense to kidnap children (the Parental Kidnapping Prevention Act of 1981). Therefore, immediately upon separation, it is *vital* to obtain temporary custody of your children in court. Even with this document in hand, guard your children to the best of your ability (see the Safety Plan in Appendix A).

Although an attorney familiar with your case can best answer your particular concerns, here are questions about child custody you may have, along with general answers.

Do Mothers Usually Get Child Custody?

Yes and no. State laws have been changing, and currently it is assumed both parents have equal rights to child custody at the onset of a divorce procedure. The paramount issue the judge weighs is the welfare of the child, not the sex of the parent. Factors that affect the child's welfare are which partner has been the primary caregiver, which partner can provide a two-parent home, and which partner can best support the child. Though more than half the time mothers are awarded custody, if an abusive male remarries and earns a good salary, he can win custody. In one tragic case a battered mother left a horrible twenty-year marriage. The judge gave her husband custody of her five children, citing that the husband had a good income, a large house, a new wife—while the battered wife was living on welfare.

After a separation or a divorce, the parent who does not have child custody usually is required to make child-support payments (should he or she have sufficient income to do so).

What Are the Main Types of Child Custody?

Sole legal custody: This is the custody you want. You will have sole legal rights to decide on all matters concerning your child. Your husband has limited rights, such as access to the your child's medical and school records. That link to you provides a way for him to track you down and keep his eye on you, but this is currently the practice. Still, you should push for sole legal custody, for it provides the least linkage to your husband. Yet it seems vital to me that in fear-laden situations, where child abuse is proven, the husband should not be able to get his hands on his children through their school or doctor. If this describes your situation, talk to your attorney to see if anything can be done to prevent your husband from accessing his children's records.

Joint legal custody: Both parents decide on issues concerning the child's welfare. (In some states, which issues can be decided upon are specified.)

Joint physical custody: The child lives with each parent; the residence time with each parent may not be exactly equal, but it will be considerable.

Certainly joint legal or physical custody is a terrifying prospect to consider if your husband is abusive to your children. Joint custody works for parents who are non-abusive, can negotiate differences, and are mature enough to put their children's interests before their own, attributes seldom present in domestic-violence cases. Often domestic-violence victims don't have the legal resources that their husbands do and are maneuvered or coerced into accepting joint custody arrangements. Professor Daniel G. Saunders states, "Recent legislation reflects the growing reservations about joint custody. Most states now have statutory clauses to take marital violence into account when making custody decisions." Yet Saunders points out that often women's charges that their children are abused are not believed in court, despite strong statistical evidence to the contrary.[5] You can see why it is important to have the best legal help possible.

IF I GET CUSTODY, WILL MY HUSBAND GET VISITATION RIGHTS?

You can request "no visitation," but no visitation is hard to get even with proof that your abuser is extremely dangerous to you or the children. The court may order supervised visitation. Colleen says, "Our courts almost have to be convinced a man is an ex-murderer before they cut off visitation. They appoint a family member or court representative to supervise visitation rather than cut it off altogether, figuring the child needs the influence of his father. Visitation requires contact between the parents, which is dangerous. I have mediated pick-up and drop-off of children, sometimes in a parking lot, when I was a new lawyer. The court didn't order it. I volunteered and didn't get paid for it."[6]

When supervised visitation is ordered, it is subject to a social worker's investigation. Even visitation that includes supervision has to be pushed for in court. Rose Hanak with 241-KIDS in Cincinnati says, "Generally if a judge grants visitation it is a routine visit without supervision. If a mother wants the visit supervised, she must let it be known that her husband has a record of child abuse and wife abuse. Supervised visitation does not come lightly or easily."[7] The mother will need medical proof, police records, and convincing witnesses to testify for her in court. Unfortunately, fathers who were not formerly abusive to the children may turn abusive out of anger over the divorce. If currently your husband has unsupervised visitation and you notice bruises, cuts, or signs of sexual abuse, call a child protective agency to investigate. Then go to court and push for either termination of visitation rights or court-supervised visitation. Hanak says, "We recommend that the mother use the court system to get visitation curtailed, not do it on her own with her husband, risking legal trouble for herself."

Finally, if all that were not enough worry, one study shows that one-fourth of abusive husbands threatened to kill their wives during a visitation period. Many abusers continue to physically abuse and harass their wives after the couples have separated, unable to let go of their lust to control. Be very careful during visitation, and if it is not supervised and your husband is violent, have a strong person at your side to protect you when your husband picks up the children.

Beware of Divorce Mediation

According to the National Center for State Courts, there are currently more than 205 state programs to mediate disputes over child custody, visitation, property division, and child support. In addition to these public programs, there are thousands of private divorce mediators.

A divorce mediator represents both parties with the object of the two sides coming to a fair and quick agreement, thus avoiding steep court costs. One objection to divorce mediation is that the mediator is not a lawyer and cannot mediate legal issues that he does not fully understand. Mediators are generally trained in social science, family therapy, or psychology. But a greater concern for abused women is that mediation assumes that both parties have equal bargaining power and have equally contributed to the collapse of the marriage. This is not the case between a victim of domestic violence and her husband.

Saunders points out that mediators often use models for mediation that assume that alcohol abuse or poor communication have caused the marriage failure; if the mother or child correct this view in a mediation session, they risk the abuser's wrath after the meeting.[8]

Another problem is that abused women are intimidated by or even terrified of their abusers. "Mediators may believe they can equalize the power difference, but battered women carry with them a terror that makes them prone to give in." Some states, realizing the safety issues and inequality of power, exempt abused women from mediation sessions for divorce settlements.[9]

I certainly recommend that you refuse divorce mediation should it be offered.

MONETARY COMPENSATION FOR ABUSE

It is sometimes possible for women to win compensation for the trauma of physical injury as well as for medical expenses and lost wages. In Georgia, a jury awarded thirty thousand dollars in punitive and compensatory damages to a woman whose husband had dragged her down the stairs by the hair because it looked "comical."[10]

You may also sue for losses due to psychological injury, though you are more likely to win compensation for physical abuse. Serious psychological injury is defined as conduct "'so outrageous in character, and so extreme in degree, as to go beyond all possible bounds of decency, and to be regarded as atrocious, and utterly intolerable in a civilized community.'... In New York, for example, the behavior of a man who destroyed the windows of his wife's house and threatened her life by displaying a bullet was found to be sufficiently outrageous."[11] Suing for compensation for abuse is a new and growing trend, one worth noting and asking your attorney about.

To each his suff'rings: all are men,
condemned alike to groan,
The tender for another's pain.

—Thomas Gray

Thirteen

Give Me Some Tender-Hearted Men

An abuser's story...

Joe's counselor arranged my interview with Joe, a twenty-five-year-old pastor of a small mission church who had been arrested for domestic violence.[1] When I interviewed people for this book, my practice was to type their comments but also to tape them in order to have verbatim quotes on hand. So far, no one had refused to be taped—except Joe. He walked into our conference room, sat his hefty frame down at the table, fastened his brown eyes on me, and laid down rules for our meeting.

He told me his fictitious name would be Joe. He told me he would like to be fictitiously born in Lansing, Michigan because it was his favorite state. He asked that my book be titled *Overcoming* because that title best described his experience. When I explained that editors generally title books, he suggested I title this chapter "Overcoming." He told me that he didn't want the book to have any contact with a certain major network, as he didn't like them. He insisted on reviewing the publisher's edited copy of his interview because editors might

237

change his quotes (a surprise as I was changing details about him to guard his anonymity).

As he zinged out commands, I felt empathy for his wife. Although the negative impact of his mandates remained, as we talked I began to see another side of Joe. I warmed toward him as he said he would have driven to my city (a long drive) "if the interview would help just one guy." He wore a good-looking striped shirt, and when I complimented him on it, he said he paid just five dollars for it and had bought eight of them. He reminded me of a kid in his enthusiasm over his good buy on shirts.

Joe told me that he had attended church four to five times a week as a child because his parents were both pastors. He became a Christian at age ten. He recalled that his grandfather cruelly abused his grandmother, deeply traumatizing her. In any case, Joe expected to grow up to serve Christ, not to abuse his wife, Helen. In fact, though he had an anger problem, he didn't realize it until one Tuesday at 9:00 A.M. He and Helen were having a trivial argument. He didn't remember the issue, but he remembered yelling, "Shut up! If you don't, I'll do something. You'll be sorry. You hear me! Shut up!"

She spoke, and anger boiled up like always when they argued, but this time it exploded in his head. He drew back his arm and slammed her in the face. She spun around, tripped over the bedroom doorjamb, and, as she scrambled to her feet, blood poured from her nose and mouth. He had never hit her before. He had yelled, raged, even pinched the back of her arm to keep her from doing something that would look stupid in public. He stared at her in shock.

He heard sobbing sounds and wheeled around to see his twin boys. They were screaming, "Mommy! Mommy!"

He knew he had to protect them from the bloody sight, and he grabbed their hands, hurried them to the car, and drove aimlessly around for an hour. He thought, *Oh, my God, am I going to hell?* He was terrified. *Above all else I must be saved,* he thought. *Oh God, will I be damned because of this sin?* He felt like a failure. He felt he had fallen from the pedestal he had put himself on.

When he returned home, Helen said, "I've called the police. They'll be here soon."

He didn't argue with her. His emotions had receded deep into his brain, and he felt nothing. *She did what she had to,* he thought. At least she had washed her face. When the police arrived a few minutes later, Helen said, "I want my husband arrested."

"Can I speak to my boys before I go?" Joe asked a police officer. "I want to explain what's happening. They saw it all."

"No."

"But I want them to know everything will be all right."

"Your wife can explain it. Let's go."

Joe was furious, his anger hot inside him again. In the squad car the tougher-looking police officer asked, "Why did you do it?"

"It's none of your business!" Joe snapped. "You're probably taping all this, and I don't have to tell you a thing without my lawyer present."

The officer used profanity, then said, "Mind your manners. You're the last person to be uppity."

Joe was put in a cell with three other men. He refused to eat and only drank water.

"Man, why don't you eat?" asked a man who shook from a drinking binge.

"I want no positive memories of this place. It's my way of telling myself I mean to never return."

The alcoholic shook his head. "Got anything to drink on ya?"

Joe turned away in disgust.

He spent two nights in jail, after which he was arraigned on charges of domestic violence. Helen bailed him out. "I promise to stay by your side," she said, "if you'll get help."

At his trial Joe received a sentence of eighty hours of community service, which he served in six days of grueling work on a road crew. He needed the work though; it distracted him from his guilt. Helen had found a therapy group for men who batter, which Joe had started to attend before the trial. He and Helen also sought individual counseling and met together with several pastors.

Joe said, "I felt it was to my benefit to get as much help as I could, but I was in agony for a long time. I knew in my mind God had forgiven me because I had turned from my evil. But my heart was heavy, and I felt distant from God. I will say I have a new respect for Helen. She got my attention through sending me to jail. I respect her ability to dial 911."

In his therapy group, Joe told no one that he was a pastor. He shrank from revealing his feelings, until the leader caught his attention with Ephesians 5:23–25: "Husbands, love your wives, just as Christ also loved the church." He asked Joe directly, "Would Jesus slap you on the head, make you fall down, and bloody your nose?"

Joe said, "The words were strong, personal, and correct. It was my turning point. "

Whenever guilt plagued Joe, which it did frequently, he took heart that God had used David and Peter after they repented from their sins, and they became his mentors. "David didn't live to build the Jewish temple because he was a man of war," Joe said. "I have chosen not to be a man of war so I can see the temple built, in this case my personal temple. I work on healing from anger and my domineering of Helen every day."

Before Joe attended the therapy group, he did not connect with his need for control or his anger. "Men are often raised to be strong and not give in to feelings, but that's wrong as far as I'm concerned. If a man can't connect with his feelings, then he can go around willy-nilly abusing and doing whatever he pleases. I had thought Helen should 'do it my way or take the highway.' "

Now Joe says that he and Helen have good communication and a better balance of power. "We go to the Bible for answers. To me that's the easiest way out of an argument. I try to accommodate her comfort zones. I used to feel if there was food on the table, then we had enough food in the house. Helen, though, had to have twenty cans of vegetables, some meat in the freezer, and two or three loaves of bread, or she felt the pantry was empty. Now when she wants groceries, we get them."

Joe adds, "Rather than look at what not to do to avoid anger, I look at what to do to be happy. When I have good thoughts, the angry ones go by the wayside."

Joe stated that he has continued private therapy. He says, "I feel I no longer abuse Helen in any way."

"Why do you feel abuse free?" I asked, because manipulative conduct is difficult to quit, requiring considerable behavioral and attitudinal changes.

"Helen comes and goes as she pleases without my telling her where to go and what to do. I consider her ideas as credible as mine. Helen controls her money without personal accountability to me. She can live for Christ and others as she is led."

"What helped you change the most?"

"Prayer—mine and others."

"How can we most help abusive men reform?"

"We need Christian counseling programs available through churches. Behavior modification is not the total solution. It helps but doesn't give that inner strength. The solution is Christ. It is Christ who strengthens me."

At home, I had trouble writing up the interview. Joe's concluding remarks were inspiring, but I couldn't get the first five minutes out of my mind. An honest report would say: "This man is quite controlling but does not realize it. He is trying hard to reform." I telephoned his therapist, who is also his support-group leader, and told him about the interview.

He said, "Joe was raised in a rigid home environment and in a rigid church. Men like Joe are usually so hurt from childhood experiences that they must control the circumstances around them to protect themselves. They don't trust; they learned early that trusting gets you hurt. Even though Joe laid out all the ground rules, he still chose to trust you. His parents urged him not to do the interview. There were limits on his trust. You're getting a look at a man who has quit using physical violence and is trying to get in touch with himself. Joe has made a long journey, but he is still very fragile." His therapist added, "Write the interview up honestly, send a copy, and we'll use it in therapy."

AN ABUSER'S CHILDHOOD

A man who abuses his wife likely grew up in a home where his father's violence seemed to be normal behavior. FBI figures show that "75 percent of men who batter saw their mothers abused by their fathers and/or were physically abused as children." Often a parent or both parents were rigid and perfectionistic, patterning their son to

become a controller. His father or both parents may have been alcoholics, robbing their son of love and attention so that he ended up
trusting no one. A father may have continually put down women, ideas
that etch into the child's mind until they are truisms. In addition, a son
may have seen his father ordering his wife around and his wife comply-
ing. The boy may have deduced that men are supposed to tell women
what to do, and if women don't obey, they should be struck.

In some cases a relative, older playmate, or authority figure (such
as a teacher or minister) may have sexually or physically abused a batterer.

Donald Dutton, director of the Assaultive Husbands' Program in
Vancouver, says, "Abusive behavior starts psychologically very young,
probably before the age of two. Typically the child has a mother who is
coping with domestic violence and cannot attach strongly to the child.
The father shames the child, and he grows up both afraid of intimacy
and desiring it. When he is around [a woman], he feels generally irritated and angry, fearful of the threat of intimacy, and yet afraid she
might abandon him. His abuse also has a sociological element. For
instance, he hits his first girlfriend and blows it with her. He hits the
second with the same result. After experiences like this, he searches
the culture for stereotypes that convince him all women are not trustworthy and no good." He digests all the negative information about
women he can to justify his abusiveness.[2]

Dutton notes that "the psychology is first, and it is primary, and it
then shapes the way that the man adjusts to whatever the culture has
to offer him.... So the psychology and the sociology interact."[3]

BREAKING AN ABUSER'S DENIAL SYSTEM

As I have mentioned in earlier chapters, abusers justify their violence through blaming their wives' behavior. If abusers attend church,
they may twist Scripture to justify their assaults. Taken out of context,
Scripture can justify almost any sin or wrong. Dan Trujillo, director of
the YWCA Amend program for batterers in Cincinnati, says, "Men
who are elders or deacons will really focus on how they don't need to be
in Amend. It's their wives' problem they got hit. Once they get their
wives' acts together all will be fine. If they find a passage to prove phys-

ical punishment is correct, and you prove it doesn't apply, they jump to another passage and another—and others. It's like playing catch up."

Kent Ernsting, marriage and family therapist at Life Way Counseling Center in Cincinnati, speaks about the intensity of abusers' denial. "I haven't yet had a man come in and say he is an abuser. Generally, a woman tells me her spouse or boyfriend is abusing her. I do have men come and say, 'I have a bad anger problem.' But they usually deny being violent. They may say, 'I grabbed her arm, and she bruises easily.'"

To attack the abuser's denial, Ernsting says, "I address his cognitive distortion that he isn't responsible for his behavior. When he says, 'She made me angry.' We have to start with, 'No one can make you feel something or do something. Your emotional responses come from your beliefs and your evaluation of the situation. You are 100 percent responsible for your behavior.'"[4]

The following letter shows an abuser's denial system at work. The letter has been altered to conceal the identity of the writer, who was convicted of domestic violence and diverted to a batterers' intervention program in lieu of jail.

> In attendance at my therapy group were men from every occupation and neighborhood in the city. I was humiliated and angry with Jody for overreacting and being the instrument for my being there. I did not throw Jody down the stairs, as she maintains. I had my hands on her shoulders and hardly pressed; it was Jody who tripped and fell backward. I learned at group that 90 percent of the men live with outright shrews like Jody, who badger them on a daily basis and frequently claw them and beat on them. The only reason men don't call 911 is we have too much pride. I can't tell you how many times Jody has attacked me.
>
> When police officers arrive at a scene, they assume it is the man's fault, because the feminists have stirred up the cause of domestic violence beyond reason. The law is currently unfair to men, and we are arrested every time our wives cry batterer. We learned in our group that to avoid unfair laws we have to walk away when our wives badger us. I am doing that. It is not easy.

Jody provokes me at every turn. If somebody would confront her with Scripture and challenge her to repent, I would not have to lose control (verbally—I'm not physical anymore with her), and these hassles would stop. But this isn't an issue I can bring up at church.

These are some things she does that drive me crazy! I live in a nut house. It is worse than hell!

She is lazy. I have checked on her. I have run white gloves over the furniture, and it stays dusty for two or three weeks. She wants a new dining-room set, and I've told her no. I can't even give her a credit card for fear that she'll buy the set behind my back. She is scheming and tricky and has no regard for the fact that I am trying to save money for the kids' college.

Her favorite scheme is to bang around the kitchen when I'm trying to watch TV or read so that I can't concentrate. She wants me to know how busy she is. It doesn't sink through her head that she is lucky I allow her the luxury of not working. Believe it or not, she harps on going to work!

She never loads the dishwasher correctly and ends up with half a load and wastes water and soap. I was not brought up to waste. We saved every penny; if Mom and Dad hadn't they wouldn't have a decent retirement now. I don't make money to throw it out the window. This is a daily irritation. She WILL NOT LEARN.

She inserts the toilet-paper roll so that the tissue pulls from the bottom up, not from the top down. I have told her repeatedly how much that practice annoys me, but she will not change. It would be very simple to change this habit. This shows me more than anything that she purposely provokes me. If she cared at all about my feelings, she would insert the roll so the paper rolls correctly.

She lets the kids' dog bark at night in the yard and will not let him in. Finally, I have to push her out of bed to get the dog in. The dog throws up and messes the carpet at least twice a week. The place smells like a kennel. I admit, I have almost killed the dog, and soon I will.

I could continue on ad infinitum, but I am getting furious just writing this down for you to read. If somebody doesn't take Jody in hand, she will be beyond help and control. If there is anything I can do to help her see the light, I would. I cannot take much more of her verbal and physical abuse. Have you got any ideas?

It is noteworthy that the writer thinks he learned in his therapy group that laws are unfairly weighted toward females. His leader would never have taught that, considering that his members arrive via the court system in lieu of a jail term. This writer's perception of the law highlights just how abusers twist information to justify violence.

In his therapy groups for abusers at the Indianapolis Salvation Army, Dan Keller finds two reasons abusers blame their wives for their violence:

1. She did something I didn't want her to do and she wouldn't stop.

2. I wanted her to do something, and she wouldn't do it.

Keller responds by telling his men this story. "A guy jerks the tablecloth off because his dinner is late by five minutes, and he shoves his wife's face in the spaghetti to teach her a lesson. So she's a quick learner and gets his meals on the table at 6:00 P.M. prompt. A few weeks later, he's in a traffic jam and gets home fifteen minutes late. His meal is on the table and lukewarm. He rakes the food on the floor because the meal's lukewarm, then he hits her.

"I tell the men that the guy's wife did as she was asked yet was punished. Most men realize it was not her fault."

THERAPIES FOR ABUSERS

Experts believe that group therapy helps abusive men the most. A YWCA Amend manual states, "Men gain most of their male identity and masculine ideals in groups. Even as boys, it is obvious that they are keenly sensitive to perceived expectations of each other as males.... Through the group counseling program, a positive peer group is established and traditional roles and expectations of women are reformed."

There is, though, an important place for private therapy, particularly if it is in conjunction with group therapy.

Dan Keller, also a former pastor, has led batterers' therapy groups in Indianapolis for twelve years. He says, "Most of the members are referrals from the prosecutor's office on a diversion program. If they complete the twenty-six-week program, they will have an arrest record but avoid a conviction. Other men see our newspaper ad or are sent by the children's bureau." There is no extended group therapy offered beyond the twenty-six weeks, but Keller is a licensed therapist and will counsel men individually.

"I don't focus on a man's behavior as much as on helping him see that what he is doing doesn't work, and if it doesn't work, why do it? I aim to turn a man around and have him assume responsibility for his thoughts, feelings, and behavior. I try to get him to honor the fact that his mate has a right to mess up her life, that he doesn't have to control her. I see men change in my groups. A man who calls his wife a bitch at the first session calls her by her name at the end. I want to set it up so a man can never say, 'I wasn't aware of what I did.'"

Dropout rates in diversion programs tend to be high. Keller says, "If I have forty men come to an orientation, by the end of the program about twenty-three have dropped out. Of these, probably 80 percent will never be physically violent. It is difficult to define if they eventually give up emotional violence though."

Dan Trujillo says the YWCA Amend program runs in three phases (phase I is four weeks, twenty hours; phase II, ten weeks, fifteen hours; phase III, long-term therapy, eighteen months average). He says, "Primarily, our clients are the victims and the children, and we work to empower victim survivors to live in nonviolent relationships. We do this through giving men the opportunity to end their violence. Abusers whose partners have them arrested, consigning them to a night or two in jail before their arraignments, pose a threat to their partners. When these abusers leave jail, their victims are no longer people, but demonic symbols. To reduce these women's risk, I teach the men that the community pressed charges, not their partners. I try to get them to see that their partners live in fear and had them arrested due to fear."

I ask them, "What if you had a daughter a. her?"

A guy will say, "I'd beat him up."

I ask, "But let's say you are two thousand miles away you want her to do?"

He will say, "Call the police."

"Yes," I say, "when someone is in fear, they have the right to the police."

Another man will say, "She probably deserved it, so I'd let him do it."

But most will say, "I'd lock him up."

I add, "Is there any better protection for your daughter than to call the police, because how does she know how far her abuser will go? One hit, a beating that sends her to the hospital, or what?"

Dan Trujillo's example causes many members to relate to a woman's fear. Many men can then take the next step and blame their violence, not their wives, for their arrest.

Trujillo says, "Maybe we should not measure the success of a program by the fact that physical abuse ends. We also want emotional abuse to stop. It takes a couple of years in group therapy to end emotional abuse." Amend offers a long-term therapy program for men who sincerely wish to be abuse free, but few men complete it. "Most victim survivors I've worked with would rather have the physical abuse," Trujillo says. "It's not as bad as the emotional stuff, which gets very disempowering and hostile. It really hurts. It destroys the self-esteem and self-respect."

Donald Dutton, director of an assaultive husbands' program, asks members of his abusers' therapy group to compose personal violence plans that state what circumstances would justify their being violent. They write statements like, "If I felt someone were attacking my family, I think it would be okay to use violence to defend my family." Or, "If someone were attacking me, I think it would be okay to use violence in self-defense." In the following weeks if a man violates his policy, Dutton points out that he violated his stated values. Dutton discusses the policies often with the men, as he wants them to "commit to the fact that this is what they want their policy to be. I think that's

nt because this way it's coming more from the man than some-
that's imposed from outside by the therapist."[5]

Kent Ernsting, a private therapist, counsels an abuser and his wife
separately, until the man admits he is abusive and begins to take
actions to change. "I don't do couples' counseling in domestic-violence
situations usually. I don't want to jeopardize the wife; what's said in
counseling can have ramifications when she goes home with this guy."

Generally, Ernsting finds that an abuser comes two to three times
then quits therapy. "They feel that they've got their tempers under
control, and they won't be violent again. I think, *Oh no, they are just
setting themselves up for the cycle of abuse.*"

When does Ernsting feel that an abuser is on the way to healing? "I
don't want to disrupt a client's recovery by making him feel he has
arrived. But when they are vulnerable, they are at a point of change.
Just as in A.A., they must admit they are powerless and need restoration. It takes guts and effort to restore themselves—and grace."

When a batterer quits physical abuse, he drops only one tool in his
store of behaviors to control his wife for his purposes. His psychological
scare tactics remain—often increasing to fill the gap that the lack of
physical abuse created. Currently experts hotly debate just how much
transformation should be expected from batterers in court-ordered
treatment programs. Isn't it enough that these men give up physical
abuse, assuring their wives safety? Wouldn't asking batterers to trans-
form to the degree that they quit coercive behavior altogether be asking more of batterers than men in the general society? These questions
remain unanswered—but heavily debated.

Christianity, though, rests on the expectation that believers will
strive to quit coercive behavior because conversion has irrevocably
changed their inner natures. Second Corinthians 5:17 says, "Therefore,
if anyone is in Christ, he is a new creation; the old has gone, the new
has come!" (NIV). It is mystical but true that Christ and the Holy Spirit
work within a Christian's new nature, motivating and enabling him to
uproot entrenched sins. It is as natural for a Christian to wish to quit
sinning as for a baby to quit crawling and start walking. It is unnatural
for one who professes to be a Christian to disregard sin. If an abuser
repents and reforms, his acts identify him as a Christian. If he does not

reform because he rationalizes his behavior as all right, we have reason to question his Christianity.

Joe is working to quit his sin. His actions toward Helen display an active, repentant process at work. He accepts that Helen has opinions that differ from his. He allows the Bible, rather than himself, to settle matters. He doesn't interfere with Helen's food choices. He believes that only through Christ can their marriage be strong.

PASTORS REACHING OUT TO ABUSERS

While Ed has faithfully attended church, he has damaged the lives of three wives and nine children, and if Caroline leaves him, the count will likely rise. If the churches Ed had attended had held him account-able for his abuse, would he have reformed? I don't know. Usually, though, abusers will not quit abusive behavior unless a crisis forces the issue. A church can create a crisis through removing an abuser from the church roll if he will not reform. This action lets the abuser know his church thinks he has a serious problem. The church can pray that he will return ready to reform. Just the fact that an abuser has attended church shows us that church is important to him. He needs to know that if he decides to reform, the church will be his ally. Psychologist Rich Meyer says, "It is in the church that abusers can most be helped. Perhaps only the church has the breadth and strength to support an abuser. A mature body of believers can pray and stand with an abuser while not sanctioning his abuse."

Here are some general ways that pastors can discover and address wife abuse:

1. When couples seek marriage counseling, look for hostility in the husband and apprehension in the wife. If you note these traits, make an appointment to see the wife and the husband sepa-rately.

2. During the husband's appointment, Dan Trujillo suggests that pastors "make statements such as, 'I have been working in churches a long time and can sense you have lots of anger and hostility.' Let him give you information." Once he opens up, "don't be afraid to ask, 'Did you hit her? Did you shove her?' Let

the abuser know you will help him in a spiritual way, but the
abuse must stop as it hurts the spiritual well-being of the
church."

3. It is best to refer the abuser to a therapy group or a therapist
    experienced in helping men who are abusive, but to remain a
    support and resource.

4. If the wife has reported abuse, make an appointment to see the
    husband alone. Dan Trujillo says, "A pastor should be straight-
    forward and not afraid to confront him. But speak in generalities
    about the abuse since the wife has already confided in you. You
    don't want to say, 'Your wife said this, or this…' as that could be
    dangerous to her. Her confidentiality must be maintained."

5. In sermons and groups be open about your sins and failings. Dan
    Keller says, "Probably the biggest secret keeper in church is the
    pastor. I was when I was a pastor. I had to have power over the
    people, so I couldn't tell them my secret sins. Now if I've got a
    secret sin, I tell it and get rid of it. If a pastor can sin, an abuser
    may think, *I could tell this guy about my anger.*"

6. Abusive men won't say outright, "I am a wife beater" or "I have
    to control my wife." They can admit to an anger problem
    though. When you first broach the subject of wife abuse in a ser-
    mon or small group, it is best to start with the concept of anger
    management. You don't want to send men running off by offer-
    ing help to wife batterers. Once a man's anger problem is estab-
    lished, you can ask, "Do you hit, yell, threaten, etc?"

7. Create a small group for men, where a member can feel secure
    enough to admit his anger. Keller says, "If I am abusive, I can't
    stand up and admit it in a large church meeting. If I meet regu-
    larly with twelve people I have learned to trust, I can. In every
    small group there can be structured time to share personal
    problems."

8. Define submission biblically in sermons and small groups.
    Trujillo says, "Our churches must work to eliminate the 'king of

the castle' idea. Reframe references of submission to include concepts of submitting only in love and kindness." Keller points out another key problem in submission. "We come to looking at the Scripture 'wives, be in subjection to your own husbands,' and somehow that becomes the husband's responsibility to force submission. It is her responsibility to submit, but only if the man loves her sacrificially."

9. Stress in sermons that God's grace is expensive, requiring repentance from habitual sins. Specify these sins, including domestic violence. Ed's church demonstrated that God's grace was cheap when they allowed him to sing in the choir after Caroline reported he was a batterer.

10. Write about males with anger problems in the church newsletter or Sunday bulletin, including an invitation to talk with men in confidence.

11. Arrange for repentant abusers to speak during Sunday service or a small group. Ernsting says, "It is a powerful thing for men to hear a story of an abuser. Then men will think, *Is this what I have done?* Not too many guys would be willing to be that vulnerable to speak and tell what they have done." But if a few men step forward, perhaps a trend will develop.

Christian men can combat wife abuse through confronting men who act abusively toward their wives in church or at social gatherings. For instance, Jody's husband frequently humiliated her in social groups. At home he was derisive and sadistic. At one party he said to Jody, "Tell them about your probation at college." Jody had not been on probation per se, but her sorority had. She flushed and fumbled for words. Seeing her shame, a man spoke up. "I don't want to hear it. You shouldn't have asked her."

You can follow up such an exchange with a telephone call, asking to meet with the man. Ask him directly if he has an anger problem. If he says he loses his temper, ask him specifically if he hits, if he yells, and if he hurts the kids. If he admits to having a bad temper, hitting, or yelling a lot, offer to help him find therapy and to support him throughout. Explain that God has given us the ability to control our anger and use it to solve problems, not cause problems. Mention, too, that we don't have to be right or have the last word—that in a marital relationship the common denominator should be love and respect, not a husband's rule and a wife's compliance.

The following self-test is for abusive men. If it's appropriate, you can copy it for a man you suspect is abusive. The test may give him a look into himself.

CHECKLIST: AM I ABUSIVE?

Look at each question in several ways. Do I do this? How would I feel if someone did this to me? How would my wife or girlfriend feel if I did this to her? Is this behavior criminal? Is this an act that God would sanction?

1. Does my mood swing from sullen and angry to happy, as if I am two different people?

2. Do I think women are inferior to men and should defer to them?

3. Am I nitpicking?

4. If I am mad at my wife, do I withdraw my affection for long periods of time?

5. Do I criticize her frequently, believing if she improved I would be happier?

6. Do I humiliate her? When I do, do I feel less stress within myself?

7. Do I rant and rave?

8. Do I want her to myself and dislike her connections with family and friends?

9. Do I resort to drinking and drugs often? (Substance abuse and wife abuse often go hand in hand.)

10. Do I destroy her property, or do I damage the house when I'm mad? Punch walls? Throw things?

11. Do I often keep tabs on where she is and make her account for time away from home?

12. Do I threaten her that if she doesn't do things my way, she will pay?

13. Have I locked her in the house or imprisoned her in any way?

14. Have I locked her out of the house?

15. Have I physically abused her? Shoved her? Hit her? Threatened her with a weapon? Choked her?

16. Have I threatened to kill her or myself?

17. Have I forced her to have sex?

18. Do I injure her during sex?

If the questions indicate that you have a problem with wife abuse and you wish to talk about it with someone, talk to the person who gave you this test, see a pastor, contact a therapy group for abusive men in your area (found through the YWCA, a women's crisis line, or the Salvation Army), or see a professional therapist. You might also contact Life Skills International, headquarters for a network of more than 102 Christian centers for men who batter. The director was formerly a batterer. Their address is P.O. Box 31227, Aurora, CO 80041, (303) 340-0598.

If the questions give you pause, but you can't yet talk to someone, put the test aside and take it again soon. It is an important step to have taken the test, indicating your concern. But it is a far more important step to contact help!

CHANCES OF RESTORATION

Though an abusive male may hope to restore his marriage, it may not be possible, for even after he stops all abusive behavior and his wife has forgiven him, relationship problems outside of the abuse remain to be addressed. One counselor says, "We don't see many couples pursue this reconciliation to the very end. The faulty relationship patterns in abusive marriages are so deeply ingrained in the husband and wife that the road to rebuilding their life is very long and rocky indeed. Few couples have the patience, the determination, and the strength to see it through. But I think that it is very important that we offer this alternative because of the value we place on the permanence of the marriage bond. There is no doubt that God's desire is for married couples to stay married."[6]

Susie Luchsinger, a Christian country music star, believes it is God's will for her marriage to continue. She had been kicked, slapped, given the silent treatment, and verbally and emotionally abused by her husband, Paul. She didn't think she could change him, but she says, "I knew that God could." All violence has now stopped. "We work daily to keep lines of communication open—it's stress management."[7]

> Once abusive men understand they have you,
> they are bored with you; you're a burden.
> And once that happens,
> these guys don't turn into sweethearts.
>
> —Caroline

A Last Look at Caroline

Fifth year of Caroline's marriage…

Midmorning Ed strode into the kitchen, smiling, letting in the scent of rotting leaves from the woods that angled down to the river and tossed its refuse all over our yard. October so far had been stormy and cool, exactly like my marriage. Ed tucked his finger under my chin and lifted my face. "Sweetheart, sometimes I forget how pretty you are."

He kissed me, and my body responded. *Maybe I am special to him after all*, I thought, as we made love. I cuddled near him afterward, allowing myself to bond with him, as always whenever he was nice.

"Sweetheart," he said in a silky voice, "I need your hundred-thousand-dollar equity in the house to pay off my debt to John McCain. We'll get a second mortgage. That way the court won't seize my business funds."

I sprang up from his side. *How calculated his act of love had been*, I thought furiously. Several years ago Ed had borrowed one hundred thousand dollars from John to pay off a loan for a boat he and his former wife had sold at a loss. Whenever John pressed Ed for the money, Ed pled that his business overhead was high but he would soon repay. Sick of Ed's excuses, John sued him. Ed lost the case and was ordered to pay John one hundred thousand dollars immediately. Ed couldn't, so the court ordered Ed's business income seized, since that was the most accessible, but if business funds could not pay the debt, the court would seize our house equity.

"All I have is that hundred thousand dollars. You tell me almost daily that you want to divorce me. It's my security. Why don't you get it from your 401k?"

"I'd have to pay a financial penalty. I need that money for my retirement."

"Well, I'd die before I'd sign a second mortgage. You have the potential to make a lot of money. I don't."

"Okay, baby, it's up to you." He swung out of bed. "I'll tell the bank to foreclose on the house so that they'll leave my business account alone. It'll be like a fire sale. The house will go to the first bidder at a discount. You'll lose your money anyhow."

I hurried toward the bathroom, refusing to give him the sadistic pleasure of one tear. I wished that I had demanded he put in one hundred thousand dollars to match mine when we bought the house. But at the time he had wanted to preserve his cash for his business, which he said would make us rich. We certainly weren't rich. Ed's business was not doing well at all.

He called after me, "You sure are easy to lay, sweetheart."

Tears poured down my face. Oh—no more! Never again!

I filled the Jacuzzi, added bubble bath, and sunk under a mountain of foam, letting the jetting water relax my body. But my mind went wild. I was certain I would lose all or most of my one hundred thousand dollars. In addition to the debt to John, Ed owed one hundred thousand dollars to the IRS. If Ed and I divorced, I would be responsible for half the IRS debt, according to an attorney friend. An honorable man would pay the full sum to the IRS, but Ed had no honor.

A few days later the court seized ten thousand dollars of Ed's business funds to partially pay John. Furious, Ed appealed at court. After hearing Ed and his attorney's arguments, the judge called Ed forward.

"The court recognizes only one standard of fairness. Funds can be seized to pay a debt, unless they are certain specified funds for needy people." He added sarcastically, "You live off River Road in a house worth a million. You're not needy."

"But my father deposited the ten thousand dollars in my business account," Ed lied, his face bright with innocence. "It was to feed my family. It's not right to appropriate money that would feed my children!"

Even Ed's lawyer blinked at the lie.

The judge replied, "All funds and properties will be seized until the loan is paid."

"I will appeal," Ed snapped back.

"You can, but I doubt you'll get anywhere."

In the car, Ed cursed me out. "If you had given me your house equity, I wouldn't be in this mess."

"Me! Whose boat was it? Who sold it at a loss? Who took the loan out? Who didn't pay it? Me? No!"

His face bloated in fury, and I cringed against the door, expecting a blow. But he gripped the wheel and shot forward in his Mercedes, dodging in and out of traffic recklessly. By the time we entered the house, I was so shaken by his driving that I wished he had hit me instead.

Within the week, probably from stress, I developed pneumonia and a cramping type of flu. I was in bed in misery when Ed walked in, sat on the bed, and shook a contract in my face. "Are you ready to sign for the second mortgage now?"

"Please go," I said weakly. "I'm too sick for this conversation."

"I have to keep a certain level of funds intact for deals I'm working on, or they'll go down the drain. You're jeopardizing my business! Caroline, sign this!"

I didn't want to sign, but I couldn't bear the strain of arguing. I was about to say okay when a cramp hit my intestines, and drawing up my legs, I dealt with the pain.

He rattled the papers at me again. "If you don't sign, I will hate you one thousand times more than I do."

When the pain had passed, I glared at him. If he had kept his mouth shut, I would have signed it. Now I never would. "Leave me alone."

I turned my head to the wall as he padded away. *Oh, God, I thought, how can it get any worse than this? You saw what Ed just did. Instead of a heart, he has a scheming tumor that thinks for him.*

I felt as if I were crazy the next morning when Ed marched in the room at 7:00, carrying a tray with hot oatmeal, toast, and juice. "Can you eat it, baby? Are you feeling better?" He was smiling and beaming as if I were adorable.

I braced myself for yet another tactic to win my one hundred thousand dollars. "Yes, much better."

He sat in my big chair. "God woke me in the middle of the night. He said two things. First that Doyle will be gone from the church in six months and second that my business will be blessed."

I stared at him in horror. If Doyle left the church in six months, Ed would gloat about being a prophet! That would be unbearable. What was worse, I would know that God spoke to men who were vain and sadistic, and that would shake my faith to the core. I could understand God speaking to Ed about repenting, but not about the future.

Ed didn't mention the prophecy again, but a week later as I dusted his dresser, I found a paper under his Bible that proved to be his prophecy list. The first two items Ed had mentioned; the last five he had not:

3. Love Caroline—be totally committed to our marriage.

4. Love the children and spend quality time with them.

5. Tithe.

6. Pay all debts.

7. Read Bible daily.

As I considered item two, the one about the business being blessed, I realized his rudimentary conscience produced the prophecy; he hoped that behaving like a Christian would eliminate his debt and propel him into wealth. I placed a penny under the cover of his Bible, where it would fall if he picked it up. Three weeks later the penny was intact.

After a mild winter, spring came hard and early to Louisville, breaking open the buds of the forsythia and shoving us from coats to shorts in just two days. I allowed Kay, who was then seventeen, to talk me into a Saturday afternoon pool party, a mixed group of four boys and five girls. I was apprehensive, but Kay promised that everyone would behave "absolutely perfectly. Mom, this is a nice crowd of kids, not the ones you don't like."

I should have known better. The boys pushed the girls into the pool, threw in the chairs, and sailed paper plates at each other and the girls.

Sybil, a mother from the neighborhood who was helping with the party, pranced around the pool screeching, "Stop it! Stop it now!"

We yelled at the boys with no effect for about five minutes.

"I'd better get my husband," I told Sybil.

She nodded. She had stopped circling the pool, and she stood still and panted, parting lips outlined in pink lipstick, which matched her pink T-shirt, nail polish, and sandals. I didn't know her well, but whenever I saw her she was totally color-coordinated.

I entered Ed's office through the side door, which faced the pool. The scent of popcorn wafted from a bowl in his lap. His feet were propped on a coffee table.

"The boys have gotten rowdy. Please come stop them."

"I told you I didn't want that party. They're acting like animals, just as I predicted. You invited them, you settle them down."

I noticed that the TV played a pornographic video.

"Ed, please turn that off. You've got your drapes open. One of the kids could see in!"

"Get out of here! If you don't quiet them down, I'm calling the police!"

"First turn off the TV!"

"You can't see inside in daylight! Get out!"

My temples pounded as I grabbed the remote and clicked the video off.

Ed's eyes narrowed as he stood. I felt the familiar fear and thought, *No, he wouldn't hit me with the kids here.*

It happened so fast. First I felt his long fingers clutching my neck, then he flung me to the floor at an angle that whipped my neck sideways. I landed full-force on my hip, and pain seared through it. I screamed for help. He jerked me to my feet, grabbed hold of my shoulders, and shook me. My neck flipped backward and forward like a disjointed puppet's. Suddenly, I caught a glimpse of horrified kids pressing their noses to the side window.

"Ed! The kids."

He released his grip and looked behind him.

"Ed, I'm badly hurt." I kept my neck rigid, afraid to move it.

Ed closed the draperies but didn't comment. Sybil ran in, her red face clashing with her pink T-shirt. "I'm humiliated!" she wailed. "This will be spread all over. I wish people like you didn't live here. People will associate you with me, and my reputation will be ruined. I'll have to move," she cried.

I looked dully at her, too dazed to be horrified. "Please call the kids' parents and have them picked up," I said. "Go in the house and use the phone."

Sybil left. Kay ran in, sneered at Ed, and said, "I'm calling the police." Ed sank on the couch, fury in his eyes, but he held his tongue. After Kay contacted the police, I called Doyle and asked him to come.

"I can't," Doyle replied. "This is police business, and I'm sure they'll handle it properly. I'll pray for you. Call me later if you still feel unsettled."

I hung up, defeated. In my desperation I had hoped that this time he would come through.

By the time the police arrived, my neck throbbed. The bone at the base of my neck had swollen to the size of a golf ball. I couldn't move my head right or left. First the police officers asked for my version of the events, then Ed's.

Ed shoved his hands in his pockets. "Caroline is mentally ill, and what you have heard is a figment of her tortured mind. I have tried to be a good husband, but she's psychotic and gets so wrought up that she falls and even self-inflicts injuries. She ran in my office, hysterical about the kids horsing around in the pool. Then she saw that I watched a video that was a little sex-oriented, and she went berserk and tripped."

An officer turned to me. "What do say about that?"

"He's lying."

"I urge you to press charges against your husband, Mrs. Stuart."

"If you do, baby," Ed hissed, "you'll be on the street."

His words scared me. I didn't have a plan for that eventuality yet. "I won't press charges."

"You could have been killed if your guests hadn't heard you screaming and called us. The best protection you have is to arrest him."

"I'm not pressing charges," I said.

"Assault is a criminal act. The next time you call us, you'll have no choice. Your husband will be arrested."

"Okay," I said. But I wondered if I would dare phone 911 and risk a divorce. I was tired. I wanted to curl up alone.

"I'd like to photograph your injuries for evidence, should they be needed in the future."

"Fine." As they took the photographs, I was shocked that the bruise on my hip and thigh was about two feet in diameter. They then drove me to an emergency ward, where my doctor met me. On hearing what happened, her eyes flamed. She was a Christian and familiar with my church. "Have you talked to your pastor about your husband's violence?"

"He puts me off. I called him tonight. He wouldn't come to my house."

"Has your pastor talked to your husband about his violence?"

"Yes, but he never holds Ed accountable."

"I'm phoning your pastor," she said angrily. "I'm going to ask him how he'll feel when he preaches at your funeral."

"Thank you," I said and wept in gratitude in her arms.

The x-rays showed no broken bones, and my doctor had me sign a release form giving her permission to phone Doyle. She then gave me a prescription for pain medication.

It was apparent that my doctor had not phoned Doyle by the Wednesday night church supper because he stopped by our table and clasped Ed's shoulder. "Hey, good buddy, how are you doing?"

Anger grasped me violently as I watched the macho in Doyle resonate with the macho in Ed, and I knew that single factor was the major reason Doyle discounted me. I wanted to scream, and I would have except the idea that good women don't yell in the fellowship hall prevailed.

Several days later when Doyle telephoned, I knew my doctor had reached him. "I've decided we will take Ed before the board, if you wish it."

"Of course, I wish it! I would love it. I would just love it!"

"You'll have to bring documents, letters, and proof, and present them to the board. You will be Ed's accuser. You know that this will end your marriage. Ed will not stand for your ridiculing him in public. Are you ready for that?"

He had thrown me off balance. "Why do I have to accuse Ed? Why can't you present the documents to the board? You know my story. I'll write it out if you wish. There are police records, pictures of bruises, and the polygraph that you can show them."

"I would like to, Caroline, and I would do it for you, but I can't. This is procedure, the way it must be done."

"I'm not ready to end my marriage yet. If you remove Ed from the church rolls without involving me, he might be shocked into repentance. Isn't that what church discipline is all about? Doyle, I beg you. Do it, but don't involve me."

"I wish I could, but I can't without involving you. Now I could do most of the speaking at the meeting, but you would have to be there to accuse."

"I can't. I don't think you're fair."

But after Doyle hung up, I realized that even if I didn't attend a board meeting to accuse Ed with domestic violence, Ed would probably consider me the culprit and end the marriage. Nonetheless, there was an outside chance he would repent. With Doyle's plan there was no chance.

The next morning Ed sipped orange juice at the counter while he glanced at the front page of the newspaper. "I'll be going to Hopper's for dinner with a client, a V.P. from a firm looking for property for a plant." His fidgeting caught my attention, for I had never seen him look uneasy. "Ah, my mother's eightieth birthday party is next week, and it's going to be a big bash. I'm making the plans. It'll be at a country club. I'll be seeing a few clients while I'm there. It would be best if you didn't come."

Feeling as if he had knifed my heart, I decided to undergo the indignity of begging to be invited rather than being left home in misery. "Ed, you can't do this. It will look bad to everyone there."

"I'm sorry, but you'll have to miss it," he said.

"But—"

"It just wouldn't work out."

"I could go and fly back right after it so you could have your appointments without worrying about me."

"No, it just won't work out," he said.

"Ed, it would work out. I really want to go."

He shook his head.

"Please," I said.

"Sorry, baby," he said and left to work.

After I wept bitterly, I sat at the kitchen table with a cup of coffee and telephoned Hildy, his first wife, with whom I had a bond, probably forged in our mutual misery over Ed, but also from her pure niceness. The stress of marriage to Ed had caused her to overeat, a habit she had not quit, and though she was fat now, pictures showed her to have once been a beauty. She worked as a sales clerk, and because she hadn't demanded much child support from Ed, she had raised her girls to adulthood on little money. I liked to daydream that I'd inherit money and give some to Hildy. She was the only wife Ed's parents liked, and I suspected she would be going to the birthday party.

She affirmed that she was, and I told her why I would not be there.

"I'm so sorry," she said. "I thought we'd both be there. It's mean of Ed, but I feel I have to go for the girls' sake. These are their grand-parents."

"Is Betsy going too?"

"I don't know. I hope not. But then Glen is their natural grand-child too. On the other hand, they despise Betsy, so she probably won't be there."

"How can Ed hurt me like this?"

"Honey, leave him. If I did—you can."

"You didn't leave him; he left you."

"It's the same thing almost. I've got hindsight now, and Ed's not worth the time of day you give him."

"I hope Betsy won't be there. I couldn't take it."

"She won't be, honey, she won't be," Hildy said soothingly.

I hung up, burning with shame that I'd begged Ed and cried on Hildy's shoulder. Where was the woman who had so fearlessly crusaded for the lives of unborn babies that she made headlines? I hated what I had become, a cripple who crawled after a worthless man. *I can't go on like this*, I thought. *I can't obsess about Betsy anymore. I will die if my major event next week is going crazy about the birthday party.*

I had to do something. A couple of months ago when stressed out over Ed, I had researched what it took to get a master's degree in social work, as a preparation for pastoral counseling. Pastoral counseling appealed to me because I could be self-employed, therefore schedule clients for the morning when my lungs were the clearest. I believed I could give my all to my clients and empathize with them, for I had been through many trials. I had even gone so far as to call my sister Audrey to ask if I could use money from Dad's trust for a master's degree, should I pursue one. (Audrey handled Dad's trust and finances because he was now incompetent.) She knew my situation with Ed, and she said I could have the money.

I poured coffee, telephoned the Kent School of Social Work, and asked them to send me an application. To celebrate a feeling of independence, I telephoned my friends and family then walked in the neighborhood to enjoy the spring flowers. I saw no "For Sale" sign at Sybil's house. *Well, maybe she's recovered*, I thought.

After Ed's mother's birthday party, Hildy phoned to say that Betsy hadn't attended.

"Believe it or not, I was okay all week," I said. "I filled out an application for a master's program, which required a lot of information. It kept my mind occupied. I'm on my way to leaving Ed—maybe."

"Hey, that's absolutely great!"

In the following weeks, Ed traveled and worked long hours, so we saw little of each other. We never slept together, which made me miserable, for I was unable to develop indifference to Ed. I no longer centered my mood entirely around him, though, for I had Kent to look forward to—if I were accepted. *I have to be—just have to*, I thought.

Early in May while Louisville focused on the Kentucky Derby, I pressed Ridly to give me a copy of Ed's itinerary; I had no idea where he was. The garbage disposal and dishwasher had quit, and I needed Ed to phone his credit-card number to the store where I planned to purchase new ones.

Ridly held a polite look on his thin, English face. "Mr. Stuart explicitly instructed me not to give his itinerary to the family."

"Ridly, I'm in an absolute mess. Please. I've had a repairman out, and he says the appliances are shot."

"He told me *explicitly* that he was not to be disturbed."

"What if one of the kids dies or is gravely ill?"

"I'm just following instructions." His eyes turned warm. "I don't like to always follow instructions, but as long as I work here I will. I can't tell you where your husband is, but I will tell you that I wish I could."

"Okay, Ridly, thanks. It just hurts that I have the position of a wife but none of the rights."

Ridly telephoned the next morning. "Ed faxed you a communication. I'm bringing it over."

"Why did he fax me?"

"I suppose," Ridly said, "because I told him you would like to speak to him. But I'm afraid that he didn't take it well."

I read the fax at the table after Ridly left.

> You had no business asking Ridly where I am. You are continually snooping into my life, and if you could just back off, Caroline, and take care of your own business, your life and mine would be much better. The reason I don't tell you where I am is that you would pester me with phone calls and interrupt meetings to see if I were working or out on the town.
>
> You have an obsession with me, and as modestly as I can say this, you behave as if I am competition for Clint Eastwood, as if every woman would love to take me home. If you would stop trailing me and relax, you would be given far more privileges. You don't need a dishwasher or disposal, because your mistreatment ruined them. My mother never had a dishwasher or garbage disposal, and she never has complained.
>
> *Leave Ridly alone! Don't ever play on his goodwill again!*

All right, Ed, I thought, *I will leave Ridly alone. Thank you for this letter, Ed! It firms my resolve to dissociate myself from you entirely one day.* Often I watched for the postman, who came at about 2:00 P.M. I would run out and take the mail from his hand. I told him I was waiting for my application at Kent to be approved, and he always assured me it would be. I would somehow feel encouraged, for he was old and experienced and probably knew what he was talking about, having seen thousands of people receive mail. But the encouragement faded quickly, for I was antsy most of the time. If I couldn't go to school, what would I do? I couldn't go back to obsessing constantly about Ed.

In June, I telephoned Kent to find out why I had not yet been contacted and learned they were still processing applications. The social-work curriculum was liberal, and I worried that they might reject me because I had specified my Christianity. About two weeks after I telephoned Kent, I ran out to the mail truck.

"Hi, Les," I said. He smiled and handed me my mail.

I shuffled through it and lifted out a white envelope with the Kent School of Social Work return address. My heart hammered.

"So you have what you're after?"

"Yes."

"Well, open it!"

I tore it open. "I'm accepted!" I screeched.

He smiled. "Well, that just shows they've got good sense."

"Oh, thank you!"

In August, Ed and I mutually decided to divorce. We went to a dissolution mediator and were advised that divorce was financially unfeasible at that time due to attorney fees and Ed's debts. The mediator suggested that we first sell the house, as Ed legally had to pay John and the IRS and his business funds would not be sufficient. I agreed. I had no choice.

Ed rented an apartment five miles away and slept there half the week and in his room at home the other half. He called it *his* apartment and did not invite me to see it. I wished my feelings were beyond injury because I now had a future career, but I often wept when he slept at *his* place.

One morning Ed strode into my bedroom while I changed into a skirt. "There's a good chance the IRS will put a lien on the house before it sells. Then you'll lose all your equity." He smiled sweetly. "Baby, give me your money now, and I can get things straightened out with the IRS and John. Then when the house sells, I'll pay your rent. You and the kids can live in an apartment above mine. As soon as I'm on my feet, I'll buy you a house. You have my word."

"No, it's unfair. The way it is, at least your business money is being used first." I tied a scarf around my neck. "Anyhow, I don't trust you."

His voice turned mean. "You'll flop in graduate school. You're too disorganized to get your books together and even get down there."

"I plan to graduate," I said.

"Don't count on it, baby."

I winced as he left. *He will always be able to hurt me*, I thought.

I grabbed my purse, rushing to Kent to register for my classes.

As I hurried to the car, I thought about Ed's last trick. *I should walk out today*, I thought. *I'd spare the children and me so much pain and cruelty*. But I wasn't ready to go. It's not that I had hope for Ed and me— or did I?

I despised my idiotic heart because it hadn't quite let go. *But I have a better grip on myself*, I thought. I had the Lord, graduate school, and when I was divorced from Ed, for I knew that was inevitable, then I would have Kitty's help, if I needed it.

I stepped into the car, shifted, and drove steadily from my house.

A final word…

Doyle did not leave the church, relieving Caroline of the horror that God might have spoken to Ed. Kay had an emotional collapse due to chemical abuse and stress. After spending a week in a psychiatric ward, Kay attended Alcoholics Anonymous and underwent private therapy to deal with fury over Ed's abuse and anger at her mother for tolerating Ed. Caroline has started graduate school and is excelling, while she and Ed wait for their house to sell. They still plan to divorce. The wild card is her lungs. Will they hold up or will they deteriorate, leading to death? She is leaving that situation with God as she proceeds toward independence.

But the fruit of the Spirit is love, joy, peace, longsuffering,
kindness, goodness, faithfulness, gentleness, self-control.
Against such there is no law.

—Galatians 5:22–23

Fifteen

A Last Look at Susan

Divorced six months...

The perky, gray-haired clerk at the office supply store slipped my legal-sized pad of paper into a bag. "Nice day," she said. "Not a cloud in the sky when I came to work."

"It's very nice," I said cheerfully, but I didn't care if it were nice or nasty outside. The legal pad represented painful probing ahead, and a good weather report couldn't dispel that.

"But it's dry," she said. "I'll have to water my lawn."

I remembered all the times Rich or I had watered our lawn, and I felt bereft. "I live in an apartment."

"Well, aren't you lucky? No maintenance at all."

I nodded then left with a wide smile at her friendliness. She had said she had to water her lawn. Was she a widow? A divorcée? I wished I had asked, for now I wanted to know. She might have given me tips on living alone.

At home I brewed a pot of coffee, sharpened a pencil, and sat at the kitchen table, poised to write. Dr. Phillips thought a letter to Rich was vital to my recovery, for it would help release my anger over Rich's brutality. I stared at the blank, yellow page for an hour, remembering scattered scenes of horror. I didn't know which episode I could write about without falling apart.

Finally I started to write. I worked on the letter for three months, until I had twenty-five legal pages. I'd write, edit, and drip tears on the pages. Sometimes I wrote six hours, not even leaving the table to eat, drink, or go to the bathroom. It was the most therapeutic thing I'd ever done, though it was always difficult. As the letter progressed, I read it to Dr. Phillips, and he cried with me.

When I finished editing the penciled copy and had typed the letter, I read it one last time.[1]

Dear Rich:

Violence and the threat of it pervaded the atmosphere of the Taylor parsonage, and more specifically, our bedroom. Remember repeatedly kicking me out of bed and sending me sailing across the room; throwing objects at me; clasping your hands around my neck while lying in bed in stone silence for what seemed to me like an eternity; holding me down on the bed "to calm me down"; twisting my hand and arm until they felt broken—one finger is permanently crooked from the 1990 brutality? And there are many, many more incidents.

My therapist said, "Susan, you're not going to make it if you don't talk about everything. You seem blocked and unable to express the deepest problems from the past." I began writing this letter. Finally I was able to read aloud to my doctor all that I had written. By far, the most recurring problem concerned sex in our marriage, and more specifically, *rape* in our marriage.

I remember feeling glad when the '60s were behind me and I would not be pregnant again and have to endure your nasty remarks and shunning attitude about my figure. All the pregnancies were the same—you seemed (and acted) ashamed of me. You also *blamed* me for deliberately getting pregnant, which, of course, was not true.

Then the sexual abuse escalated after we moved once again in the early '70s. It is *rape* when a violent, angry husband rips off his wife's undergarments and brutally assaults her. It is also called *rape* when that same husband performs anal sex on his wife while she's crying and telling him how painful it is. *Rape* is when you acted furious those countless times and "manhandled" me and said things like "Your body is mine," or "I married you and I'm entitled to your body." Then you would proceed to do what you pleased no matter what I said or did. Everything about you reeked of fury and contempt.

Not all of our sex life consisted of rape, though. There were times when you *were* the gentlest man I could imagine. That's what made it so confusing. I came into the marriage a normal woman with normal human drives, including the sex drive. Within the first year of our marriage it became clear to me that you gained much more pleasure from anger-driven sex than you did from mutual, loving sex. My attempts to discuss this with you were futile. Though I had never been sexually active with anyone else, instinctively I knew that what was happening to me was not right. The man I had fallen in love with and married was relating to me with anomalous behavior, both inside the bedroom and out.

1) You'd be kind and caring to the family and me; our love-making would be tender. I remember how precious it was to have such a gentle, loving mate. Every time this phase came along, I convinced myself that it would last forever.

2) When you inevitably became so angry following your niceness, I would ask you what was wrong or what had I done to cause your wrath. At this phase the children came to me privately and asked the same question every time: "What's wrong with Dad?" For years I'd make up some credible-sounding "reason": "He's preoccupied, had a hard day, doesn't feel good, behind on his sermon, etc."

The day came when I said, "Don't ask me. Ask your dad what's wrong with him."

Usually they didn't bother. One or the other would say to

me, "You and Dad must have had another fight." This pierced me through my soul, because I couldn't (wouldn't) tell them what went on inside the four walls of our bedroom.

I once thought your sickness resulted from a sickness in your mind. I know now that you *chose* that behavior and used it for your own controlling purposes. You managed consistently to treat parishioners with utmost dignity and respect. I cannot recall a time that you disabled one of their cars or took away their keys. *Never*, to my knowledge, did you rape another woman besides me or beat another child (teenager) and verbally brutalize her. I recently found this list of vile things that you called Colleen in college: "ungrateful, puke, bitch, attack dog, leech, sponge, mother's shadow, crow's feet, whore," and more. You knew too well what would happen to you had you treated outsiders the way you treated your family. Besides, you didn't need to because it was your wife (and family) that you wanted to keep close reins on. We were also your parishioners, but that was different.

The time came, Rich, somewhere in the late '70s, that the tons of hurt shoved inside of me turned to anger and hate. I remember the day that I *knew* I could no longer say to you, "I love you," because the love that I came into the marriage with was overtaken by all that this letter is about. The following quotes from *License to Rape* say exactly what I feel. "My whole body was being abused. I felt if I'd been raped by a stranger, I could have dealt with it a whole lot better.... When a stranger does it, he doesn't know me; I don't know him. He's not doing it to me as a person, personally. With your husband, it becomes personal. You say, this man knows me. He knows my feelings. He knows me intimately, and then to do this to me—it's such a personal abuse." Then this next quote says what I cried out to you so many times: "I felt like a prostitute afterward.... What I was engaged in was nothing but prostitution. I was buying another hour of peace and quiet—that was all it was."[2]

Surely, Rich, my words must ring in your ears, "Just get it over with so you'll leave me alone for a while."

My quest for wholeness since our final separation in December, 1990, has led me through ways that I knew nothing of. I write the next part with trepidation, remembering your insistence that I "keep that religion stuff" out of our conversations. Psalm 23 has been my mainstay. Throughout the separation, divorce proceedings, my ovarian cancer, multiple losses (husband, home, health, hair, church, and job), I have found hope in this psalm.

I have always been afraid of you, Rich; you know that. Remember when you said to the doctor in my presence, "I really wanted to kill her"? You seemed to delight in intimidating and brutalizing me with your words, both spoken and written. You undoubtedly led certain people to believe that the separation and divorce happened because "Susan needed to be her own person and be independent." You also said that Susan was in "that time of her life" and had emotional problems. At least when I talked about reasons with close friends and family, I told the truth—that *ongoing abuse caused the breakup.*

Your ability as an orator and persuasive speaker is outstanding. I'm the first to say you preached wonderful sermons. I remember so many times trying to disconnect the abusive you from your sermons. I honestly tried to practice what you preached. When I tried to talk about the gross discrepancies between what you said and what you did, you invariably said, "I'm just doing my job. If I knew how to do anything else, I'd be doing it. Just get off my back. It's a job and it pays the bills."

You said to me in the final few years of our marriage that you wished I were "the same girl that you married."

I am and I'm not. I'm older, wiser, deafer, and weaker from chemotherapy. I'm not impressed with money and the things it can buy. I still believe in a personal God, and my faith is stronger. My capacity to love is greater. I'm a kinder, gentler person than I was back then. I now know what it's like to face death, and I have no fear of it. I also know what it's like to face life and to love it.

I wake up early like always and love the morning, but the

compulsion to jump out of bed is gone. I'm still the maternal one, the homemaker, the creator who practices George Washington Carver's motto to "start where you are with what you have and make something of it."

My three children and four grandchildren bring me far more joy than sorrow. I believe more strongly than ever that the most important and worthwhile occasions happen with family. The woman I am now is slowly learning to trust. I was too serious back then. I like my body better. I didn't have a private therapist back then, couldn't have afforded it, and wouldn't have told even a therapist about us anyhow. I now have a therapist and will for as long as I need to. My insurance pays some of it. I can't afford not to have one to help me untangle the knots on the underside of the tapestry of my life. The finished product will be beautiful, I just know it will.

As I mailed the letter at the post office, I thought, *Up to now this has been my document, between my past and me. Soon it would be Rich's too. How would he react? "Trash!" "Lies!" "You've made me see the light; I'll devote my life to atonement."* Then I realized that it didn't matter what he thought. The letter was not for Rich, but for me; my stark statement to a cruel man, for the record. My attempt to close out my past, not his.

I was towel-drying my hair when the telephone rang. Rich's voice was crisp and hurried. "I got your letter. It's very well written. You have a gift in writing—you always did."

"Thanks."

"Well, I've got a meeting."

"Okay. Take care."

"I will—ah…well, I do have to go."

I never would know what he had been about to say. I would often wonder about it. I had a way to go to complete healing, I thought, or was it possible that one never healed totally from all that carnage?

*R*omance…

I arrived at my church between the 9:30 and 11:00 services, planning to attend the coffee time in the fellowship hall. My church was the same denomination as Rich's, but my church was smaller and cozier. I liked the sanctuary being wider than it was long so that everyone had a good view of the pulpit. Even after six months of attendance, though, it seemed strange that people didn't greet me as the minister's wife. It was different, as well, that Rich wasn't here; I would often glance around, half-expecting he lurked in the wings.

I liked the minister, but due to Rich's example I feared that hypocrisy lay under his gracious manner. Was he as kind to his wife and children at home as he was at church? Was his biblical insight a pulpit-only thing as it had been with Rich?

I spotted a row of people wearing nametags in front of a table in the entrance hall, and I realized it was new-member Sunday. I started down the row, shaking hands. At the end I faced a tall man with thick, white hair and a bushy mustache to match, a gentle-looking person whom I had noticed before. He always sat alone, so I supposed that his wife sang in the choir. He smiled and tousled the hair of the two small children who clung to his long legs. *He's really good-looking,* I thought.

"Hi, buddies," I said to the children.

He introduced himself as Porter Harrison and the children as his grandchildren, visiting him for the day.

"Welcome to the church," I said.

That smile again, stretching under that white mustache.

"Did you recently move here?" I asked.

"No. After my wife died, I needed a new church; I couldn't take the memories of all we did as a couple at the last church."

"I'm sorry. How long has it been?"

"Just three months. She had cancer of the pancreas. She thought for months that she was just tired. She was a commercial artist with a big contract that she had to finish, and she believed she could push herself through. By the time she went to the doctor, it was too late, and she died after four weeks."

"It's been so recent," I said softly. "It must be very hard."

His eyes showed his pain. "Is—uh—is your husband here? I've seen you, but I haven't seen him."

"No, we're divorced."

At that he blushed, and I warmed inside. *I think he thinks I'm nice*, I thought.

I left for the fellowship hall, and the next Sunday during coffee time Parker joined me. I learned he was sixty-one and planning to retire from his engineering position in four years then do part-time consulting. He had three married daughters, and he lived in a two-year-old, semi-Victorian house with a tennis court and pool. His wife, Tilly, had drawn the floor plans and designed the landscaping. The mention of a tennis court caught my interest; I loved to play.

It became a habit, having coffee at church with Parker. One Sunday while talking to a group of women, I glanced at the entrance to the fellowship hall, anticipating Parker's arrival, wondering why he was late. *I hope he's not sick*, I thought.

He finally appeared. As he stopped and greeted several people, I felt a twinge of impatience and realized I was becoming interested in Parker. It felt strange to have an interest in a man other than Rich, almost as if I wore the wrong set of clothes. I liked the genuine smile that Parker flashed while he conversed with people. I liked his name. I wondered what it would be like to go out with him.

He joined me, and as we walked to the coffee urn, I asked, "What was Tilly like?"

"She was organized. She paid all our bills and made all the purchases for the house. She handled our home and her commercial-art business admirably. Everyone said that Tilly was larger than life. She'd have one goal she was working on and ten more down the road." Parker filled his cup.

"What did she look like?"

"Tall, willowy. She looked younger than her years—far younger than me."

I flirted a little. "You certainly don't look your age."

He blushed. I loved it that he blushed, for Rich would never in his life have the sensibilities to blush.

"Well, what about you?" he asked. "What—uh—you were divorced—and..." He shifted his feet, definitely uneasy about intruding on my personal life.

I dropped my eyes, flooded with shame for enduring Rich's mistreatment. I wondered, would a man who loved God and seemed as naive as a child, who had a wife who evidently babied him, understand domestic violence of the horrible sort I had? I doubted it.

"I—yes. We were married for more than thirty-two years. But it was an unhappy marriage." Though likely it sounded as if my unhappiness had been mild, I could go no further.

A few days later Parker telephoned to invite me for ice cream at a shop near my apartment. The hot fudge in the bottom of our sundae dishes dried as we talked for two hours. The next week he invited me to a movie, after which we rode up on my elevator. "Would you like to come in for coffee?" I said.

"No, thanks. It's late, and I have some things to do at home."

At my door he kissed me, only a moment, but I knew we had a future.

"I'll call you," he said. He didn't set a date, unlike Rich, who had staked claims on me weeks in advance when he had first dated me. I knew Parker would call, because he had said he would. I sailed to my bedroom and threw my purse on the bed, feeling like a schoolgirl. I ran to the kitchen table and wrote a poem about him.

The next morning Parker telephoned, and from then on we saw each other almost daily.

One night Parker invited me to dinner, my first visit to his house. As I neared his street, I realized that the last time I had been in this area was after a six-hour dinner with Rich, which he had wanted to extend to an all-night event, even though he was dating Rita. At about this location, I had felt betwixt and between, wondering if I should try it again with Rich. I had trembled as I realized the horror that would inflict on me. Yet being without Rich had been killing me inch by inch. I had wept bitterly. Suddenly a voice had spoken, not audibly, but clearly in my mind. *Susan, I have something better for you.*

Awed, I had thought, *God, this can't be you?* Yet the voice had been so clear, and I believed it was God. For the first time, I had felt hope for my future.

At home, I had gotten out my journal and written *Susan, I have something better for you.* Then cancer, chemo, and my divorce slammed at me in rapid order, mocking the voice I had thought was God. Often

I would read my journal entry and think, *God, I did hear your voice. What I heard was not a mockery.*

As I pulled into Parker's drive, I realized I had heard God's voice within a mile of Parker's home. *Oh, dear God,* I thought joyfully, *you did have something better for me.*

Parker ushered me into a house warm with the heat of cooking and thick with the scent of roast beef. His foyer, I noticed, divided the living room on the right from a sitting room on the left and led to a curving staircase to the second floor. I saw immediately that Tilly had loved antiques, just like me.

"Can I take your purse?" Parker asked.

"No, I'll keep it." I nervously fingered it. It contained a copy of the letter I had sent Rich. I had reached the point with Parker where I felt it only fair that he should know about the domestic violence. He needed to decide if he wanted to continue seeing a woman still recovering from trauma.

After salad, roast beef with horseradish sauce, and oven-baked potatoes, we had coffee in the sitting room. I felt comfortable among the antiques, but I knew if it were my house, I would want sunnier colors. My hand trembled as I reached into my purse for the letter. "Parker, you have to know about my marriage and its effect on me before you get serious about me."

I tensely watched Parker's face as he read. He wiped away tears. *Oh, this is too hard for him,* I thought. I had to look away from Parker. I was so afraid of being thrown away again.

Parker handed me the letter, his eyes drawn. "No one should have to go through that." He pulled me into his arms. His big hands stroked my back for a long time, as if to impart life.

"I've agonized over why I stayed. I don't think I'm the kind to be exploited. I'm sure it was love addiction with Rich. Plus I believed enough in miracles to feel he'd change."

"I don't see how anyone could injure a woman, especially a clergyman," Parker said angrily. "They tell us how to live, yet they do that!"

"Rich is a cruel man. Being a pastor was just a job to him."

"You're so confident and happy now."

"It's taken me a long time to become well enough to give you a letter like that."

Parker later told me he had thought such violence occurred mainly in the motorcycle culture, until he read my letter. He never knew anyone who admitted to being battered, nor had he heard or read much about domestic violence. It frustrated him that he could do nothing to fix my past.

In a stroke of chance, we saw Rich and his wife in a lobby after a play while the letter was fresh in Parker's and my minds. They were several yards away, involved in conversation, and they didn't see us.

"It's them," I said, pointing out Rich and his chic new wife. My heart beat staccato from the anxiety of just looking at him.

"I don't want to meet him," Parker said, heading for the exit in a state of high distress. I ran after his tall figure to keep up. I had never seen Parker behave so abruptly. He reached back and pulled me along to the car. While we drove from the lot, his hands clenched the wheel. "I didn't want to be introduced. I would have had to be civil. It would have been difficult, but I would have been. I didn't want to try."

"You're wonderful," I said, touched that he cared so much for me. I reached over and stroked his face. "Tilly was fortunate to have a man like you."

While we dated, I felt as happy as I had in college, and maybe that is why I felt so young. We went to the symphony, Disney World, and the theater—and we played tennis and often ate ice cream, which we both loved. At times I wondered if we would marry, but I didn't feel rushed to do so. I was able to put the relationship in God's hands and enjoy it as it was.

Although my love for Parker grew during the next year, I was terrified that I would be discarded again. I needed infinite assurances that Parker's love wouldn't disappear. One night at his place during a TV show, I flung my arms around Parker's neck and wept. "I'm so glad you're not mad at me."

"What are you talking about?"

"I'm so grateful that you're not angry with me."

He shook his head. "But I've never been mad at you."

"But you do love me, don't you?"

"Why, yes, darling. You know that. I've told you many times."

Parker flicked off the show. "Honey, what's wrong? What brought this on?"

"I don't know exactly. I suddenly felt so grateful that you weren't like Rich. You've never been rough or angry. I was suddenly amazed that you weren't mad at me. Rich had been angry for so long."

"But I'm not Rich."

I gazed at him. "No, you are not!"

"I love you so much, darling," he said, cupping my face in his hands.

I wept. "Your moods don't change—ever. You're pleasant when you leave me, and you're happy when you return. When Rich left the house, I never knew if he'd return in a rage or in a good mood."

"I'll never be mad at you. I'll be irritated at times, but I'll tell you."

Parker left the room, returned with a velvet box, got down on his knees with a gleam in his eye, and did the perfect thing for the moment. The box contained a diamond ring. "Will you marry me?"

"Oh, yes, darling. Yes! Yes!"

We were married in April in a simple service surrounded by three hundred friends and family members, including Colleen and Lillie, who had stuck by me through it all. Magnolias filled the church and perfumed the air. I wore a long white suit and hat, and Parker wore a conservative brown suit with a tan tie. Parker did not take his eyes from mine while the vows were read. *Oh, how I love this man*, I thought with joy. *Thank you, dear God, for him. Yes, you had something so much better for me.*

A final word…

Susan and Parker returned from their honeymoon cruise to Parker's house, where they now live. Susan has redecorated the house to express her and Parker's taste as a couple, and Parker loves the effect.

Susan still sees Dr. Phillips (though infrequently), a process she believes will continue for some time. She hopes her story will help women realize they must not keep silent about abuse as she did. "Talking about it gives it validity and verifies your knowledge of reality," she says. "If you don't talk about it, you allow yourself to live in an illusion."

Parker gives this advice to husbands who marry victims of domestic violence: "Talk about it with her when she wants to. Be sympathetic and reiterate that you would never do anything like that. Just hold her."

*E*pilogue

You have had an intimate look at Caroline's and Susan's lives, as well as the lives of other abused women. There is no "the end," because life is not like that. We stop our days in the middle of muddled relationships, so everything and everyone around us is not tied up in a neat bundle marked, "Okay, nicely finished."

If you are abused, you likely related to situations in this book and thought, *Oh, that could be me!* If you are not abused, you likely know someone who is abused and felt great concern for her.

Caroline and Susan finally realized that their marriages gave them nothing but pain and suffering with no relief ahead on their landscapes. The only way out was to take control of their lives inch by inch. The Safety Plan in Appendix A can guide you to safety and independence step by step until finally your life is controlled by *you*, not your abuser.

Appendix A

*T*he Safety Plan

The following safety plan is a revised version of one provided by Barbara Hart and Jan Stuehling of the Pennsylvania Coalition against Domestic Violence.[1] This resource is meant to be copied, written on, handed out, and filed in ministers' offices. Working through the Safety Plan decreases your odds of injury and can even save your life, but it also represents an act of taking control of your life. Keep your safety plan in a secret place; it contains information your husband could use against you.

Memorize important parts of your safety plan. Mark Twain wrote that navigating a steamboat on a dark river was like walking down a hall passage with your eyes shut. But he knew every snag and bend in the river and could navigate it blindfolded. You need to know your safety plan so well that you will take the safest turn even in the dark.

The Safety Plan contains six steps. If you have already separated from your husband, skip steps one and two but do steps three through six.

Name:_____

Date:_____

   The following steps represent my plan for increasing my safety and preparing in advance for the possibility of further violence. Although I do not have control over my husband's violence, I do have a choice about how to respond to him and how to best get myself and my children to safety.

STEP 1
SAFETY IN A VIOLENT ENVIRONMENT

   I cannot always avoid violent incidents. In order to increase my safety, I can, though, use a variety of strategies.

A. If I decide to leave in an emergency, I will practice how to get out safely. What doors, windows, elevators, stairwells, or fire escapes would I use? I can teach these strategies to my children:

_____

_____

_____

_____

B. I can teach my children to call 911.

C. I can teach my children to flee the house or hide during a violent situation. I must instruct them to never try to break up a violent incident.

D. I can keep my purse and car keys or copies ready and put them

_____

if I have to leave quickly.

E. I can tell the following people about the violence and request they call the police if they hear suspicious noises coming from my house or see a certain signal initiated, as the porch light on during the day.

_____

_____

_____

F. I will use _____ as a code word to signal my children or my friends to call for help.

G. When I expect my husband and I are going to have an argument, I will try to move to a space that is least risky, such as:

_____

_____

_____

_____

I will try to avoid arguments in the bathroom, garage, kitchen, near weapons, or in rooms without an outside exit. If possible I will run from the house or to a room with an inside door lock. I can buy a rope ladder for the room with the lock and also install a telephone so that I can call 911.

H. During an attack, I can wrap my arms around my head to protect it from blows and curl up to protect my stomach. Generally, I will not verbally defend myself or argue with him during a beating, for he is irrational and might become more violent. If I feel that I can act in self-defense (hit, run, scream for help because it is nearby) to save further injury, I will. After an attack I will see a doctor to assess the injuries. I may be more severely hurt than I realize. I recognize the importance of reporting this assault to the police.

Step 2A
Safety When Preparing to Leave Your Husband

Leaving is a risky time, for your husband might retaliate, so plan carefully how you will depart. Size up the enemy. Of course, don't tell him you are leaving. Leave when he is out, or if that is not possible, tell him you are going on an errand.

A. I can use some or all of the following safety strategies: I will decide with whom I can leave the following items: money, an extra set of car and house keys, clothes for the children and myself. If I don't have a car, I will determine in advance if I can take a bus, train, or borrow a car.

B. Places to go if I leave my home: If you choose a private home, phone the owner and ask permission. A shelter may be listed here as an option as well. Call in advance and find out the procedure.

_____

_____

_____

_____

_____

C. I will decide where I can hide important documents in my house to grab quickly when I flee.

_____

_____

_____

D. If possible, I will try to take the following items when I leave. Those that I can gather in advance, I will hide.

- The Safety Plan
- My birth certificate
- Children's birth certificates
- Social Security cards
- School and vaccination records
- Money
- Checkbook, ATM card
- Credit cards
- Keys: house, car, office
- Driver's license and car registration

- Medications
- Welfare identification
- Work permits
- Passport(s)
- Marriage license
- Divorce papers
- All medical records
- Lease/rental agreement
- House deed mortgage-payment book
- Bankbooks
- Insurance papers
- Small saleable objects
- Address book
- Photographs
- Jewelry
- Children's toys and/or blankets
- Items of special sentimental value

E. Telephone numbers I need to know:

- Crisis hotline: memorize it!

   National Domestic Violence Hotline

   (800) 799–SAFE (7233)

   _____

- Police station, school security force, and work security force

   _____

   _____

   _____

- Children's schools and my school (if applicable)

  _____

  _____

  _____

- My work number and my supervisor's home number

  _____

  _____

- Battered Women's crisis and shelter numbers

  _____

- Minister, if he is supportive

  _____

- County registry where I can register my restraining order. (There may not be such a system available to you. If there is, it is easier for a police officer to arrest your husband should he violate his restraining order.)

  _____

- Other telephone numbers

  _____

  _____

  _____

  _____

  _____

F. I will open a savings account by the following date_____ to increase my independence.

G. I can keep change for phone calls on me at all times. I understand that if I use my telephone credit card, the following month the telephone bill will tell my batterer whose numbers I called. To keep my telephone communications confidential, I must either use coins or I might borrow a friend's telephone credit card number for a limited time.

H. I will review the Safety Plan every month to reevaluate the safest way to leave my residence. Review dates:

_____

_____

_____

_____

_____

I. Names of violence-against-women advocates or friends who will help me review this plan periodically.

_____

_____

J. I will rehearse my escape plan and, as appropriate, practice it with my children.

STEP 2B
I AM NOT READY TO LEAVE YET

But I can do the following things to prepare for my future, should I leave:

A. Return to school to update skills.

B. Explore sources of supplemental aid.

C. Find out about free day care, should I need it.

D. Find out how to apply for welfare, as well as what income and services to expect. Write a projected budget.

E. Find out how to apply for assisted housing. You can call your local YWCA, Coalition of Labor Union Women, Department of Human Services, or Social Service organizations for information about these programs. Other ideas for increasing my independence are:

_____

_____

_____

_____

_____

_____

_____

STEP 3
SAFETY IN MY OWN RESIDENCE AND OUTER ENVIRONMENT, AFTER LEAVING

There are many things I can do to increase my safety in my residence. It may be impossible to do everything at once, but safety measures can be added step by step.

A. I can change the locks on my doors and windows as soon as possible. I can install solid-core doors with dead bolts.

B. I can install an electronic security system. I can use window bars and poles to wedge against doors. I can buy an alarm device (about $9.99) to attach to the doorknob. The alarm buzzes loudly if someone breaks in, alerting both me and my neighbors (I'll tell them about it) that someone is in the house. I can get a dog that barks loudly. *It is vital to know if your abuser has broken in. One woman reports that her abuser crawled in through an upstairs window and brandished a knife at her, threatening to cut off her hands. Fortunately she escaped.*

C. I can purchase rope ladders to escape from second-floor windows.

D. I can install smoke detectors and purchase fire extinguishers for each floor in my residence. *Your abuser might set your house on fire.*

E. I can install an outside lighting system that lights up when a person nears my house.

F. I can trim back bushes and vegetation around my house.

G. I can ask a couple at church to stay with me if I am particularly frightened.

H. I will have my children memorize a few telephone numbers to phone collect should my husband abduct them (list numbers):

_____

_____

_____

_____

I. I will tell people who take care of my children which people have permission to pick them up. I will stress that my husband is not permitted to do so. The people I will list for pick-up permission are:

- At school

_____

_____

_____

_____

- At day care

_____

_____

_____

- At babysitter's

_____

_____

_____

_____

- At Sunday school

_____

_____

_____

_____

- At my parents' or other relatives'

_____

_____

_____

_____

- Others

_____

_____

_____

_____

J. I can inform the listed contacts, as well as friends and neighbors, that my husband no longer resides with me and they should call the police if he is observed near any of the listed settings or my residence. Should my neighbors not know him, I can provide a photograph. (List friends and neighbors.)

_____

_____

_____

_____

STEP 4
SAFETY WITH A RESTRAINING ORDER

I realize that many batterers obey restraining orders, but no one can be sure who will and who will not. I realize that I must be particularly careful as violence can escalate when there is a restraining order. I also recognize that I have a fifty-fifty chance of being stalked. I will take the following actions to help the enforcement of my restraining order.

A. I will keep it on or near my person. If I change purses, the order will be transferred first.

B. I will give copies of it to police departments in the communities where I live, work, visit family or friends, and to the county registry of restraining orders (if one exists).

C. For further safety, if I often visit other counties in my state, I can file my restraining order with the court in those counties. I will register my restraining order in the following counties:

_____

_____

_____

D. If I move to a new state, I will call the district attorney and list my restraining order, for it is valid in any state. I must always have it on my person.

E. I can call the local violence-against-women program if I am not sure about any items concerning my restraining order.

F. I will inform the following people that I have a restraining order in effect (my employer, my minister, my closest friends, relatives):

_____

_____

_____

_____

_____

G. If my husband destroys my copy of the restraining order, I can get another copy from the courthouse located at:

_____

_____

H. If my husband violates the restraining order, I can call the police to report the violation, contact my attorney, call my advocate, and/or advise the court of the violation.

I. If the police do not help, I can contact my advocate or attorney and file a complaint with the chief of police.

J. I can also file a private criminal complaint at the district attorney's office or police station in the jurisdiction where the violation occurred. Each item my abuser violated is a crime, and I can charge him with each violation. I can call a violence-against-women advocate to help with this procedure.

STEP 5
SAFETY ON THE JOB AND IN PUBLIC

I must decide whom I will tell that I am separated from my husband, explaining why I am at risk to be injured. (If possible, choose people who will appreciate your need for safety.)

A. I can inform my boss, the security supervisor, and the following people at work of my situation:

_____

_____

_____

_____

_____

B. I can ask_____ to help screen my phone calls at work.

C. When leaving work, I can take these actions to be sure I get safely into my car:

- Have two people walk me to my car.

- Wear a bracelet that blares an alarm when the button is pressed.

- Carry a container of mace.

D. When driving home, if my husband follows me, I can do the following:

- Invest in a cellular phone and call 911.

- If all else fails and I am trapped and must pull over, I can lock the doors, lean on the horn, and yell fire, hoping to attract help.

E. If I use the public transit and my husband appears, I can:

- Carry a cellular phone and call 911.

- Inform the driver of my problem and ask him to radio for help.

F. I can shop at different grocery stores and shopping malls and go at different hours than I did when I lived with my husband.

G. I can choose a new bank and go at different hours than I did when living with my husband.

H. I will list ways to prevent my husband from abducting the children at school or attacking me there. (You might have to change schools to be safe. If you have moved to a different school district to escape your husband, inform your children's principal of the risk and ask how his staff can best keep your children's presence secret from your husband. Stress the gravity of your situation. Many times husbands track down their wives through learning where the children go to school.)

_____

_____

_____

_____

_____

I. I will inform my pastor that my husband might show up and harm me or abduct our children. With my pastor's help, I will develop safety measures at church. You might have to change churches, difficult as that may be, because church is one place your husband knows where to find you.

_____

_____

_____

J. To assure my safety in public (eating out, walking, going to church), I can also:

_____

_____

_____

_____

STEP 6
SAFEGUARDING MY SPIRITUAL AND EMOTIONAL HEALTH

Battering and/or verbal degradation has emotionally exhausted you. The process of building a new life for yourself takes courage and incredible energy.

A. If I feel down and ready to return to an abusive situation, I will do the following things to avoid it:

_____

_____

_____

_____

B. When I have to communicate with my husband in person or by telephone, I will do the following things to lessen emotional turmoil:

_____

_____

_____

_____

C. I will memorize scriptures that assure me the Lord is with me. I will meditate on these verses when I am afraid. For example, 2 Samuel 22:49: "He delivers me from my enemies. You also lift me up above those who rise against me; You have delivered me from the violent man." List scriptures:

_____

_____

_____

_____

_____

_____

_____

_____

D. When others try to control or abuse me, I will tell them that their behavior upsets me. Some things I can say are:

_____

_____

_____

_____

_____

E. Daily, I will commit _____ amount of time to Bible reading and _____ amount of time to inspirational reading to gain spiritual and emotional strength.

F. For spiritual support and practical advice, I can call:

_____

_____

_____

_____

G. Character traits I can work to develop to make me stronger spiritually and emotionally are:

_____

_____

_____

_____

_____

_____

H. I can attend workshops and support groups at a women's crisis center, and I can strengthen my relationships with Christians through Bible study groups and church. List of groups:

_____

_____

_____

_____

*O*rganizations That Help

DOMESTIC VIOLENCE

National Domestic Violence Hotline
(800) 799–SAFE (7233)
Immediate help in English or Spanish twenty-four hours a day. A nationwide database that links individuals and services. There is access to translators in 139 languages. The best bet if you need immediate help is to dial 911, but if it is not an emergency, phone this number.

The National Coalition against Domestic Violence
P. O. Box 18749
Denver, CO 80218-0749
(303) 839-1852 M–F 8:00 A.M. to 5 P.M.
Provides the telephone number of the shelter nearest you and will send you an information packet with fact sheets on domestic violence.

Face to Face Program
> (800) 842-4546 Call twenty-four hours a day.
> The Academy of Facial Plastic and Reconstructive Surgery and the National Coalition against Domestic Violence will provide free reconstructive surgery to domestic-violence victims.

Family Renewal Shelter
> Keith Galbraith, director
> Barbara Nixon, assistant director
> P. O. Box 98318
> Tacoma, WA 98498-0318
> (253) 475-9010
> A Christian-oriented program. They shelter Christian and non-Christian women.

National Resource Center on Domestic Violence
> (800) 537-2238
> Supplies comprehensive information and resources, as well as policy development and technical assistance to those providing services to battered women, their children, and other victims of domestic violence.

Center for Prevention of Sexual and Domestic Violence
> 936 N. 34th St.
> Suite 200
> Seattle, WA 98103
> (206) 634-1903
> Visit their Web site (http://www.cpsdv.org).
> Marie Fortune, director. An interfaith organization that educates and trains clergy and lay leaders to deal with domestic-violence problems.

Connection
> A Project of the Spokane Council of Ecumenical Ministries
> 245 E. 13th Avenue
> Spokane, WA 99202

(509) 535-1813

Connection is a newsletter that seeks to communicate insights and to connect groups concerned about clergy families facing divorce, abuse, misconduct, and everyday trials of family living.

Department of Justice Information Center
(800) 421-6770

Provides a copy of the Violence against Women Act, signed into law by President Clinton on September 13, 1994. The Violence against Women Act of 1998 is pending in Congress, and if passed it will reauthorize the act of 1994, and, it is hoped, increase benefits.

Local Organizations

Listed in the white business pages of telephone directories under such titles as YWCA, Hospitals, Women's Services, Battered Women, Crisis Intervention, Women Helping Women. They can provide information about shelters, support groups, legal aid, court advocacy, job training, housing, day care, and therapy groups for victims and abusers.

CHILD ABUSE

Childhelp, USA
(800) 422-4453 Call twenty-four hours a day.

For victims, offenders, and parents. The hotline offers crisis intervention as well as information regarding child abuse, adult survivors of child abuse, parenting, and other related issues. Refers you to similar agencies across North America.

Parents Anonymous National
(909) 621-6184

For parents who feel like hitting their children.

Missing Youth

Operation Lookout, National Center for Missing Youth
(800) 782-SEEK
(800) 782-7335

LEGAL DEFENSE

Call local legal-aid offices listed in telephone directories. Also call women's crisis agencies for referrals.

LAAW
> 3524 S. Utah Street
> Arlington, VA 22206
> (703) 820-8393
> Women (and men) in an abusive relationship in need of legal representation. Assistance is provided regardless of race, nationality, gender, social status, or education level.

National Clearinghouse for the Defense of Battered Women
> 125 S. Ninth Street
> Suite 302
> Philadelphia, PA 19107
> (215) 351-0010
> Gives legal information to women charged with crimes due to self-defense while assaulted.

HELP FOR BATTERERS

Life Skills International
> Paul Hegstrom
> P. O. Box 31227
> Aurora, CO 80041
> (303) 340-0598
> Headquarters for a network of more than 102 counseling centers, four of which are in London. The educational programs, which apply a Christian perspective, are offered for abusers and victims of abuse (children and women). The director, Paul Hegstrom, is a former batterer. Cost is determined on a sliding scale. Life Skills International may have a therapy group program near your area.

Battered Women's Justice Project
> (800) 903-0111
> The Domestic Abuse Intervention Project department provides materials to help those wishing to develop batterers' programs.

Notes

INTRODUCTION

1. "The Letter Box," *Virtue*, November/December 1993, 10.
2. Ibid., 8.
3. "A Safe Place," *Virtue*, January/February 1994, tear-out sheet.
4. Ibid., 67.
5. Muriel Canfield, "The Secret Scars," *Virtue*, July/August 1993, 33.
6. James Alsdurf and Phyllis Alsdurf, *Battered into Submission* (Downers Grove, Ill.: InterVarsity Press, 1989), 10.
7. American Psychological Association, "Violence and the Family: Report of the American Psychological Association Presidential Task Force on Violence and the Family," 1996, 10.
8. American Medical Association. 1992 Diagnosis Treatment Guidelines on Domestic Violence. In National Domestic Violence Statistics.
9. Canfield, "The Secret Scars," 33.

10. Los Angeles Police Department recording.

11. The Nicole Brown Charitable Foundation, Fall 1997, Internet: http://www.nbscf.org/html/core.htm.

12. Canfield, "The Secret Scars," 32–34.

13. Lenore E. Walker, "Spouse Abuse: A Basic Profile," in Anne L. Horton and Judith A. Williamson, ed., *Abuse and Religion* (Lexington, Mass.: D.C. Heath and Company, 1988), 16.

14. Canfield, "The Secret Scars," 34.

15. Liz Kelly, "How Women Define Their Experiences of Violence," in K. Yllo and M. Bograd, *Feminist Perspectives on Wife Abuse* (London: Sage Publication Limited, 1988), 127. Copyright 1988 by Kersti Yllo. Reprinted by permission of Sage Publications.

CHAPTER 1: THE LIE-DETECTOR TEST

1. Susan Forward and Craig Buck, *Obsessive Love* (New York: Bantam Books, 1992), 10.

2. "Domestic Violence Fact Sheets," National Woman Abuse Prevention Project, which is no longer operative in former location. Request Domestic Violence Fact Sheets from the National Coalition against Domestic Violence, P.O. Box 18749, Denver, CO 80218-0749, (303) 839-1852.

3. Domestic Unit, 1996, "Domestic Violence Statistics," Internet: http://www.nvc.org/edir/domestic.htm.

4. Based on material from the Domestic Abuse Project, 206 West Fourth Street, Duluth, Minnesota, 55806.

5. *Rivera Live*, CNBC, 11 May 1995.

6. Interview with author.

7. Material derived from Michele Ingrassia and Melinda Beck, "Patterns of Abuse," *Newsweek*, 4 July 1994, 29–30. Statistics originate from Amy Holtzworth-Munroe, a psychologist at Indiana University, and were found in "The Coordinated Community Response and Research on Men Who Batter," Fernando Mederos, Ed.D., April 1998.

8. Alsdurf and Alsdurf, *Battered into Submission*, 71.

9. Interview with author.

10. "Violence between Intimates," Bureau of Justice Statistics, NCJ-149259, November 1994, 4.

11. Interview with author.

12. "TV Violence," *CQ Researcher*. 3, no. 12 (26 March 1993): cover page.

13. Ibid., 272.

14. "TV Violence," *CQ Researcher*, 268.

15. Ibid., 267.

16. Ibid., 276.

17. Ibid.

18. Eric Gongola, "Sports Can Turn Dreams to Nightmares," *The Standard-Times*, Internet: http://www.s-t.com/projects/DomVio/sports-dreams/ html, 2.

19. Paul Tournier, *The Violence Within* (San Francisco: Harper & Row Publishers, 1978), 45.

CHAPTER 2: ME TARZAN, YOU JANE

1. Pia Mellody with Andrea Wells Miller and J. Keith Miller, *Facing Love Addiction* (New York: Harper San Francisco, 1992), 11.

2. Susan Forward and Joan Torres, *Men Who Hate Women and the Women Who Love Them* (New York: Bantam Books, 1986), 88–89.

3. "NCADV Fact Sheet," National Coalition against Domestic Violence, which is no longer operative in former location. Request Domestic Violence Fact Sheets from The National Coalition Against Domestic Violence, P.O. Box 18749, Denver CO 80218-0749, (303) 839-1852.

4. George Cooper, *Lost Love* (New York: Random House, 1994), 52.

5. Judith Lewis Herman, M.D., *Trauma and Recovery* (New York: Basic Books, 1992), 75.

6. Seminar, "Abusive Relationships: Issues and Challenges," October 27–28, 1994, Cincinnati, Ohio.

7. "Domestic Violence Fact Sheets," National Woman Abuse Prevention Project, which is no longer operative in former location. Request "Domestic Violence Fact Sheets" from the National Coalition against Domestic Violence, P.O. Box 18749, Denver CO 80218-0749, (303) 839-1852.

8. "A Safe Place," *Virtue*, January/February 1994, tear-out sheet.

9. Alsdurf and Alsdurf, *Battered into Submission*, 158.

10. National Council on Child Abuse & Family Violence, 1155 Connecticut Ave., N.W., Suite 400, Washington, D.C., 20036, (202) 429-6695.

11. Alsdurf and Alsdurf, *Battered into Submission*, 36.

12. Ibid.

CHAPTER 3: UNDER DADDY'S FOOT

1. "Domestic Violence and Children," Internet.

2. Signs of physical and sexual abuse and neglect are adapted from National Council on Child Abuse and Family Violence literature, 1155 Connecticut Avenue, N.W., Suite 400, Washington, D.C. 20036, (202) 429-6695.

3. Childhelp USA, *Child Abuse in America*, 15757 N. 78th Street, Scottsdale, AZ 85260, (602) 922-8212.

4. NCADV Fact Sheet, National Coalition against Domestic Violence, *Domestic Violence Fact Sheets*, which is no longer operative in former location. Request Domestic Violence Fact Sheets from the National Coalition against Domestic Violence, P. O. Box 18749, Denver, CO 80218-0749, (303) 839-1852.

5. In David E. Clevenger, "Family Violence/Children," *Facets*, American Medical Association Alliance, Inc. (March 1992): 12.

6. NCADV Fact Sheet. (Lenore Walker, *The Battered Woman Syndrome*, 1994). This location is no longer operative. Request Domestic Violence Fact Sheets from the National Coalition against Domestic Violence, P. O. Box 18749, Denver, CO 80218-0749, (303) 839-1852.

7. Ibid.

8. Interview with author.

9. Mark Hansen, "Liability for Spouse's Abuse," *ABA Journal* (February 1993): 16.

10. Mary Pellauer, "Counseling Victims of Family Violence," *Lutheran Partners*, July/August 1986, 19.

11. Ibid.

CHAPTER 4: WHEN CHURCH IS A HAVEN OF REJECTION

1. Linda Midgett, "Silent Screams: Do Evangelicals Hear the Cries of Battered Women?" *Working Together* 15, no. 2 (Winter 1995): 6.

2. LynnNell Hancock, "Why Batterers So Often Go Free," *Newsweek*, 16 October 1995, 62.

3. Alsdurf and Alsdurf, *Battered into Submission*, 84.

4. "Abuse in the Christian Home," *Working Together*, Center for the Prevention of Sexual and Domestic Violence, Winter 1995, vol. 15, no. 2, 4.

5. Myriam Miedzian, *Boys Will Be Boys* (New York: Doubleday, 1991), 7.

6. William Oscar Johnson, "A National Scourge," *Sports Illustrated* 80 (June 1994): 92.

7. Interview with author.

8. Alsdurf and Alsdurf, *Battered into Submission*, 140.

CHAPTER 5: WHEN A CHRISTIAN HOME IS HELL

1. Robin Norwood, *Women Who Love Too Much* (New York: Pocket Books, Simon & Schuster, 1985), 8.

2. Rebecca Emerson Dobash and Russell Dobash, *Violence against Wives: A Case against Patriarchy* (New York: The Free Press, 1979), 126. Copyright © 1979 by The Free Press, a Division of Simon and Schuster, 126. Reprinted with the permission of the publisher.

CHAPTER 6: SPEAKING OF THE UNSPEAKABLE: MARITAL RAPE

1. In Liz Kelly, "How Women Define Their Experiences of Violence," 114.

2. Herman, *Trauma and Recovery*, 57–58.

3. David Finkelhor, Ph.D., and Kersti Yllo, Ph.D., *License to Rape* (New York: Holt, Rinehart and Winston, 1985), 122.

4. Mitch Finley, "A Doctor Responds," *Facets*, American Medical Association Alliance, Inc. (March 1992): 23.

5. Elizabeth Post, "Etiquette for Every Day," *Good Housekeeping*, April 1995, 28.

6. *Harvard Law Review*, The Harvard Law Review Association (May 1993): 6–7.

7. Finkelor and Yllo, *License to Rape*, 124–25.

8. Ibid., title page.

9. Abused Women's Aid in Crisis, 100 W. 13th Ave., Anchorage, AK 99501.

10. Finkelor and Yllo, *License to Rape*, 117–34.

11. The following information provided by Mary Stamp is based on a September 9, 1995 interview, written communication, and information in "Clergy Families in Crisis Project" literature. You can reach Mary Stamp through Clergy Family in Crisis Project, 245 East 13th Ave., Spokane, WA 99202, (509) 642-5156.

12. Interview with author.

13. Stamp, "Clergy Families in Crisis Project."

CHAPTER 7: LAMB IN THE PULPIT; LION AT HOME

1. Fifteen to 25 percent of pregnant women are battered. (Evan Stark and Anne Flitcraft, 1992). NCADV Fact Sheet, National Coalition against Domestic Violence, which is no longer operative in former location. Request Domestic Violence Fact Sheets from the Nation Coalition against Domestic Violence, P. O. Box 18749, Denver, CO 80218-0749, (303) 835-1852.

2. Ibid., 18.

3. Kent Ernsting, marriage and family therapist at Life Way Counseling Center, Cincinnati, OH.

4. Herman, *Trauma and Recovery*, 114.

5. Mitch Finley, "A Doctor Responds," *Facets*, American Medical Association Alliance, Inc. (March 1992): 23.

6. James F. Masterson, M.D., *The Search for the Real Self* (New York: The Free Press, 1988), 91.

7. Ibid., 90–106.

8. Ibid., 97.

CHAPTER 8: GIVE ME LIBERTY

1. Anonymous, "Wife Writes a 'Victim Impact Statement,'" *Connection* (Fall 1997): 4–5.

2. Richard I. Worsnop, "Depression," *CQ Researcher* (9 October 1992): 859.

3. Tim Lahaye, *Anger Is a Choice* (Grand Rapids: Zondervan Publishing House, 1982), 51.

4. Lois Johnson, "Daylight for Depression," *Total Health*, December 1994, 14.

5. Donald F. Tapley, M.D., Robert J. Weiss, M.D., and Thomas Q. Morris, M.D., *The Columbia University College of Physicians and Surgeons Complete Home Medical Guide* (New York: Montague Books, 1985), 711.

6. Johnson, "Daylight for Depression," 14.

7. Ibid., 86.

8. Judith Herman, M.D., *Trauma and Recovery* (New York: Basic Books, 1992).

CHAPTER 9: THE DANGEROUS DEPARTURE

1. Defined as "To call [an accused person] before a court to answer the charge made against him or her by indictment, information, or complaint" by the *American Heritage Dictionary*, s.v.

2. "Domestic Violence," Bureau of Justice Statistics, NCJ-149259, November 1994, 5.

3. Stark and Flitcraft, 1988, NCADV Fact Sheet.

4. Ibid.

5. Interview with author.

6. Christine Kennedy, crisis-team coordinator for Women Helping Women in Cincinnati, has provided significant information for this chapter.

7. Adapted from "Court Preparation and Advocacy Volunteer Manual," Women Helping Women, 216 E. Ninth St., Cincinnati, OH, 45202.

8. Interview with author.

9. Susan Schechter, *Women and Male Violence* (Boston: South End Press, 1982), 2.

10. Adapted from questions on *Phil Donahue Show*, 23 October 1995.

11. Faith McNulty, *The Burning Bed* (New York: Avon Books, 1989).

12. Ann Jones, *Women Who Kill* (New York: Holt, Rinehart and Winston, 1980), 289.

CHAPTER 10: SENTENCING YOURSELF TO LIFE

1. Lee H. Bowker, "The Effect of Methodology on Subjective Estimates of the Differential Effectiveness of Personal Strategies and Help Sources Used by Battered Women," in Gerald T. Hotaling, David Finkelhor, John T. Kirkpatrick, and Murray A. Straus, ed., *Coping with Family Violence* (Newbury Park, Calif.: Sage Publications, 1988), 91. Copyright 1988 by Sage Publications, Inc. Reprinted by permission of Sage Publications, Inc.

2. Interview with author.

3. Candace A. Hennekens, *Healing Your Life* (Chippewa Falls, Wisc.: ProWriting Services and Press, 1991), 35–36, 42.

4. Richard I. Worsnop, "Depression," CQ *Researcher* (9 October 1992): 860.

5. Forward and Torres, *Men Who Hate Women and the Women Who Love Them*, 209–10.

6. "Set Yourself Up for Success," *Cooking Light* (Birmingham: Oxmoor House, 1993), 23.

7. Fred Littauer, *The Promise of Healing* (Nashville: Thomas Nelson Publishers, 1994), 242–43.

CHAPTER 11: LET'S BE THERE FOR HER

1. Anne L. Horton, "Practical Guidelines for Professionals Working with Religious Spouse Abuse Victims," in Anne L. Horton and Judith A. Williamson, ed., *Abuse and Religion* (Lexington, Mass.: D.C. Heath and Company, 1988), 92.

2. The shelter where I volunteer provided the majority of the questions.

3. Mitch Finley, "A Doctor Responds," 23.

4. Some material is based on information from the National Clearinghouse for the Defense of Battered Women in Canfield, "The Secret Scars." Other material is derived from research, interviews, and seminars.

5. Robert Hicks, *Failure to Scream* (Nashville: Thomas Nelson, 1993), 85.

6. Interview with author.

7. Abigail McCarthy, "Hitting Home," *Commonweal*, 11 October 1991, 566.

8. *National Crime Victimization Survey* Bureau of Justice Statistics, August 1995.

9. Kenneth W. Petersen and Esther Olson, *No Place to Hide* (Wheaton, Ill.: Tyndale House, 1982). Printed with the verbal permission of Kenneth W. Peterson.

10. Adapted from *Reaching Rural Battered Women*, Project for Victims of Family Violence, Fayetteville, Arkansas.

CHAPTER 12: LEGAL MEDICINE THAT HELPS

1. Sidney M. De Angelis, *You're Entitled!* (Chicago: Contemporary Books, 1994), 107.

2. *60 Minutes*, 30 April 1995.

3. De Angelis, *You're Entitled!*, 190.

4. "Guidelines for Child Custody Evaluations in Divorce Proceedings," *American Psychologist*, July 1994, 677.

5. Daniel G. Saunders, "Child Custody Decisions in Families Experiencing Woman Abuse," *Social Work* 39, no. 1 (January 1994): 56.

6. Interview with author.

7. Interview with author.

8. Saunders, "Child Custody Decisions," 53.

9. Ibid., 55.

10. *Harvard Law Review*, The Harvard Law Review Association (May 1993): 5.

11. Ibid.

CHAPTER 13: GIVE ME SOME TENDER-HEARTED MEN

1. The interview is printed with permission from Joe and his counselor. Some details are fictionalized to conceal Joe's identity.

2. Donald Dutton, *Fresh Air with Terry Gross*, WHYY FM, Philadelphia, PA, 25 October 1995.

3. Ibid.

4. Interview with author.

5. Dutton, *Fresh Air*.

6. Terry Davidson in Holly Wagner Green, *Turning Fear to Hope*, (Nashville: Thomas Nelson Publishers, 1984) 204.

7. Correspondence with author.

Chapter 15: A Last Look at Susan

1. This is an excerpt from Susan's letter. The actual letter is nine single-typed pages long.

2. Finkelhor and Yllo, *License to Rape*, 118, 120.

Appendix A: The Safety Plan

1. Barbara J. Hart and Jan Stuehling, PCADV, 1992. Address: PCADV, 524 McKnight Street, Reading, PA, 19601. Adopted originally from "Personalized Safety Plan," Office of the City Attorney, City of San Diego, California.

Printed in the United States
6176